FIVE PLAYS OF STRINDBERG

SCHOLARS PROGRAM
The Ralph Engel Collection
bequeathed by
Ralph Engel, Professor of English
Scholars Program
1969 - 1975

ELIZABETH SPRIGGE was educated in London and Ontario and has written a number of novels and children's books. Her two biographies, *The Strange Life of August Strindberg* and *The Life and Work of Gertrude Stein,* are both highly successful, authoritative works. She has also done much translating from the Swedish, including her previous Anchor collection of *Six Plays of Strindberg* (1955). Miss Sprigge was co-founder of the *avant-garde* Watergate Theatre Club in London and has lectured and broadcast on literature and the theatre in many parts of the world.

Five Plays of
STRINDBERG

in New Translations by
ELIZABETH SPRIGGE

ANCHOR BOOKS
DOUBLEDAY & COMPANY, INC.
GARDEN CITY, NEW YORK

COVER DESIGN BY ANTONIO FRASCONI

All performance rights strictly reserved. Address inquiries to author's agent, Willis Kingsley Wing, 24 East 38th Street, New York 16.

Library of Congress Catalog Card Number 60–13053

Copyright © 1960 by Elizabeth Sprigge
All Rights Reserved
Printed in the United States of America

A word of thanks to my Swedish friend Anna Sturge, for comparing every word of these translations with the original and ensuring their fidelity, and to Ita Cope, whose knowledge of theatre has been of great assistance in the preparation of this volume.

Contents

CREDITORS

A Tragi-Comedy

FOREWORD

Creditors is one of the most brilliant of Strindberg's short plays. It was written in 1888, the same year as *Miss Julie,* the year following *The Father,* the first of his so-called Naturalist plays.

At the time of writing it Strindberg was thirty-nine. His first marriage—to Siri von Essen, whom he had once adored and who had borne him children—had finally crashed. True, they were still living under the same roof in Copenhagen, but Strindberg no longer considered her his wife. He thought of her as his housekeeper and former mistress, and if he referred to his marriage at all, it was as an affair too ludicrous to be taken seriously. Hypersensitive and deeply wounded by his failure as a husband, Strindberg dreaded ridicule and judged it better to do the laughing himself.

Before writing *Creditors* he finished his autobiographical novel, *A Fool's Defence,* based on his relations with Siri and her former husband, Baron Carl Gustav Wrangel, and describing the wife's anxiety to be rid of her present husband, "the troublesome creditor." Both in the novel and in *Creditors* he called the former husband Gustav, Baron Wrangel's second name, and referred to him as "an idiot," and it is evident that the play grew directly out of this book. *Creditors* also contains other biographical details, such as the reference to the death of Tekla's child by Gustav.

Another influence on this play was Strindberg's current interest in hypnosis, which also appears in *Miss Julie.*

The Father had been accepted by Antoine for his Théâtre Libre in Paris, and *Creditors* was intended for this *avant-garde* theatre and for the Scandinavian Experimental Theatre Strindberg was now hoping to have himself. He felt that in *Creditors* he had taken "the new form" even further than in his earlier plays. *The Father* and *Miss Julie* are described by him as tragedies; *Creditors* is called a tragi-comedy, and Strindberg wrote to his publisher that the play was "humane, good-humoured, with all three characters sympathetic." This is characteristic and revealing, for although on occasion Strindberg recognised his own virulence, he more often saw the softer, even sentimental side there was to his nature. And this side should never be forgotten in the production of any of his plays. Strindberg's heroines were conceived as good, feminine women and his heroes as fine, intellectual men, who have only grown evil through the demoralising influence of sex warfare. When, for instance, Laura in *The Father* is played from the first line to the last as a vixen, so that one cannot believe that she and the Captain were once a happily married couple, the point of the plot is lost. And it is relevant that he intended Siri to play the part of Tekla when *Creditors* was performed in Scandinavia, although this she did not in fact do.

This, however, is not to say that one can regard *Creditors* as "humane" or "good-humoured." The content is serious, but the tone is ironical and the whole work reflects the cynicism of Strindberg's outlook at this time. The dialogue has sharpened since the earlier plays, possibly owing to Strindberg's growing admiration for the Paris theatre, and there is ample opportunity for satirical production, so long as it is remembered that he pillories people not from cruelty, but from his misery at mankind's wickedness and folly. He caricatures life's tragedy.

Many of Strindberg's recurrent themes appear in *Creditors*, such as Adolf's statement that he had birth-pangs while his wife was in labour, and Gustav's assertion that a child resembling a former husband is no proof that the child is his.

Strindberg's scheme for a Scandinavian Experimental Theatre petered out from excess of strain (his wife, in spite of their estrangement, was in charge of the management) and lack of funds, after single performances of *Miss Julie* and *Creditors*, and Strindberg did not achieve a real theatre of his own until 1907, five years before his death.

In 1893, however, by which time Strindberg was coming

to the end of his second marriage, following the great success in Paris of *The Father* and *Miss Julie,* Lugné Poë, founder of the Théâtre Nouveau, put on *Creditors* with himself in the part of Adolf. The play was enthusiastically received and in the same year was produced at the Residentz Theatre in Berlin, where it gained more laurels. Since then it has often been performed on the Continent and several times in London, the latest production being that of the 59 Theatre Company in 1959.

E. S.

CHARACTERS

TEKLA

ADOLF, *her husband, a painter*

GUSTAV, *her divorced husband, a schoolmaster, travelling under an assumed name*

Non-speaking parts, appearing once briefly: TWO LADIES *and a* WAITER

SCENE: *A sitting-room in a hotel at a Swedish watering-place in the eighties*

CREDITORS

At the back a door to a verandah, with a view of the land-
scape. On the right a door leading to another room.

Centre right a table with newspapers on it, and beyond that
a sofa. To the left a chair beside a small modelling stand.

GUSTAV *is sitting on the sofa, smoking a cigar.*

ADOLF *is at the modelling stand, working on a wax figure.*
His crutches stand beside him.

ADOLF. . . . and for all this I have you to thank.

GUSTAV, *puffing at his cigar.* Oh nonsense!

ADOLF. But certainly. For the first days after my wife went off
on this trip, I just lay on a sofa, unable to do anything but
long for her. It was as if she had taken my crutches with
her, so I couldn't move at all. Then when I'd slept for a
couple of days, I came to and began to pull myself together.
My mind, which had been working deliriously, began to
calm down. Old thoughts that I had had in the past rose
up again; the desire to work, to create, came back, and my
eyes regained their old power of looking at things truthfully and boldly. And then you turned up.

GUSTAV. You were wretched enough when I first met you, I
admit, and you had to use your crutches; but that doesn't
make me responsible for your recovery. You needed a rest
and you needed male company.

ADOLF. Yes, that's true enough, like everything you say. I used
to have men as friends in the old days, but after I was married they seemed superfluous. I was content with the one
person I had chosen. Then I found myself in new circles,
where I made many acquaintances, but my wife was jealous

of them—she wanted to have me to herself. But what was
worse, she also wanted to have my friends to herself. And
so I was left alone with my jealousy.

GUSTAV. You're given to that disease, aren't you?

ADOLF. I was afraid of losing her and tried to prevent it. Was
that unreasonable? But I was never afraid of her being un-
faithful.

GUSTAV. A married man never is afraid of that.

ADOLF. No, isn't it extraordinary? What I was afraid of was
that these friends would get an influence over her and so
indirectly have power over me. And that I couldn't stand.

GUSTAV. So your opinions differed, your wife's and yours.

ADOLF. Having heard so much, you'd better hear it all. My
wife has an independent nature—what are you smiling at?

GUSTAV. Go on. She has an independent nature. . . .

ADOLF. So she won't accept my ideas. . . .

GUSTAV. Only everybody else's.

ADOLF, *after a pause.* Yes. It really has seemed as if she hated
my ideas just because they were mine, and not because she
found them preposterous. You see, quite often she has
brought out some former opinion of mine and forced it on
everyone as her own. Yes, and then on other occasions, when
some friend of mine passed on views he had got directly
from me, she'd think them fine. Everything was fine as long
as it didn't come from me.

GUSTAV. In other words, you are not very happy.

ADOLF. Yes, I am happy. I have the person I chose and I have
never wanted anyone else.

GUSTAV. And never wanted to be free?

ADOLF. No, I can't say that. At times it has seemed to me that
it would be—well, a rest to be free. But the moment she
leaves me, I am consumed with need for her—as I need my
own arms and legs. It's really extraordinary. I sometimes feel
she isn't a separate being at all, but an actual part of me
. . . an intestine that carries away my will, my will to live.
It's as if I'd given into her keeping my very solar plexus that
the anatomists talk of.

GUSTAV. Perhaps, by and large, that is what has happened.

ADOLF. And where would we be then? After all, she's an independent being with a mind of her own. And when I first met her I was just a boy artist whose education she took in hand.

GUSTAV. But before long you were shaping her thoughts and educating her, weren't you?

ADOLF. No. She stopped growing and I went on.

GUSTAV. Yes, it's curious how her writing deteriorated after that first book, or anyhow did not improve. But that time she had an easy subject—it's supposed to be a portrait of her husband, you know. Did you ever meet him? He seems to have been a bit of an idiot.

ADOLF. I never met him because he'd gone away for six months, but he must have been a prize idiot, to judge from her description. *Pause.* And her description was accurate. You can be sure of that.

GUSTAV. I am. But why did she take him?

ADOLF. Because she didn't know him. People never do seem to know one another until afterwards.

GUSTAV. Then people shouldn't marry until—afterwards! But he was a tyrant, of course.

ADOLF. Of course?

GUSTAV. Well, all married men are that. *Feeling his way.* And you not least.

ADOLF. I? Who allow my wife to come and go as she pleases?

GUSTAV. Oh, then you certainly are the least! Perhaps you ought to lock her up. Do you like her spending whole nights away?

ADOLF. No, I certainly do not.

GUSTAV. You see! *Turning.* Actually you'd be ridiculous if you did.

ADOLF. Ridiculous? Can a man be ridiculous because he trusts his wife?

GUSTAV. Certainly he can. And you already are. Utterly ridiculous.

ADOLF, *vehemently*. What? That's the last thing I mean to be.
. . . And things will have to be changed.

GUSTAV. Don't get so excited. You'll have another attack.

ADOLF. And why isn't *she* ridiculous when I spend nights
away?

GUSTAV. Why? That's no concern of yours—that's how it is—
and while you're wondering why, there's your disaster.

ADOLF. What disaster?

GUSTAV. Well, her husband was a tyrant and she took him so
as to get her freedom. A girl can only get that by providing
herself with a chaperon—in other words, a husband.

ADOLF. Of course.

GUSTAV. And now you are the chaperon.

ADOLF. I?

GUSTAV. Well, you're her husband, aren't you?

ADOLF *looks bewildered*.

Isn't that right?

ADOLF, *uneasily*. I don't know. You live with a woman for
years and you never think about her or your relationship
with her—and then—suddenly you begin to wonder and the
whole thing starts. . . . Gustav, you are my friend, the only
friend I have of my own sex. During this week you've given
me back my will to live. It's as if I'd been charged by your
magnetism. You've been like a watchmaker, mending the
works in my head and winding up the spring again. Can't
you hear for yourself how much clearer my thoughts are
and how lucidly I'm talking? And it seems to me that my
voice has got back its old ring.

GUSTAV. Yes, I think it has. I wonder why.

ADOLF. Perhaps one gets used to lowering one's voice when
talking to a woman. Certainly Tekla always used to accuse
me of shouting.

GUSTAV. So you lowered your voice and bowed to the apron
strings.

ADOLF. Don't put it like that. *Reflects*. As a matter of fact, it's
worse than that. But don't let's talk about it now . . . Where
was I? Yes, you came here and opened my eyes to the truth

of my art. As a matter of fact, I had felt my interest in painting waning for some time, as paint didn't seem the right medium for what I wanted to express. But it was only when you gave me the reason for this, and explained that painting could not be the proper form for creative art to-day, that I saw the light and realised it would be impossible for me ever to work in colour again.

GUSTAV. Are you really convinced that you won't paint any more? That you won't have a relapse?

ADOLF. Absolutely convinced. I've proved it. When I went to bed that night after we had that conversation, I went through all your arguments, point by point, and I knew you were right. But when I woke after a sound night's sleep with a clear head, it came to me in a flash that you might be mistaken. I jumped out of bed, grabbed my brushes, and began to paint. But it was all over. I no longer had any illusions. It was only daubs of paint, and I was amazed to think that I had believed and made others believe that a painted canvas was anything more than a painted canvas. The veil had fallen from my eyes and it was just as impossible for me to go on painting as it was for me to become a child again.

GUSTAV. And then you realised that the naturalistic trend of today with its demand for realism and tangibility could only find its proper form in sculpture, which gives you body, projection in three dimensions.

ADOLF, *hesitating*. The three dimensions . . . yes, that's to say, body.

GUSTAV. And so you became a sculptor. Or rather you were one already, but you had gone astray, and it only needed a guide to put you on the right road. . . . Tell me, are you getting great satisfaction now from your work?

ADOLF. Now I'm living.

GUSTAV. May I see what you are doing?

ADOLF. A female figure.

GUSTAV, *looking at it*. Without a model? And so lifelike.

ADOLF, *flatly*. Yes, but all the same it's like someone. It's extraordinary how that woman is in my body, just as I'm in hers.

GUSTAV. Not really so extraordinary. You know what transfusion is?

ADOLF. Blood transfusion? Yes.

GUSTAV. Well, you seem to have bled yourself. But looking at this figure I understand several things I only suspected before. You have made love to her passionately.

ADOLF. Yes, so passionately that I couldn't tell if she were I, or I, she. When she smiles, I smile; when she weeps, I weep. And when she—can you imagine it?—when she was giving birth to our child, I felt the pains in my own body.

GUSTAV. You know, my dear friend—it gives me great pain to say this—but you have the first symptoms of epilepsy.

ADOLF, *agitated*. What? How can you say such a thing?

GUSTAV. Well, I've seen the symptoms before—in a younger brother I had, who indulged in amorous excesses.

ADOLF. How . . . how did it show itself, this thing?

GUSTAV. It was terrible to witness. If you're feeling at all weak, I won't upset you by describing it.

ADOLF, *urgently*. No, go on, go on!

GUSTAV. Well, the boy had got himself married to an innocent young girl with curls and dove's eyes—the face of a child and the soul of an angel. But none the less, she managed to usurp the prerogative of the male . . .

ADOLF. What's that?

GUSTAV. Initiative, of course. With the result that the angel nearly carried him off to heaven. But first he had to be crucified and feel the nails in his flesh. It was horrible.

ADOLF, *breathlessly*. But what happened?

During the following passage GUSTAV *graphically illustrates his words and* ADOLF *listens so intently that he unconsciously imitates* GUSTAV's *gestures.*

GUSTAV, *slowly*. We would be sitting talking, he and I, and when I'd been speaking for a while, his face would turn as white as chalk, his arms and legs would grow stiff, and his thumbs would be twisted into the palms of his hands, like this! *Gesture, imitated by* ADOLF. Then his eyes would grow bloodshot and he would begin to masticate, like this! *Gesture, imitated by* ADOLF. The saliva rattled in his throat; his chest was constricted as if in a vice; the pupils of his eyes flickered like gas jets; his tongue worked till he foamed at the mouth, and then . . . he sank . . . slowly . . . down . . . backwards . . . into his chair, as if he were drowning. And then . . .

ADOLF, *in a whisper.* Stop!

GUSTAV. And then . . . Are you ill?

ADOLF. Yes.

  GUSTAV *fetches a glass of water.*

GUSTAV. There. Drink this, and we'll talk about something else.

ADOLF, *feebly.* Thank you. . . . Go on now.

GUSTAV. Then, when he came to, he didn't remember anything at all. He had been completely unconscious. Has this ever happened to you?

ADOLF. Well, I do have attacks of giddiness sometimes, but the doctor says it's anaemia.

GUSTAV. Yes, but that's the beginning, you know. You must believe what I say. It will turn into epilepsy if you don't take care of yourself.

ADOLF. What ought I to do then?

GUSTAV. To begin with, you should practise complete sexual abstinence.

ADOLF. How long for?

GUSTAV. Six months at least.

ADOLF. I can't do that. It would destroy our married life.

GUSTAV. Goodbye to you then.

ADOLF, *covering the wax figure.* I couldn't do that.

GUSTAV. Not to save your life? But tell me—as you have taken me so far into your confidence—isn't there anything else, any secret wound that's troubling you? It's rare to find only one reason for discord when life is so varied and so rich in opportunities for destruction. Isn't there some skeleton in your cupboard that you're hiding from yourself? . . . You said just now, for example, that you had a child which was sent away. Why doesn't it live with you?

ADOLF. My wife didn't want it to.

GUSTAV. And her reason? Out with it.

ADOLF. When the child was about three years old it began to look like him, her former husband.

GUSTAV. Ah! Have you ever seen her former husband?

ADOLF. No, never. I just had a brief glance at a bad portrait, but I couldn't see any likeness.

GUSTAV. Portraits never are like the person anyway, and he may have changed since it was done. But I hope this didn't arouse your suspicions?

ADOLF. Certainly not. The child was born a year after our marriage, and her husband was abroad when I first met Tekla here—it was at this very place—actually in this house. That's why we come here every summer.

GUSTAV. Then you couldn't possibly have any suspicions. And you wouldn't need to in any case, for the children of a widow who remarries are often like her dead husband. It's vexing, of course—that's why they used to burn the widows in India, you know . . . But tell me, have you never felt jealous of him, of his memory? Wouldn't it sicken you to meet him out somewhere and hear him—with his eyes on your Tekla—saying "we" instead of "I"? *We!*

ADOLF. I can't deny that thought has haunted me.

GUSTAV. There you are. And you'll never get rid of it. There are discords in life, you see, that never can be resolved. So you had better just put wax in your ears and work. Work, grow older, and pile up new impressions against the cupboard door, so that the skeleton can't get out.

ADOLF. Excuse me interrupting you, but it's amazing how like Tekla you are sometimes when you are talking. You have a way of blinking your right eye as if you were taking aim, and when you look at me your eyes have the same effect on me as hers do sometimes.

GUSTAV. No, really?

ADOLF. And then you said that "No, really?" in just the indifferent tone she uses. She says "No, really?" very often too.

GUSTAV. Perhaps we are distantly related, as all human beings come from the same stock. But it's strange anyhow, and it will be interesting to meet your wife and see this likeness.

ADOLF. But you know she never picks up an expression from me. She seems rather to avoid my vocabulary and I have never seen her use any of my mannerisms. Although married couples are supposed to become rather alike.

GUSTAV. Yes, and do you know why not? That woman has never loved you.

ADOLF. What the devil do you mean?

GUSTAV. I . . . I beg your pardon, but, you see, a woman loves by taking, by receiving, and if she doesn't take anything from a man, she doesn't love him. She has never loved you.

ADOLF. Do you think she's unable to love more than once?

GUSTAV. Yes, one only lets oneself be taken in once. After that one keeps one's eyes open. You have never been taken in, but you had better beware of those that have. They are dangerous, those.

ADOLF. Your words cut into me like knives, and I feel something pierced inside me without my being able to prevent it. Yet the piercing is something of a relief, like the lancing of boils which would not come to a head. . . . She has never loved me. . . . Then why did she take me?

GUSTAV. Tell me first how she came to take you, and if it was you who took her, or her, you.

ADOLF. God knows if I can answer that. . . . Or say how it came about. It didn't happen all in one day.

GUSTAV. Shall I try to guess how it came about?

ADOLF. You couldn't do that.

GUSTAV. Oh, with the help of all you have told me about yourself and your wife, I think I can reconstruct the course of events. Listen now and you'll see. *Lightly, almost jokingly.* The husband had gone abroad to study, and she was alone. At first she found her freedom rather pleasant, then she had a sense of emptiness. Yes, I think she felt pretty empty when she had been living by herself for a fortnight. Then *he* turned up and gradually the emptiness was filled. By comparison the absent one began to fade, for the simple reason that he was at a distance—you know, the law of quadratics. But when they felt passion stirring they were troubled—for themselves and their consciences and for him. To protect themselves, they sheltered behind their fig leaves, played brother and sister, and the more physical their emotions became, the more spiritual they declared their relationship to be.

ADOLF. Brother and sister? How do you know that?

GUSTAV. I guessed it. Children play at being papa and mamma, but when they are older they play at being brother and sister, in order to hide what must be hidden . . . And then they took a vow of chastity, and then they played hide-and-seek, till they found one another in a dark corner where they were sure of not being seen. *With mock severity.* But they felt that there was *one* who could see them in the darkness . . . and they grew frightened, and in their terror the figure of this absent one began to haunt them—to assume gigantic proportions, to be changed, to become a nightmare which disturbed their amorous slumbers, a creditor who knocked at the doors. They saw his dark hand between theirs as they sat at table; they heard his harsh voice in the stillness of the night, which should only have been broken by the beating of their hearts. He did not stop them from possessing one another, but he spoiled their happiness. And when they discovered his invisible power to spoil their happiness, and at last fled—but fled in vain—from the memories that pursued them and the debts they left behind them, and the public opinion they dared not face, they hadn't the strength to carry their own guilt, and so a scapegoat had to be brought in from outside to be sacrificed. They were freethinkers, but they hadn't the courage to go and speak openly to him and say: "We love one another." No, they were cowards, and therefore the tyrant had to be slaughtered. Is that right?

ADOLF. Yes. But you have forgotten how she improved me, how she inspired me with new thoughts. . . .

GUSTAV. I haven't forgotten that. But can you tell me why

she didn't improve the other one too—into a freethinker?

ADOLF. Oh, he was just an idiot!

GUSTAV. Yes, of course. He was an idiot. But that's a somewhat ambiguous term, and in her novel his idiocy seemed to consist mainly of his not understanding her. Excuse the question, but is your wife really so profound? I haven't seen anything profound in her writing.

ADOLF. Nor have I. But I must confess that I too have some difficulty in understanding her. It's as if the mechanism of our brains didn't interlock, as if something goes to pieces in my head when I try to understand her.

GUSTAV. Perhaps you are an idiot too.

ADOLF. No, I don't think I'm that, and I nearly always think she's wrong. . . . Will you read this letter, for instance, that I got today?

Takes a letter from his pocket-book and hands it to GUSTAV.

GUSTAV, *glancing through it.* Hm! The handwriting seems familiar.

ADOLF. Rather masculine, do you think?

GUSTAV. Well, I have seen *one* man at least who writes something like that. . . . She calls you "brother," I see. Do you still play that comedy for each other? With the fig leaves still in place, though withered. Aren't you less formal when you address her?[1]

ADOLF. No, I think respect is lost if one does that.

GUSTAV. I see. Is it to make you respect her then that she calls herself your sister?

ADOLF. I want to respect her more than I respect myself. I want her to be my better part.

GUSTAV. Why not be the better part yourself? Surely that would be less tiresome than someone else being it. You don't want to be inferior to your wife.

ADOLF. Yes, I do. I enjoy always being a little beneath her. For instance, I taught her to swim, and now I like to hear her boasting that she's better at it and braver than I am. At first I pretended to be weak and timid just to give her

[1] NOTE. Literally: "Don't you '*tutoyer*' her?"   E.S.

courage, but one fine day I found that I really was weaker and less brave than she. It was as if she had actually taken my courage.

GUSTAV. Have you taught her anything else?

ADOLF. Yes—but this is between ourselves. I taught her to spell, which she couldn't do before. And do you know what happened then? When she took on our correspondence, I stopped writing and—would you believe it?—over the years, with lack of practice, I've even forgotten bits of my grammar. But do you imagine that she remembers it was I who taught her at the start? No, it's I, of course, who am the idiot now.

GUSTAV. Ah, so you are the idiot after all!

ADOLF. That's just a joke, of course.

GUSTAV. Yes, naturally. But all this is pure cannibalism. Do you know what I mean? Well, savages eat their enemies so that they'll get their strength for themselves. She has eaten your soul, this woman, your courage, your knowledge . . .

ADOLF. And my faith. It was I who urged her to write her first book. . . .

GUSTAV, *grimacing*. Is that so?

ADOLF. It was I who boosted her even when I found her writing cheap. It was I who took her into literary circles, where she could sip honey from the ornamental plants. It was I who, through personal influence, kept the critics at bay and blew up her self-confidence, blew so hard that I lost my own breath. I gave, I gave, I gave—until I had nothing left for myself. You know—I'm telling you everything now—it really seems to me that one's soul is pretty extraordinary. When my artistic success threatened to put her in the shade and ruin her reputation, I tried to bolster up her courage by belittling myself and making my work seem inferior to hers. I talked so much about the insignificant part played on the whole by painters, talked so much and invented so many reasons for this, that one fine day I found I had convinced myself of the futility of painting. So all you had to do was to blow down a house of cards.

GUSTAV. Excuse me for reminding you, but at the beginning

of our talk you declared that she never took anything from you.

ADOLF. She doesn't now. There's nothing left to take.

GUSTAV. Now the snake, being full, vomits.

ADOLF. Perhaps she took more from me than I realised.

GUSTAV. You can be sure of that. She took when you weren't looking, and that's known as stealing.

ADOLF. Perhaps she didn't educate me after all.

GUSTAV. But you, her. Very likely. And she tricked you into believing the opposite. May I ask how she set about your education?

ADOLF. Well, first of all . . . hm!

GUSTAV. Yes?

ADOLF. Well, I . . .

GUSTAV. No, surely it was *she*.

ADOLF. Really, I don't know now.

GUSTAV. You see!

ADOLF. Anyhow, she ate up my faith and that sank me, until you came and gave me a new faith.

GUSTAV, *smiling*. In sculpture?

ADOLF, *uncertainly*. Yes.

GUSTAV. You really believe in it? In this abstract, antiquated art from the childhood of the human race. You believe you can work in pure form, in three dimensions—eh? In the realistic vein of today and produce the necessary illusion without colour—without colour, mind you. Do you really believe you can do that?

ADOLF, *crushed*. No.

GUSTAV. And nor do I.

ADOLF. Then why did you say so?

GUSTAV. Because I pitied you.

ADOLF. Yes, I am to be pitied. For now I am bankrupt. Finished. And the worst thing of all is that I haven't got her.

GUSTAV. What use would she be if you had?

ADOLF. She would be what God was for me before I became an atheist. Something I could reverence.

GUSTAV. Reverence be blowed! Cultivate something else instead. A little wholesome contempt, for example.

ADOLF. I can't live without something to look up to. . . .

GUSTAV. Slave!

ADOLF. Without a woman to respect and worship.

GUSTAV. Oh hell! You'd better take God back if you need something to genuflect to. What an atheist! All fuddled up in this superstition about woman. Do you know what that mysterious, sphinx-like profundity in your wife really is? It is pure stupidity. Look here, she doesn't even speak correctly! You see, something's wrong with the mechanism. The watch-case looks expensive, but the works inside are cheap. It's the skirts that do it, nothing else at all. Put a pair of trousers on her and draw a moustache under her nose with a bit of charcoal. Then sober yourself up and listen to her again and you'll see how different it sounds. Nothing but a phonograph, repeating your own words and other people's, a bit thinned down. . . . Have you ever looked at a naked woman? Yes, of course you have. A youth with breasts on his chest, an immature man, a child that's shot up but not developed, a chronic anaemic, who has haemorrhages regularly thirteen times a year! What can you expect of such a creature?

ADOLF. If all you say is true, then how is it that I think of her as my equal?

GUSTAV. Hallucination. The hypnotising power of skirts. Or —because you actually have become equal. The levelling process is complete. Her capillary capacity has equalised the water level. . . . Look here . . . *Takes out his watch* . . . we have been talking for six hours and your wife ought to be here soon. Hadn't we better stop, so that you can have a rest?

ADOLF. No, don't leave me! I daren't be alone.

GUSTAV. It's only for a little while. Then your wife will be here.

ADOLF. Yes, she will be here. . . . It's quite extraordinary. I am longing for her to come; yet I am afraid of her. She caresses me; she is tender, but there is something suffocating about her kisses, something weakening and numbing.

It's as if I were a circus child being pinched behind the scenes by the clown, so as to look rosy to the audience.

GUSTAV. My dear friend, it gives me great pain to see the state you are in. Without being a physician I can tell that you are a dying man. One only has to look at your last pictures to perceive this quite clearly.

ADOLF. What did you say? How do you mean?

GUSTAV. The colour is a washy blue, pallid, thin, with the canvas showing through, yellow as a corpse. It's as if I saw your sunken, putty-coloured cheeks sticking out . . .

ADOLF. Stop it! Stop it!

GUSTAV. Well, that's not just my personal opinion. Haven't you seen today's paper?

ADOLF, *shuddering.* No.

GUSTAV. It's there on the table.

ADOLF, *stretching out his hand, but not daring to take the paper.* Does it say that?

GUSTAV. Read it. Or shall I?

ADOLF. No.

GUSTAV. I'll go if you like.

ADOLF. No! No! No! . . . I don't know. . . . I think I'm beginning to hate you and yet I can't let you go. . . . You pull me out of the hole where I've fallen through the ice, but as soon as I'm out, you hit me on the head and push me under again. As long as I kept my secrets to myself I still had my vitals, but now I am empty. There's a picture by some Italian master—of a torture—a saint whose intestines are being wound out on a winch. The martyr is lying there watching himself growing thinner and thinner, as the roll on the winch gets thicker. . . . Well, it seems to me as if you had swelled since you emptied me out, and when you go you'll take my vitals with you and leave an empty shell.

GUSTAV. Oh, the things you imagine! But anyway isn't your wife coming home and bringing your heart with her?

ADOLF. No, not now. Not since you have burnt her to ashes for me. You have left everything in ashes—my art, my love, my hope, my faith.

GUSTAV. They were pretty well done for already.

ADOLF. But they might have been saved. Now it's too late. Incendiary!

GUSTAV. We have cleared the ground a bit, that's all. Now we will sow in the ashes.

ADOLF. I hate you! I curse you!

GUSTAV. That's a good sign. You still have some strength left. Now I'll pull you out of the ice again. Listen! Will you listen to me and obey me?

ADOLF. Do what you will with me. I'll obey.

GUSTAV, *rising*. Look at me!

ADOLF, *gazing at* GUSTAV. Now you are looking at me again with those other eyes that draw me to you.

GUSTAV. And now listen to me.

ADOLF. Yes, but talk about yourself. Don't talk about me any more. I am like an open wound and cannot bear to be touched.

GUSTAV. But there's nothing to say about me. I am a teacher of dead languages and a widower, and that's all there is to it. Now take my hand.

ADOLF, *doing so*. What terrific power you must have! It's like taking hold of an electric generator.

GUSTAV. And remember, I have been as weak as you are now. . . . Stand up!

ADOLF *rises and falls on* GUSTAV's *neck*.

ADOLF. My bones are as weak as a baby's. And my mind is all at sea.

GUSTAV. Walk about a bit.

ADOLF. I can't.

GUSTAV. You must, or I'll hit you.

ADOLF, *straightening himself up*. You'll *what*?

GUSTAV. I said I'll hit you.

ADOLF *starts back from him, furious*.

ADOLF. You . . . !

GUSTAV. That's better. You've got some blood to your brain

and your self-confidence has come back. Now for some electric current. . . . Where is your wife?

ADOLF. Where is she?

GUSTAV. Yes.

ADOLF. She is . . . at . . . a meeting.

GUSTAV. Are you quite certain?

ADOLF. Quite.

GUSTAV. What sort of meeting?

ADOLF. An orphanage committee.

GUSTAV. Did you part friends?

ADOLF, *hesitating*. No, not friends.

GUSTAV. Enemies, eh? What did you say that made her so furious?

ADOLF. You're uncanny. You terrify me. How do you know?

GUSTAV. It's quite simple. There are three known factors and from them I can deduce the unknown . . . What did you say to her?

ADOLF. I said . . . only two words, but they were terrible, and I regret them, regret them very much.

GUSTAV. You shouldn't regret. What were these words?

ADOLF. I said: "You old flirt."

GUSTAV. What else?

ADOLF. I didn't say anything else.

GUSTAV. That's what you tell me, but you're forgetting the rest—perhaps because you daren't remember it. You've put it in a secret drawer, but now you've got to bring it out.

ADOLF. I don't remember what . . .

GUSTAV. But I know what you said. This. "You ought to be ashamed of flirting, considering you are so old that you can't get any more lovers."

ADOLF. Did I say that? I suppose I did. But how on earth can you know about it?

GUSTAV. I heard her telling the story on the boat on my way here.

ADOLF. Who to?

GUSTAV. To the four youths she was with. Of course, she always did have a fancy for innocent youths, so as to . . .

ADOLF. There's no harm in that.

GUSTAV. . . . so as to play brother and sister instead of papa and mamma.

ADOLF. You have seen her then.

GUSTAV. Yes, I have. But *you* have never seen her when you weren't seeing her—seen her, I mean, when you weren't there. And that's why—you follow me?—a husband can *never* know his wife . . . Have you got a picture of her?

Mystified, ADOLF *takes a photograph from his pocket-book.*

You weren't there when this was taken?

ADOLF. No.

GUSTAV. Look at it. . . . Is it like the portrait you painted of her? . . . No! The features are the same, but the expression is different. But you can't see that because you force your own image of her in between. Look at this as a painter now, without considering the original. . . . What does it represent? I can't see anything but a study of a coquette, out to attract. Do you see that cynical expression of the mouth, which you are never allowed to see? Do you see those glances aimed at a man who is not you? Do you see how low the dress is cut, how cunningly the hair is combed up, and how the sleeve has managed to slip back?

ADOLF. Yes, I do see it—now.

GUSTAV. Beware, my boy!

ADOLF. What of?

GUSTAV. Her revenge. Don't forget that when you said she couldn't attract a man, you wounded her in the most vital and sacred spot. If you had said that what she wrote was trash, she would have laughed at your bad taste—but as it is, believe you me, it will not be her fault if she hasn't taken her revenge already.

ADOLF. I must know.

GUSTAV. Find out.

ADOLF. Find out?

GUSTAV. Use your eyes. I'll help you if you like.

ADOLF. Well, as I'm going to die anyway, let it come. Now's as good a time as another. What are we to do?

GUSTAV. First for a piece of information. Hasn't your wife any point that's specially vulnerable?

ADOLF. Scarcely. She's like a cat with nine lives.

The hoot of a steamer is heard.

GUSTAV. Ah! That was the steamer hooting in the Sound. She will be here at any moment.

ADOLF. I must go down and meet her.

GUSTAV. No. You must stay here. You've got to be rude. If she has a clear conscience you'll get a hailstorm about your ears. If she's guilty she'll cover you with caresses.

ADOLF. Are you quite sure of that?

GUSTAV. Not quite, for the hare sometimes doubles back—but I'll look out for that. *Points to the door on the right.* I'll take up my position in my room there and watch while you play your scene in here. And when you've finished yours, we'll change roles. I'll go into the cage and engage the serpent, while you take your place at the key-hole. Afterwards we'll meet in the park and compare notes. But stand up for yourself! If you begin to weaken I shall knock twice on the floor with a chair.

ADOLF. Very well. . . . But don't go away. I must know you're in that room there.

GUSTAV. You can take my word for it that I shall be. . . . But don't be alarmed later on, when you watch me dissecting a human soul and exposing its entrails on the table. They say it's rather hard for a novice to take, but when you've seen it once it doesn't worry you. . . . But one thing you must remember. Not a single word about meeting me or having made any new acquaintance during her absence. Not one word. I'll seek out her vulnerable point for myself. Hush! She is already here—she's in her room. . . . She's humming. . . . That means she's in a rage. Now, pull yourself together and sit down there in your chair. Then she'll have to sit on the sofa, and I shall be able to watch you both at the same time.

ADOLF. It's only an hour till dinner time, and no new guests have arrived or the bell would have rung. That means we shall be alone, I'm sorry to say.

GUSTAV. Are you such a coward?

ADOLF. I am nothing. . . . Yes, I am afraid of what is going to happen now. But I can't stop it happening. The stone is rolling, but it wasn't the last drop of water that set it rolling, nor the first one either—it was all the drops together.

GUSTAV. Let it roll then. . . . There will be no peace until it has. Goodbye for now.

ADOLF *nods.*

Exit GUSTAV.

ADOLF *stands still holding the photograph. Then he tears it up and throws the pieces under the table. He sits down on his chair, pulls nervously at his tie, runs his fingers through his hair, fidgets with his lapels, and so on.*

TEKLA *enters, goes straight up to him, and kisses him. She is friendly, frank, gay, and attractive.*

TEKLA. Hullo, little brother! How are you?

ADOLF *is almost won over by her manner and speaks reluctantly and as if joking.*

ADOLF. What mischief have you been up to that makes you come and kiss me like that?

TEKLA. I'll tell you. I've spent a frightful lot of money.

ADOLF. Did you have a good time then?

TEKLA. Yes, very. But not at that old crèche meeting. That was just shit—as the Danes would say. But how has my little brother amused himself while Squirrel was away?

TEKLA's *eyes roam round the room as if she is looking for someone or suspecting something.*

ADOLF. I've been bored stiff.

TEKLA. Didn't anyone come to keep you company?

ADOLF. No, I've been quite alone.

TEKLA, *watching him as she sits down on the sofa.* Who has been sitting here?

ADOLF. There? Nobody.

TEKLA. That's odd. The sofa's still warm and here's a hollow that seems to have been made by an elbow. Have you had some lady friends?

ADOLF. You know I haven't.

TEKLA. But you're blushing. Little brother, I believe you're telling fibs. Come over here and tell Squirrel what's on your conscience.

She draws him to her. He sinks down with his head on her knees.

ADOLF, *smiling.* You're a devil. Did you know that?

TEKLA. No, I don't know anything about myself.

ADOLF. I see. You never give a thought to your own reactions.

TEKLA, *warily.* On the contrary, I never think about anything but myself—I'm a terrible egoist. You're very philosophical all of a sudden!

ADOLF. Put your hand on my forehead.

TEKLA, *soothingly.* Have you been having another brain-storm? Poor head! Let me see what I can do. *Kisses his forehead.* There, is it better now?

ADOLF. Yes, it's better now.

Pause.

TEKLA. Well, tell me how you have been amusing yourself? Have you painted anything?

ADOLF. No, I've done with painting.

TEKLA. What? Done with painting?

ADOLF. Yes. But don't nag me about it. It's not my fault I can't paint any more.

TEKLA. But what will you do then?

ADOLF. I'm going to be a sculptor.

TEKLA. O Lord, another whole lot of new ideas!

ADOLF. Yes, but don't be cross. . . . Take a look at that figure over there.

TEKLA *uncovers the wax figure.*

TEKLA. Well I never! Who is it supposed to be?

ADOLF. Guess!

TEKLA, *gently.* Is it meant to be Squirrel? Aren't you ashamed of yourself?

ADOLF. Isn't it a good likeness?

TEKLA. How can I tell when it hasn't got a face?

ADOLF. Yes, but there's so much else—beautiful!

TEKLA, *caressing his cheek.* Hold your tongue or I'll kiss you.

ADOLF, *backing.* Now, now! Somebody might come in.

TEKLA. What do I care? Mayn't I kiss my own husband then? Surely that's my legal right.

ADOLF. Yes, but do you know what? Here in the hotel they don't believe we're married, because we kiss so often. And the fact that we quarrel sometimes makes no difference— lovers are known to do that too.

TEKLA. Yes, but why should we quarrel? Why can't you always be as nice as you are now? Tell me. Don't you want to be? Don't you want us to be happy?

ADOLF. Oh, I do! But . . .

TEKLA. What is all this business anyhow? Who has put it into your head that you're not going to paint any more?

ADOLF. Who? You're always suspecting there's someone behind me and my thoughts. You're jealous.

TEKLA. Yes, I am. I'm afraid someone may come and take you away from me.

ADOLF. You're afraid of that? When you know no woman can cut you out, and that I can't live without you.

TEKLA. It's not a woman I'm afraid of, but your friends who put ideas into your head.

ADOLF, *looking at her searchingly.* You really are frightened. What frightens you?

TEKLA, *rising.* Someone has been here. Who has been here?

ADOLF. Don't you like me to look at you?

TEKLA. Not like that. That's not how you usually look at me.

ADOLF. How was I looking at you then?

TEKLA. Under your lids.

ADOLF. And under *yours!* Yes, I want to see what's behind them.

TEKLA. Look as much as you like. There's nothing to hide. But —you're talking in a different way too—you're using strange expressions—— *Searchingly.* You're philosophising. Why? *Going up to him threateningly.* Who has been here?

ADOLF. Only my doctor.

TEKLA. Your doctor? Who's that?

ADOLF. The doctor from Strömstad.

TEKLA. What's his name?

ADOLF. Sjöberg.

TEKLA. What did he say?

ADOLF. He said—well, among other things, he said I was on the brink of epilepsy.

TEKLA. Among other things? What else did he say?

ADOLF. Well, something very upsetting.

TEKLA. Tell me.

ADOLF. He said we were not to live together as man and wife for a time.

TEKLA. Did he then! I can well believe it. They want to separate us. I have noticed that for a long time.

ADOLF. You can't have noticed what's never happened.

TEKLA. Haven't I though!

ADOLF. How can you see what doesn't exist? Or is your imagination so distraught by fear that you see what has never existed? What is it you are so afraid of? That I shall borrow somebody else's eyes so as to see you as you are, instead of as you appear to be?

TEKLA. Keep your fancies in check, Adolf! They come from the beast in the human soul.

ADOLF. Wherever did you learn that? From those innocent youths on the boat? Eh?

TEKLA, *without losing her composure.* Well, as a matter of fact, there is a lot to be learned from youth.

ADOLF. I think you're beginning to be infatuated by youth.

TEKLA. I always have been. That's why I fell in love with you. Do you mind?

ADOLF. No, but I'd rather be the only one.

TEKLA, *lightly.* My heart is so big, you see, little brother, that there's room in it for many more than you.

ADOLF. Little brother doesn't want any other brothers.

TEKLA. Come to Squirrel then, and get your hair pulled for being so jealous—no, envious is the word.

Two knocks are heard from GUSTAV's *room.*

ADOLF. No, I don't want to fool now. I want to talk seriously.

TEKLA, *as if talking to a baby.* O Jesus, does he want to talk seriously then? It's frightful how serious he's grown.

She takes his face in her hands and kisses him.

Now just a little smile.

ADOLF *unwillingly smiles.*

There!

ADOLF. You devilish woman! I really believe you can cast spells.

TEKLA. You see! So don't start any trouble or I'll spirit you away.

ADOLF, *rising.* Tekla! Will you pose a moment for me—in profile? So I can put the face on your figure.

TEKLA. Of course I will.

She turns her head so that he can see her profile. He gazes at her and pretends to model.

ADOLF. Don't think about me now. Think about somebody else.

TEKLA. I'll think about my latest conquest.

ADOLF. The chaste youth?

TEKLA. Exactly. He had such a sweet little moustache and cheeks like a peach. They were so smooth and rosy one wanted to bite them.

ADOLF, *grimly.* Keep that expression on your face!

TEKLA. What expression?

ADOLF. A cynical, brazen one I have never seen before.

TEKLA, *making a face.* Like this?

ADOLF. Yes, like that. *Rises.* Do you know how Bret Harte describes an adultress?

TEKLA, *smiling.* No, I have never read Bret whatever-you-call-him.

ADOLF. As a pallid creature who never blushes.

TEKLA. Never? But when she meets her lover she's bound to

blush, though her husband and Mr. Bret aren't there to see it.

ADOLF. Are you sure?

TEKLA, *as before.* Of course. As the husband is incapable of bringing the blood to her head, he can't ever see that charming spectacle.

ADOLF, *furiously.* Tekla!

TEKLA. You little ninny!

ADOLF. Tekla!

TEKLA. You should call me your squirrel, then I'd blush beautifully for you. Don't you want me to?

ADOLF, *disarmed.* I'm so furious with you, you little monster, I could bite you.

TEKLA, *playfully.* Come and bite me then. Come on!
She stretches out her arms to him. ADOLF *takes her in his arms and kisses her.*

ADOLF. Yes, I will bite you to death!

TEKLA, *teasing him.* Now, now! Somebody might come in.

ADOLF. What do I care? What do I care about anything in the world, so long as I've got you?

TEKLA. And if you hadn't got me any more?

ADOLF. Then I should die.

TEKLA. But you're not afraid of that happening because I'm so old no one else would have me.

ADOLF. Oh Tekla, you have not forgotten those words of mine! But I take them all back.

TEKLA. Can you explain why you're so jealous and yet at the same time so confident?

ADOLF. No, I can't explain anything. But it's possible the thought that another man once possessed you still rankles in me. Sometimes it seems to me that our love is nothing but a fiction, a self-defence, a passion held to as a matter of honour. But there's nothing I would hate more than for *him* to know I'm not happy. Oh! Though I've never seen him, the mere thought of somebody waiting for my downfall obsesses me. Somebody who's raining curses on my head every day of the year, and would laugh his head off at my ruin. The mere idea of that haunts me, drives me to you, fascinates me, cripples me.

TEKLA. Do you think I'd allow him that satisfaction? Do you think I want to make his prophecy come true?

ADOLF. I don't want to think so.

TEKLA. Then why don't you keep calm?

ADOLF. You go on upsetting me with your coquettishness. Why do you play these tricks?

TEKLA. They're not tricks. I want to be liked, that's all.

ADOLF. But only by men?

TEKLA. Of course. A woman's never really liked by other women, you know.

ADOLF. Tell me—have you heard from him—recently?

TEKLA. Not for the last six months.

ADOLF. Do you ever think about him?

TEKLA. No. When our child died there was no further link between us.

ADOLF. And you haven't seen him anywhere?

TEKLA. No, he's said to be living somewhere on the west coast. But why are you worrying about all that now?

ADOLF. I don't know. But these last days, while I've been alone, I've found myself thinking how he must have felt, when he was left alone that time.

TEKLA. I believe you have a bad conscience.

ADOLF. I have.

TEKLA. I suppose you feel like a thief.

ADOLF. Pretty nearly.

TEKLA. That's beautiful! Men can steal women just as children and chickens are stolen. So you only think of me as one of his goods and chattels. Thank you very much.

ADOLF. No, I think of you as his wife. And that's more than property. It's something that can't be replaced.

TEKLA. Of course it can! If you were to hear he had married again, all those silly ideas would go out of your head. After all, haven't you replaced him in my life?

ADOLF. Have I? And did you love him once?

TEKLA. I most certainly did.

ADOLF. And then . . . ?

TEKLA. I got tired of him.

ADOLF. Supposing you were to get tired of me too.

TEKLA. I shan't do that.

ADOLF. Supposing somebody else came along who had the qualities you want in a man *now*. Then you'd give me up.

TEKLA. No.

ADOLF. Supposing he captivated you. So you couldn't give him up. Then you'd leave me, of course.

TEKLA. No, that's not true.

ADOLF. Surely you couldn't love two men at the same time.

TEKLA. Yes. Why not?

ADOLF. I don't understand.

TEKLA. Things can be, even though you don't understand them. All people are not made alike, you know.

ADOLF. Now I begin to see.

TEKLA. No, really?

ADOLF. No, really?

Pause. ADOLF *seems to be struggling with some memory he cannot grasp.*

Tekla, you know your frankness is beginning to trouble me.

TEKLA. But that used to be the virtue you put highest—and you taught it to me.

ADOLF. Yes, but it seems to me you're hiding something now behind your frankness.

TEKLA. That's the new tactics, you see.

ADOLF. I don't know why, but I'm beginning to dislike this place. If you don't mind, we'll go home—this evening.

TEKLA. What sort of whim is this? I've only just arrived. I don't want to start on another journey.

ADOLF. But I do.

TEKLA. What's it got to do with me what you want? You can go.

ADOLF. I command you to come with me by the next boat.

TEKLA. Command me! What sort of talk's that?

ADOLF. Do you realise that you are my wife?

TEKLA. Do you realise that you are my husband?

ADOLF. Yes, there's a difference between the one and the other.

TEKLA. So that's the line you're taking. You have never loved me.

ADOLF. Haven't I?

TEKLA. No, for to love is to give.

ADOLF. To love as a man is to give, but to love as a woman is to take. And I have given, given, given!

TEKLA. Oh? What have you given?

ADOLF. Everything.

TEKLA. That's a lot. And if it's so, then I've taken it. Are you giving me the bills for your gifts now? And if I have taken them, that's a proof that I loved you. A woman only takes gifts from her lover.

ADOLF. Her lover, yes. You used the right word. I have been your lover, but never your husband.

TEKLA. Well, isn't that much pleasanter—to escape being the chaperon? But if you're not satisfied with that position, you can take yourself off. I don't want a husband.

ADOLF. No, I've noticed that. And lately, when I've watched you sneaking away from me like a thief and making friends of your own, among whom you could flaunt my feathers and glitter with my jewels, I've tried to remind you of your debt. Then at once I became the unwelcome creditor whom one only wants to get rid of. You wanted to repudiate your notes of hand, and so as not to increase your debt to me, you stopped pillaging my treasure chest and started on other people's. I became your husband without wanting to be, and then you began to hate me. But now, as I mayn't be your lover, I am going to be your husband, whether you want it or not.

TEKLA, *playfully*. My sweet idiot, don't talk such nonsense!

ADOLF. You know it's risky to go round thinking everyone's an idiot but yourself.

TEKLA. Well, everyone does.

ADOLF. And I'm beginning to suspect that he—your former husband—possibly wasn't such an idiot after all.

TEKLA. O God, I believe you're beginning to sympathise with him!

ADOLF. A little bit, yes.

TEKLA. Well I never! Perhaps you would like to make his acquaintance and have a heart to heart. What a beautiful picture! But I'm beginning to be rather drawn to him too, as I'm tired of playing nursemaid. He was at least a man, although he had the disadvantage of being my husband.

ADOLF. Look here, don't talk so loud! People will hear us.

TEKLA. What does it matter if they take us for a married couple?

ADOLF. So now you're beginning to be infatuated by virile men and chaste youths all at the same time.

TEKLA. As you see, my infatuations haven't got any limits. My heart is open to everybody and everything, big and small, beautiful and ugly, young and old. I love the whole world.

ADOLF. Do you know what that means?

TEKLA. No, I don't know anything. I only feel.

ADOLF. It means that you are getting old.

TEKLA. There you go again! Take care!

ADOLF. Take care yourself!

TEKLA. What of?

ADOLF, *picking up one of his tools.* This knife.

TEKLA, *lightly.* You shouldn't play with such dangerous things, little brother.

ADOLF. I'm not playing now.

TEKLA. Oh, this is serious, is it? Dead serious. Then I'll show you—that you're under a delusion. That's to say, you'll never be able to see it, you'll never know it, but the whole rest of the world will know it, everyone but you. But you will suspect it; you will have a sense of it, and you will never have another moment's peace. You will feel that you're ridiculous, that you're deceived, but you'll never have proof of it—a married man never does have that. That's what you'll find out.

ADOLF. You hate me then?

TEKLA. No, I don't. And I don't believe I ever shall. But that
of course is because you are a child.

ADOLF. Now, yes. But do you remember how it was when the
storm broke over us? Then you would lie crying like a small
baby; then you would have to sit on my lap while I kissed
your eyes to sleep. It was I who was the nurse then. I had
to see that you didn't go out without doing your hair, had
to send your shoes to the cobbler and see that there was
food to cook. I had to sit by your side and hold your hand
for hours at a time. You were frightened, frightened of the
whole world, because you hadn't a single friend left and you
were crushed by public opinion. I had to talk courage into
you until my mouth was dry and my head ached. I had to
imagine I was strong and force myself to believe in the future. And at last I managed to bring you back to life, although you seemed half dead. Then you admired me. Then
I was the man—not the athlete you had left, but the man of
will-power. The mesmerist who instilled new energy into
your flabby muscles and charged your empty brain with
new electricity. And then I gave you back your reputation,
provided you with new friends, surrounded you with a little
court of people whom I tricked, out of their friendliness to
me, into admiring you. I set you over me and my house,
and then I painted my most beautiful pictures—rose-red and
azure blue against golden backgrounds, and there wasn't
one exhibition then where you did not hold the place of
honour. Sometimes you were St. Cecilia, sometimes Mary
Stuart, Karin Månsdotter,[2] or Ebba Brahe.[3] I made everyone interested in you and compelled the booing mob to see
you with my own infatuated vision. I plagued people with
your personality and forced you on them, till you had won
their all-important good opinion—and could stand on your
own feet. But by the time you could do that, my strength
was finished and I collapsed from exhaustion. In lifting you
up, I had overstrained myself. I was taken ill, and my illness infuriated you, coming now when at last life had begun

[2] Mistress, later wife, of Erik XIV of Sweden.
[3] Loved by King Gustavus Adolfus.

to smile on you. Sometimes, it seemed to me, you had a secret longing to be rid of your creditor and witness. . . . Your love begins to take on the character of an overbearing sister's, and for want of a better I have to learn the new part of little brother. Your tenderness remains; it even increases, but it has in it a suggestion of pity that's not far from contempt—and which changes into open scorn when my talent wanes and your sun rises. But somehow your fountain of inspiration seems to dry up when mine can no longer replenish it, or rather when you want to show that you don't draw on mine. And so both of us sink. And then you have to have somebody to blame. Somebody new. For you are weak and can never shoulder your own guilt. . . . So I became the scapegoat to be sacrificed alive. But when you cut my sinews, you didn't realise you were also crippling yourself, for the years had joined us as twins. You were an offshoot of my tree, but you tried to make your shoot grow before it had any roots. That's why you couldn't develop on your own. And my tree couldn't spare its vital branch—so both of them died.

TEKLA. What you mean to say by all this is that you wrote my books.

ADOLF. No, that's what *you* mean to say, so as to prove me a liar. I don't express myself as crudely as you do, and I have talked for these five minutes so as to get in all the half-tones and nuances and variations. But your barrel-organ has only one note.

TEKLA. Yes, yes, but the gist of it all is that you wrote my books.

ADOLF. There isn't any gist. You can't reduce a chord to a single note. You can't express a varied life in a single number. I didn't say anything so crude as that I wrote your books.

TEKLA. But that's what you meant.

ADOLF, *furiously*. That's not what I meant.

TEKLA. But the sum of it . . .

ADOLF, *distraught*. There can't be a sum if you don't add things up. If you divide and the figure doesn't go into the other one evenly, you get a quotient which is a long, un-ending, decimal fraction. I haven't added it up.

TEKLA. No, but I can add it up.

ADOLF. No doubt you can, but I haven't.

TEKLA. But you wanted to.

ADOLF, *exhausted, closing his eyes.* No, no, no! Don't talk to me any more! I shall have an attack. Be quiet! Go away! You destroy my brain with your clumsy pincers—you claw my thoughts and tear them to pieces.

ADOLF seems almost to lose consciousness and sits staring in front of him, rolling his thumbs.

TEKLA, *tenderly.* What is it? Adolf, are you ill?

He motions her away.

Adolf!

He shakes his head.

Adolf!

ADOLF. Yes?

TEKLA. Don't you think you were unfair just now?

ADOLF. Yes, yes, yes, yes, I admit it.

TEKLA. And do you apologise?

ADOLF. Yes, yes, yes, I apologise. If only you won't talk to me.

TEKLA. Then kiss my hand.

ADOLF, *kissing her hand.* I'll kiss your hand. If only you won't talk to me.

TEKLA. And now go out and get some fresh air before dinner.

ADOLF. I certainly need it. *Rises.* And then we'll pack and go.

TEKLA. No.

ADOLF. Why not? There must be some reason.

TEKLA. I've promised to go to the concert tonight. That's the reason.

ADOLF. Oh, so that's it!

TEKLA. That's it. I've promised to be there and . . .

ADOLF. Promised? I expect you only said you might go. That doesn't stop you from saying now that you can't.

TEKLA. No, unlike you, I keep my word.

ADOLF. One can keep one's promise without having to stand by every casual word one says. Perhaps someone made you promise to go.

TEKLA. Yes.

ADOLF. Even so, you can be released from your promise, as your husband is ill.

TEKLA. No, I don't want to be. And you aren't so ill that you can't come with me.

ADOLF. Why do you always want to have me with you? Do you feel more at ease then?

TEKLA. I don't know what you mean.

ADOLF. That's what you always say when you know I mean something you don't like.

TEKLA. Really? What is it I don't like now?

ADOLF. Stop it, will you! Don't start that again! Goodbye for the moment. And think what you are doing.

Exit ADOLF *by the door to the verandah, turning to the right.* TEKLA *is left alone.*

After a moment GUSTAV *enters and goes straight to the table, as if looking for a newspaper. He pretends not to see* TEKLA. *She is agitated but controls herself.*

TEKLA. Is it you?

GUSTAV. It is I. Please excuse me.

TEKLA. How did you get here?

GUSTAV. By land. But I'm not going to stay. I . . .

TEKLA. Do stay. . . . Well, it's been a long time.

GUSTAV. Yes, a long time.

TEKLA. You have changed a lot.

GUSTAV. And you are as charming as ever. And even younger. But you must excuse me. I am not going to spoil your happiness by my presence. If I had known you would be here, I should never . . .

TEKLA. If you don't think it's improper, I should like you to stay.

GUSTAV. There's nothing against it from my point of view, but I'm afraid whatever I say is bound to offend you.

TEKLA. Sit down for a moment. You won't offend me. You have that rare quality—you always had it—of tact and courtesy. . . .

GUSTAV. You flatter me. But one can't expect your husband to regard my qualities so leniently.

TEKLA. As a matter of fact, he was expressing his sympathy for you just now.

GUSTAV. Oh? Well, of course everything vanishes in time—like one's name cut in a tree. Even hatred can't stay in one's mind for ever.

TEKLA. He has never disliked you. How could he when he's never seen you? And as for me, I've always dreamt of seeing you two once as friends, or at least of seeing you meet once in my presence, shake hands, and part.

GUSTAV. And it has been my secret desire to see if she whom I loved better than my life was in truly good hands. I have certainly heard good accounts of him and I know his work well, but even so I should have liked, before I grew old, to take his hand and look into his eyes and beg him to guard the treasure providence has put into his keeping. At the same time I should have liked to put an end to the instinctive hatred there was bound to be between us, and give my soul some peace and humility to live by for the rest of my sorrowful days.

TEKLA. You have spoken my very thoughts. You have understood me. Thank you for that.

GUSTAV. Oh, I am a poor man—I was too insignificant ever to put you in the shade. The monotony of my life, the drudgery of my work, and the narrowness of my horizon were not for your adventurous spirit. I realise that, but you, who have studied the human soul so deeply, must realise what it cost me to confess this to myself.

TEKLA. It is noble, it is great to be able to acknowledge one's own weaknesses, and not everyone is capable of it. *Sighs.* But yours was always an honest, faithful, trustworthy nature —which I respected, although . . .

GUSTAV. I wasn't like that then—not at that time—but suffering purifies one, sorrow ennobles one—and I have suffered.

TEKLA. Poor Gustav! Can you forgive me? Tell me. Can you?

GUSTAV. Forgive you? What are you saying? It is for me to ask your forgiveness.

TEKLA, *fencing.* Why, I believe we're both crying. At our age!

GUSTAV, *parrying.* Our age! Ah yes, I am old! But you get younger and younger.

Unobtrusively he sits down on the chair, left, whereupon TEKLA *seats herself on the sofa.*

TEKLA. Do you think so?

GUSTAV. And you know how to dress.

TEKLA. I learnt that from you. Don't you remember how you found the best colours for me?

GUSTAV. No.

TEKLA. Yes. Don't you remember? Hm, I even remember a time when you were cross with me if I didn't wear some touch of scarlet.

GUSTAV. I wasn't cross. I was never cross with you.

TEKLA. Oh yes, you were! When you tried to teach me how to think. Don't you remember that? I couldn't do it at all.

GUSTAV. Of course you could think. Everyone can do that. And now you are quite intelligent—in your writing at least.

TEKLA *is embarrassed and rushes on with the conversation.*

TEKLA. It's delightful to see you again anyway, dear Gustav. Specially in such a peaceful way.

GUSTAV. Well, I never was exactly rowdy. You always had a peaceful time with me.

TEKLA. Yes, a bit too peaceful.

GUSTAV. Oh! But you see that's how I thought you wanted me to be. That's how it seemed when we were engaged.

TEKLA. One doesn't know what one wants then. Besides, I'd been told by Mamma to make a good impression on you.

GUSTAV. Well, you live in a whirl now. The artistic life is always dazzling, and your husband doesn't seem to be exactly lethargic.

TEKLA. One can have too much of a good thing, you know.

GUSTAV, *once again changing his tactics.* I say! I do believe you are still wearing my earrings.

TEKLA, *embarrassed.* Well, why shouldn't I? We've never quarrelled—so I thought I might wear them as a token . . . as a reminder that we were not enemies. . . . Besides, you know, it's impossible to get earrings like this nowadays. *She takes one off.*

GUSTAV. That's all very well, but what does your husband say about it?

TEKLA. Why should I care what he says?

GUSTAV. Don't you care? But you do him a wrong by that. It could make him ridiculous.

TEKLA, *quickly, as if to herself.* He is that already.

She has difficulty in putting her earring on again.

GUSTAV *rises.*

GUSTAV. Perhaps you'll let me help you . . .

TEKLA. Thank you so much.

Putting the earring on, GUSTAV *pinches her ear.*

GUSTAV. Supposing your husband could see us now!

TEKLA. Yes, what a wail there would be!

GUSTAV. He's very jealous then?

TEKLA. Jealous? I should say he is.

Sounds from the adjacent room.

GUSTAV. Who has that room next door?

TEKLA. I don't know. . . . Well, tell me how you are getting along and what you are doing.

GUSTAV. Tell me how *you* are getting along.

Trying to think how to answer, TEKLA *inadvertently uncovers the wax figure.*

I say! Whoever's that? By Jove, it's you!

TEKLA. I don't think so.

GUSTAV. Well, it's just like you.

TEKLA, *cynically.* In your view.

GUSTAV. That reminds me of the story . . . "How could Your Majesty see that?"

TEKLA *bursts out laughing.*

TEKLA. You're impossible! Do you know any new stories?

GUSTAV. No, but surely you should.

TEKLA. Oh, I never hear anything funny now!

GUSTAV. Is he prudish?

TEKLA. Well—in speech he is.

GUSTAV. But not in—other ways?

TEKLA. He's not well just now.

GUSTAV. Poor dear! But little brother shouldn't go poking his nose into other people's wasps'-nests.

TEKLA, *laughing.* You're quite impossible!

GUSTAV. Do you remember once, when we were newly married, we stayed in this very room? Eh? It was furnished differently then. There was a chest of drawers against that wall, and the bed was over there . . .

TEKLA. Stop it!

GUSTAV. Look at me!

TEKLA. Well, that I can do.

They gaze at one another.

GUSTAV. Do you think one can forget something that has made a very deep impression?

TEKLA. No. Memories have tremendous power. Specially youthful ones.

GUSTAV. Do you remember when I first met you? You were a charming little girl—a small slate on which parents and governesses had made some scrawls, which I had to wipe off. Then I wrote new texts to suit my own ideas, until you felt your slate was full. That's why, you see, I shouldn't like to be in your husband's place—but that's his business. It's also why I have so much pleasure in seeing you again. Our thoughts match so well. Sitting here talking with you is like opening bottles of old wine of my own tapping. Yes, I have my own wine again, but it has matured. And now that I have a fancy to marry again, I have purposely chosen a young girl, whom I can educate to my own way of thinking. For the woman, you see, is the man's child, and if she is not, he becomes hers, and that makes a topsy-turvy world.

TEKLA. You're going to marry again?

GUSTAV. Yes, I mean to tempt fortune once more, but this time I shall harness the mare better, so she won't bolt.

TEKLA. Is she pretty?

GUSTAV. To me she is. But I may be too old. And curiously enough, now that chance has brought you and me together once more, I am beginning to doubt if it is possible to play that game again.

TEKLA. How do you mean?

GUSTAV. I feel that my roots are still in your soil, and the old wounds are opening. You are a dangerous woman, Tekla!

TEKLA. Oh! But my young husband says I shan't be able to make any more conquests.

GUSTAV. In other words, he no longer loves you.

TEKLA. I don't understand what he means by love.

GUSTAV. You have played hide-and-seek so long that now you can't find each other. That's what happens. You have gone on playing the innocent until now he doesn't dare. . . . Yes, you see, change has its disadvantages. It has its disadvantages.

TEKLA. Is that a reproach?

GUSTAV. By no means. To a certain extent, whatever happens has to happen. If it didn't happen, something else would. This did happen and there it is.

TEKLA. What an enlightened man you are! I have never met anyone with whom I so much liked exchanging ideas. You are so free from moralising and preaching, and make so few demands on people, that one feels at ease in your company. You know, I'm jealous of your wife to be.

GUSTAV. You know, I'm jealous of your husband.

TEKLA, *rising*. And now we must part. For ever.

GUSTAV. Yes, we must part. But not without taking leave. Eh?

TEKLA, *uneasily*. No.

GUSTAV, *following her*. Yes! We must take leave of each other. We must drown our memories in an intoxication so deep that when we wake we shall have forgotten those memories. There is such an intoxication, you know. *Puts his arm round her.* You have been dragged down by a sick soul who has infected you with his own disease. I will breathe new life into you. I will make your talent bloom again like an autumn rose. I will . . .

TWO LADIES *in travelling dress come on to the verandah. Seeing the couple, they look surprised, point at them, laugh, and go off.*

TEKLA, *freeing herself.* Who was that?

GUSTAV, *indifferently.* Some visitors.

TEKLA. Go away! I'm frightened of you.

GUSTAV. Why?

TEKLA. You take away my soul.

GUSTAV. And give you mine in exchange. Anyhow, you haven't got a soul. That's just an illusion.

TEKLA. You say the most impertinent things in a way that makes it impossible to be angry with you.

GUSTAV. That's because you know I have the first mortgage. Now tell me. When and where?

TEKLA. No. It wouldn't be fair on him. He really does still love me, and I don't want to do any more harm.

GUSTAV. He doesn't love you. Do you want proof of it?

TEKLA. How could you give me that?

GUSTAV *picks up the pieces of photograph from the floor.*

GUSTAV. Here you are. See for yourself.

TEKLA. Oh, this is scandalous!

GUSTAV. You see for yourself. So . . . when and where?

TEKLA. The deceitful wretch!

GUSTAV. When?

TEKLA. He is going tonight by the eight o'clock boat.

GUSTAV. Then . . .

TEKLA. Nine o'clock.

Noises from the room are heard.

Whoever can have taken that room and be making such a din?

GUSTAV. Let's see. *Peers through the key-hole.* A table has

been overturned and a water carafe smashed. That's all.
Perhaps they have shut up a dog in there. . . . Nine o'clock
then.

TEKLA. Very well. He has only himself to blame. . . . To
think of him being so false, when he's always preaching hon-
esty and making me tell the truth. . . . But wait a moment
. . . How was it? . . . He received me rather coldly—he
didn't come down to the jetty—and then he said something
about the youths on the boat, which I pretended not to take
in. . . . But how could he have known about them? . . .
Wait a minute . . . After that he began philosophising
about women—and you seemed to be haunting him. . . .
And then he talked about becoming a sculptor, and how
sculpture was the art of today—just as you used to say once.

GUSTAV. No, really?

TEKLA. No, really! Ah, now I understand! Now I begin to see
what an absolute monster you are. You have been here
stabbing him to death. It was you who had been sitting
on the sofa. It was you who made him think he had
epilepsy and must live as a celibate—and that he must show
he was a man by taking a stand against his wife. Yes, it
was you! How long have you been here?

GUSTAV. I have been here for a week.

TEKLA. So it *was* you I saw on the boat.

GUSTAV. It was me.

TEKLA. And then you thought you would trap me.

GUSTAV. I have done so.

TEKLA. Not yet.

GUSTAV. Yes.

TEKLA. You stole on my lamb like a wolf. You came here with
a fiendish scheme to destroy my happiness, and you were
carrying it out when my eyes were opened and I foiled it.

GUSTAV. It wasn't quite as you say. This is what actually happened. I admit I had a secret hope things would go wrong
with you, but I was pretty certain no interference on my
part would be needed. Besides, I was too much taken up
with other things to have time for intriguing. Then, when
I happened to be away and at a loose end, I saw you on the

boat with those young men, and I decided the time had come to have a look at you. I came here, and your lamb immediately threw himself into the arms of the wolf. I won his sympathy through a kind of reflex action I won't be so discourteous as to try and explain. At first I was sorry for him, as he seemed to be in the same fix as I once was. But then he began to probe old wounds—the book, you know, and the idiot—and I was seized with the desire to pull him to pieces and mix the pieces up so thoroughly that he could never be put together again. And thanks to your conscientious groundwork, I succeeded. But I still had you to deal with. You were the mainspring of the works and had to be twisted to bits. What a buzz! When I came in here, I didn't really know what I was going to say. I had various schemes, but as in chess, my play depended on your moves. One thing led to another, chance helped, and so I had you ditched. Now you're caught.

TEKLA. No.

GUSTAV. Yes, you are. The last thing you wanted has happened. The world—in the guise of two lady travellers, whom I did not send for, being no intriguer—the world has seen you reconciled with your former husband, creeping repentantly back into his faithful arms. Isn't that enough?

TEKLA. It should be enough for your revenge. But tell me, you who are so enlightened and just, how can you, who think whatever happens has to happen and we are not free to act . . .

GUSTAV, *correcting her.* Not entirely free.

TEKLA. It's the same thing.

GUSTAV. No.

TEKLA. . . . how can you, who hold me guiltless since I was driven by my nature and the circumstances to behave as I did, how can you believe you have any cause for revenge?

GUSTAV. For that very reason. Because my nature and the circumstances drove me to seek revenge. Which makes it quits, doesn't it? But do you know why you two were bound to get the worst of it in this fight?

TEKLA *looks scornful.*

And why you let yourselves be tricked? Because I'm stronger than you and wiser too. It's you who have been the idiot —and so has he. And now you can see that one isn't necessarily an idiot because one doesn't write novels or paint pictures. Bear that in mind.

TEKLA. Have you no feelings at all?

GUSTAV. None. That's why I can think, you know, a process of which you have little experience. And act—as you have recently discovered.

TEKLA. All this merely because I wounded your vanity!

GUSTAV. There's no *merely* about that. You'd better stop wounding people's vanity. It's their most vulnerable spot.

TEKLA. You vindictive creature! Shame on you!

GUSTAV. You wanton creature! Shame on you!

TEKLA. It's my nature, isn't it?

GUSTAV. It's *my* nature, isn't it? One should learn something of human nature in general before giving one's own nature free rein. Otherwise one may get hurt, and then what a wailing and gnashing of teeth!

TEKLA. Can't you ever forgive?

GUSTAV. Yes. I have forgiven you.

TEKLA. Have you?

GUSTAV. Certainly. Have I lifted a finger against you in all these years? No. And now I only came here to have a look at you—and then you went to pieces. Have I reproached you or moralised or preached? No. I played a bit of a joke on your spouse and that was enough to burst his bubble. And now here am I, the plaintiff, defending myself. Tekla, have you nothing to reproach yourself with?

TEKLA. Nothing at all. Christians say our actions are ruled by providence, and others call it fate. So we're guiltless, aren't we?

GUSTAV. Up to a point, yes. But there's always a place where the guilt creeps in. And the creditors present themselves sooner or later. Guiltless but responsible. Guiltless before Him, who no longer exists. Responsible to oneself and one's fellow creatures.

TEKLA. So you came here to dun me.

GUSTAV. I came here to recover what you had stolen, not what you had had as a gift. You stole my honour and I could only regain it by taking yours. Wasn't that my right?

TEKLA. Honour! Hm! Well, are you satisfied now?

GUSTAV. Yes, I am satisfied. *Rings the bell.*

TEKLA. And now you are going home to your fiancée.

GUSTAV. I have no fiancée. And I shall never have one. And I am not going home, for I have no home. Nor do I want one.

A WAITER *enters.*

Will you bring my bill, please. I am leaving by the eight o'clock boat.

The WAITER *bows and goes out.*

TEKLA. Without atonement?

GUSTAV. Atonement? You use so many words that have lost their meaning. Atonement? Are we perhaps all three to live together? It's you who should do the atoning, by making good my losses—but you can't. You did nothing but take, and what you took you have devoured, so you can't return it. Will it satisfy you if I say: Forgive me for your having clawed my heart to pieces. Forgive me for your having disgraced me. Forgive me for having been the daily laughing-stock of my pupils for seven years. Forgive me for setting you free from the domination of your parents, for releasing you from the tyranny of ignorance and superstition, for setting you over my house, for giving you friends and a position, for making a woman of the mere child you were. Forgive me, as I forgive you! . . . So, I have cancelled my note of hand. Now go and settle your account with the other one.

TEKLA. What have you done with him? I'm beginning to suspect—something terrible.

GUSTAV. Done with him? Why, do you love him?

TEKLA. Yes.

GUSTAV. Just now it was me. Was that true?

TEKLA. It was true.

GUSTAV. Do you know what you are then?

TEKLA. You despise me?

GUSTAV. I pity you. It's a trait—I don't say a fault but a trait —which has disastrous consequences. Poor Tekla! Do you know I feel almost remorseful, although I am as free from guilt as—as you are. But perhaps you will enjoy knowing just how I felt that time. . . . Do you know where your husband is?

TEKLA. I think now I do know. . . . He is in that room there. And he has heard everything. And seen everything. And he who sees his familiar spirit dies.

ADOLF *appears in the verandah doorway. He is white as a corpse. There is a bleeding scratch on one cheek. His eyes are staring without expression and he is frothing at the mouth.*

GUSTAV, *backing.* Well, there he is! Settle up with him now and see if he is as generous as I have been. . . . Goodbye.

GUSTAV *goes towards the other room and stops.*

TEKLA *runs to* ADOLF *with arms outstretched.*

TEKLA. Adolf!

ADOLF *leans against the verandah door and collapses on the floor.*

TEKLA *throws herself across his body, caressing him.*

TEKLA. Adolf! My darling child! Are you still alive? Oh speak, speak! Forgive your wicked Tekla! Forgive, forgive, forgive! You must answer me, little brother. Can you hear? . . . No, O my God, he doesn't hear! He is dead. O God in heaven! O God, help us, help us!

GUSTAV. She really does love him too. Poor creature!

CRIME AND CRIME

A Comedy

FOREWORD

Crime and Crime was written early in 1899. Although the play is set in Paris, it was now four years since Strindberg, after the terrible ordeals there, described in *Inferno,* had returned to live in Sweden. He refers to *Advent,* the play preceding *Crime and Crime,* as a Swedenborgian drama, and this treats mystically of sin and retribution. In *Crime and Crime* Strindberg further develops the Swedenborgian view that crime is its own punishment; but this time the treatment is realistic, and the play is something of a psychological thriller at one level and a spiritual adventure at a deeper one. It is extremely autobiographical: the scenes set in places Strindberg himself frequented, and the hero a playwright, with much of his own strange temperament, at the moment of his first brilliant success in the Paris theatre. Although Maurice's play is spoken of as redeeming slandered human nature, which could not be said of *The Father,* even if true of some of the later plays, Strindberg was certainly thinking of the fame which came to him overnight with the first performance of *The Father* in Antoine's Théâtre Libre. And the sense of guilt and mutual torture dominating *Crime and Crime* were among Strindberg's deepest obsessions, as was too belief in the destructive power of evil thought. During the *Inferno* period he had practised black magic and believed that he had once caused the illness of one of his children, although he had not actually, like Maurice, "wished the life out of" the child.

Madame Cathérine, Henriette, and the Abbé all have their origins in people who played a part in Strindberg's Paris life. He called *Crime and Crime* his "boulevard" play, and surely its swift action and dialogue were influenced by the French theatre. Although Strindberg never again lived there, his attachment to France remained, and he continued to correspond with Antoine, Lugné Poë, and other Frenchmen connected with literature and the theatre.

E. S.

CHARACTERS

MAURICE, *a playwright*
JEANNE, *his mistress*
MARION, *their daughter, aged five*
EMILE, *Jeanne's brother, a workman*
ADOLPHE, *an artist*
HENRIETTE, *his mistress*
MADAME CATHÉRINE, *proprietress of the Crémerie*
THE ABBÉ
A KEEPER, *in the Cemetery*
THE WOMAN, *in the Cemetery* (*non-speaking*)
THE COMMISSAIRE
FIRST DETECTIVE
SECOND DETECTIVE
THE HEAD WAITER (*non-speaking*)
A WAITER
A KEEPER, *in the Luxembourg Gardens*
A SERVING GIRL

The whole action of the play takes place in Paris in the nineties

ACT I

SCENE 1

SCENE: *The upper end of the cypress avenue in the cemetery at Montparnasse. Seen in the background are burial chapels and stone crosses bearing the inscription:* O Crux! Ave spes unica! *Also the ivy-clad ruin of a windmill.*

A well-dressed WOMAN *in mourning is kneeling beside a flower-decked grave, murmuring prayers.*

JEANNE *is walking to and fro, as if expecting somebody.*

MARION *is playing with some withered flowers she has picked up from a rubbish heap on the path.*

The ABBÉ *is walking at the far end of the avenue, reading his breviary.*

The KEEPER *enters.*

KEEPER, *to* JEANNE. Look here, this isn't a playground.

JEANNE, *meekly.* I'm only waiting for someone who's bound to be here soon. . . .

KEEPER. That's as it may be, but no one's allowed to take any flowers. . . .

JEANNE, *to* MARION. Put the flowers down, dear.

The ABBÉ *approaches and is saluted by the* KEEPER.

ABBÉ. But, Keeper, surely the child may play with those flowers which have been thrown away?

KEEPER. The regulations forbid anyone to touch any flowers, even those that have been thrown away. They are supposed to be contagious—whether it's true or not.

ABBÉ, *to* MARION. In that case, there is nothing for us to do but obey. What is your name, my little friend?

MARION. I'm called Marion.

ABBÉ. And what is your papa's name?

MARION *bites her fingers and does not answer.*

The KEEPER *goes out.*

To JEANNE. Pardon my question, Madame. I did not mean to intrude. I was simply talking to calm the little girl.

JEANNE. I realised that at once, Reverend Father, and I was wishing you would say something to calm me too, for I am very troubled after waiting here for two whole hours.

ABBÉ. Two hours—for him? How human beings can torture one another! *O Crux! Ave spes unica!*

JEANNE. Yes, what do they mean—those words which are written all over this place?

ABBÉ. They mean: O Cross! Our only hope!

JEANNE. Is it our only one?

ABBÉ. Our only sure one.

JEANNE. I shall soon believe that you are right, Father.

ABBÉ. May I ask why?

JEANNE. You have already guessed. When a man keeps a woman and child waiting for two hours in a cemetery, the end is not far off.

ABBÉ. And when he does abandon you, what then?

JEANNE. The river.

ABBÉ. Ah, no, no!

JEANNE. Yes, yes!

MARION. I want to go home, Mamma. I'm hungry.

JEANNE. Be patient just a little longer, my darling, and then we will go.

ABBÉ. Woe, woe upon them who call evil good and good evil!

JEANNE. What is that woman doing at that grave?

ABBÉ. She appears to be talking to the dead.

JEANNE. But can you do that?

ABBÉ. She seems to be able to.

JEANNE. Then won't there be an end to the misery even when this is over?

ABBÉ. Do you not know that?

JEANNE. Where can you find out?

ABBÉ. Hm! Next time you feel you need some enlightenment on this well-known question, come and find me in the Chapel of Our Lady in the Church of Saint-Germain. *Looking off.* Here comes, surely, the one you are expecting.

JEANNE, *embarrassed.* It's not him, but I know this one too.

ABBÉ, *to* MARION. Goodbye, little Marion. May God keep you! *Kisses the child. To* JEANNE. In Saint Germain-des-Prés.

Exit the ABBÉ.

Enter EMILE.

EMILE. Why, Sister, what are you doing here?

JEANNE. Waiting for Maurice.

EMILE. Then you'll have to wait a long time, for I saw him lunching on the boulevard with some friends an hour ago. And how's dear little Marion? *Kisses the child.*

JEANNE. Were there women with him?

EMILE. Yes, of course, but that doesn't mean anything. He writes plays and his new one's opening tonight. They were probably some of his actresses.

JEANNE. Did he recognise you?

EMILE. No. He doesn't know who I am and there's no reason why he should. I know my place as a workman and I don't want any favours from those above me.

JEANNE. But suppose he leaves us high and dry?

EMILE. Now, look, when that happens it will be time enough for me to introduce myself. But surely you don't expect anything of the kind, because he really thinks the world of you, and above all he's set on the child.

JEANNE. I don't know—I just feel something frightful is going to happen to me.

EMILE. Has he promised to marry you?

JEANNE. No, he hasn't promised, but he's led me to hope.

EMILE. Hope, eh? Don't you remember what I said at the start? Don't hope, for those on top don't marry beneath them.

JEANNE. But it does happen.

EMILE. Of course it does. But would you be happy in his set? I bet you wouldn't—you wouldn't even understand what they were talking about. I eat there sometimes—in the kitchen—at the place he has his meals, and I can't make out a word they say.

JEANNE. Really, you eat there?

EMILE. Yes, in the kitchen.

JEANNE. To think he's never invited me there.

EMILE. You can give him credit for that. It shows he has some respect for Marion's mother, for the ladies who go there are a queer lot.

JEANNE. Oh . . . !

EMILE. But Maurice doesn't bother with the ladies. No, there's something *straight* about that chap.

JEANNE. I think so too, but when a woman comes along, men lose their heads.

EMILE, *smiling*. You're telling me. But listen. Are you short of money?

JEANNE. No, not that.

EMILE. Then all's well so far. Look! Over there, down the avenue. There he comes! And I'll be on my way. Goodbye, little girl.

JEANNE. Is he coming? Yes, it is him.

EMILE, *going*. Now don't drive him crazy with your jealousy, Jeanne.

JEANNE. Of course I won't.

Exit EMILE.

Enter MAURICE.

MARION *runs to him and he catches her up in his arms.*

MARION. Papa, Papa!

MAURICE. My pet, my darling! *Turning to* JEANNE. Jeanne, can you forgive me for keeping you waiting so long? Can you?

JEANNE. Of course I can.

MAURICE. But say it so I can hear that you forgive me.

JEANNE. Come here and I'll whisper it to you.

MAURICE *comes close to her.*

JEANNE *kisses him on the cheek.*

MAURICE. I didn't hear.

JEANNE *kisses him on the mouth.*

I heard then. . . . Well . . . I suppose you know this is the day on which my fate will be decided. My play is to be presented and has every chance of success—or failure.

JEANNE. I'll pray for you; then you'll have a success.

MAURICE. Thank you. Even if that doesn't help, it can't do any harm. . . . Look down there in the valley, in the sun haze. There lies Paris. Today Paris does not know who Maurice is, but within twenty-four hours it will know. The cloud of smoke which has hidden me for thirty years will disperse as I blow upon it, and I shall be seen. I shall take shape and begin to be somebody. My enemies, that's to say all those who wish they could do what I have done, will writhe with pain, and that will give me pleasure—to see them suffering what I have suffered.

JEANNE. Don't talk like that, don't!

MAURICE. But that's how it is.

JEANNE. Yes, but don't talk about it. . . . And then?

MAURICE. Then we'll be in clover, and you and Marion will bear the name I have made famous.

JEANNE. You do love me then?

MAURICE. I love you both, one as much as the other, or Marion even a little more.

JEANNE. I'm glad of that, for you may tire of me, but not of her.

MAURICE. You don't trust my feeling for you?

JEANNE. I don't know, but I'm afraid of something, something terrible. . . .

MAURICE. You're tired and depressed by this long wait. Once more, please forgive me. What have you to be afraid of?

JEANNE. The unknown—that you can have a presentiment about without a real reason.

MAURICE. Well, the only presentiment I have is—success, and

with real reasons: the sure instincts of theatre folk and their experience of the public, not to mention their personal acquaintance with the critics. So now you must be calm and . . .

JEANNE. I can't, I can't! Do you know, there was an Abbé here just now who talked so kindly to us. You haven't wiped out my faith, but you have smeared it over like when you whiten windows, so I couldn't get at it. But this old man passed his hand over the chalk and the light came through, and you could see again that the family was at home inside. I shall pray for you this evening in Saint-Germain.

MAURICE. Now it's I who am frightened.

JEANNE. Fear of God is the beginning of wisdom.

MAURICE. God? What is that? Who is He?

JEANNE. He who gave joy to your youth and strength to your manhood. And it is He who will support us in the terrors that lie ahead.

MAURICE. What lies ahead? What do you know? Where have you learnt this? This that I don't know.

JEANNE. I can't tell. I haven't dreamt anything, seen anything, heard anything. But during these two dreadful hours, I have lived through such an eternity of pain that I am ready for the very worst.

MARION. I want to go home now, Mamma. I'm hungry.

MAURICE. You shall go home, my darling. *Hugs her.*

MARION, *whimpering.* Oh, you hurt me, Papa!

JEANNE. We must go home to dinner. So goodbye, Maurice. And good luck!

MAURICE, *to* MARION. How could I hurt you? You know I only want to be kind to my little girl.

MARION. Come home with us then, if you're kind.

MAURICE, *to* JEANNE. You know, when I hear the child talk like that, I feel I ought to do as she says. But then reason and duty step in. . . . Goodbye, little daughter.

He kisses the child, who puts her arms round his neck.

JEANNE. When do we meet again?

MAURICE. Tomorrow, my dear, we shall meet. And never more to part.

JEANNE *embraces him.*

JEANNE. Never, never more to part.

She makes the sign of the cross on his forehead.

May God keep you!

MAURICE, *moved in spite of himself.* My own beloved Jeanne!

JEANNE *and* MARION *move right.*

MAURICE *moves left.*

Both turn at the same moment and kiss hands to one another.

Turning back. Jeanne, I'm ashamed of myself. I'm always forgetting you, and you are the last to remind me. Here is your ticket for tonight.

JEANNE. Thank you, my dear, but—you must be at your post alone, and I shall be at mine—with Marion.

MAURICE. Your wisdom is as great as your goodness of heart. Yes, I swear no other woman would sacrifice a pleasure in order to do her man a service. I need to be quite free tonight, and a man doesn't take his wife and children to the battlefield with him. This you understood.

JEANNE. Maurice, don't think too highly of a simple woman like me, then you won't have to lose your illusions. . . . And now you will see I am as forgetful as you were. Here is a tie and a pair of gloves I've bought you. I thought you might do me the honour of wearing them on your great day.

MAURICE, *kissing her hand.* Thank you, my love.

JEANNE. And then, Maurice, don't forget, as you so often do, to go to the barber. I want you to look handsome, so that others will like you too.

MAURICE. You aren't jealous at all, are you?

JEANNE. Don't use that word. It rouses bad thoughts.

MAURICE. Do you know, at this moment I could forego tonight's victory—yes, it will be a victory. . . .

JEANNE. Hush, hush, hush!

MAURICE. And come home with you.

JEANNE. But you mustn't. Go! Your fate is waiting for you.

MAURICE. Goodbye then. And let come what may.

Exit MAURICE.

JEANNE, *alone with* MARION. *O Crux! Ave spes unica!*

SCENE 2

SCENE: *The Crémerie. The same afternoon.*

Right, a buffet, on which stands an aquarium containing goldfish, a palm, vegetables, fruits, preserves, etc.

Back, a door to the kitchen, where workmen are gathered, with a further door to the garden.

Left, a raised counter and shelves holding many kinds of bottles.

Down right, one long marble-topped table against the wall, and another parallel with it, nearer in. Wicker chairs stand beside the tables. The walls are covered with paintings.

MADAME CATHÉRINE *is sitting at the counter.*

MAURICE *is leaning against the counter with his hat on, smoking a cigarette.*

MME CATHÉRINE. So tonight the balloon goes up for you, eh, Monsieur Maurice?

MAURICE. Yes, tonight.

MME CATHÉRINE. Are you nervous?

MAURICE. Cool as a cucumber.

MME CATHÉRINE. Well, I wish you luck, you deserve it, Monsieur Maurice, after fighting difficulties such as yours.

MAURICE. Thank you, Madame Cathérine. You have been very kind to me. Without your help, by now I'd be down and out.

MME CATHÉRINE. We won't talk about that now. Where I see hard work and the will to get on, I help, though, mind you, I don't like to be exploited. . . . Can we trust you to come back here when the play's over and let us drink a glass of wine with you?

MAURICE. Of course you can trust me. I've already given you my promise.

Enter HENRIETTE, *right.*

MAURICE *turns, raises his hat, and gazes at* HENRIETTE, *who regards him appraisingly.*

HENRIETTE, *to* MME CATHÉRINE. Isn't Monsieur Adolphe here?

MME CATHÉRINE. No, Madame. But he will be here soon. Please take a seat.

HENRIETTE. Thank you. But I would prefer to wait for him outside.

Exit HENRIETTE.

MAURICE. Who . . . was . . . that?

MME CATHÉRINE. That was Monsieur Adolphe's lady friend.

MAURICE. Was . . . that . . . she?

MME CATHÉRINE. Haven't you ever seen her before?

MAURICE. No, he has been hiding her from me, just as if he were afraid I would take her from him.

MME CATHÉRINE. Aha! Well, what do you think of her looks?

MAURICE. Her looks? Let me see. I don't know . . . I didn't see her, for it was as if she had flown straight into my arms. She came so close that I had no view. And she left her impression on the air. I can still see her standing there.

He goes towards the door and mimes putting his arm round someone's waist.

Ow! *Mimes having pricked his finger.* She has pins in her waistband. She is one of the kind that stings.

MME CATHÉRINE, *smiling.* You and your ladies—you're crazy!

MAURICE. Yes, I'm crazy, crazy! But I tell you what, Madame Cathérine—I'm going to leave before she comes back, for if I don't, if I don't . . . Oh, she is a terrible woman!

MME CATHÉRINE. Are you scared?

MAURICE. Yes, I'm scared for myself and scared for some others . . .

MME CATHÉRINE. Well then, go.

MAURICE. Listen. When she drifted out of that door, it made a little whirlwind which sucked me in too. . . . You may laugh, but look how that palm on the buffet is still trembling! She is a devil of a woman.

MME CATHÉRINE. Well then, go, my dear man, before you're
stark staring mad.

MAURICE. I want to go, but I can't. . . . Do you believe in
destiny, Madame Cathérine?

MME CATHÉRINE. No, I believe in the good God, who protects
us from evil powers, if we ask Him nicely.

MAURICE. So, anyway there are evil powers. . . . Isn't it *them*
I hear in the entrance now?

MME CATHÉRINE. It certainly is. She rustles so much it's like
the draper tearing off a length of material. Go on! Get out!
Through the kitchen.

MAURICE *dashes to the kitchen door and collides with* EMILE
coming out.

EMILE. A thousand pardons! *Backs into the kitchen, shutting
the door.*

Enter ADOLPHE, *followed by* HENRIETTE.

ADOLPHE. Why, there's Maurice! Good day to you! Let me
introduce you! My dear friend, Mademoiselle Henriette, and
my oldest and best friend, Monsieur Maurice.

MAURICE, *bowing stiffly.* Enchanted.

HENRIETTE. We have seen one another before.

ADOLPHE. Really? But when, if I may ask?

MAURICE. Just now. In here.

ADOLPHE. Oh, I see! Well, now you mustn't go until we've
had a talk.

MME CATHÉRINE *signals to* MAURICE.

MAURICE. I only wish I had time.

ADOLPHE. Make time. We are not staying long.

HENRIETTE. I won't disturb you, if you gentlemen want to talk
business.

MAURICE. Any business we have is too bad to talk about.

HENRIETTE. Then we'll talk about something else.

She takes MAURICE'S *hat and hangs it up.*

Be kind now and let me make the acquaintance of the great
author.

MME CATHÉRINE *signs to* MAURICE, *but he pays no attention.*

ADOLPHE. That's right, Henriette, you take him prisoner.

They seat themselves at a table.

HENRIETTE, *to* MAURICE. You certainly have a good friend in Adolphe, Monsieur Maurice. He never talks about anything but you, so much so that I often feel quite put in the shade.

ADOLPHE. I like that! I may tell you, Maurice, that Henriette doesn't give me a moment's peace about you. She has read everything you have written and is always wanting to know where you got *this* from and where that. She has asked me what you look like, how old you are, what you care about most. In a word, I've had you morning, noon, and night. We've been as good as living together, the three of us.

MAURICE, *to* HENRIETTE. Good gracious! Why didn't you come here and take a look at this prodigy? Then your curiosity would have been satisfied at once.

HENRIETTE. Adolphe didn't want me to.

ADOLPHE *looks embarrassed.*

Not that he was jealous . . .

MAURICE. Why should he be, when he knew my affections were otherwise engaged?

HENRIETTE. He may not have trusted the constancy of your affections.

MAURICE. I don't see why not. I'm famous for my fidelity.

ADOLPHE. It wasn't that. It . . .

HENRIETTE, *interrupting, to* MAURICE. Perhaps because it's never been put to the test. . . .

ADOLPHE. Oh really, you know . . . !

HENRIETTE, *interrupting.* Well, the world has never yet seen a faithful man.

MAURICE. Then it's going to see one.

HENRIETTE. Where?

MAURICE. Here.

HENRIETTE *laughs.*

ADOLPHE. Well, that sounds . . .

HENRIETTE, *interrupting and continuing to address herself to* MAURICE. Do you think I'd trust my dear Adolphe for more than a month or so?

MAURICE. It's not my business to challenge your lack of confidence, but I'd go bail for Adolphe's fidelity.

HENRIETTE. You needn't do that. . . . My tongue just ran away with me, and I take it back. Not only so I don't feel less high-minded than you, but because it really is so. . . . It's a bad habit of mine only to see the worst, and I go on doing it, even when I know better. But if I could be with you two for a while longer, I would grow good again in your company. Forgive me, Adolphe.

She lays her hand against his cheek.

ADOLPHE. You always talk so ill and behave so well. What you really think, I don't know.

HENRIETTE. Who does know that?

MAURICE. If we had to answer for our thoughts, who would stand a chance?

HENRIETTE. Do you have evil thoughts too?

MAURICE. Yes, of course. Just as I do the cruellest things—in dreams.

HENRIETTE. In dreams, ah! Just think I . . . no, I'm ashamed to talk about it. . . .

MAURICE. Go on, go on!

HENRIETTE. Last night I dreamt I was coolly dissecting the muscles of Adolphe's chest. I'm a sculptor, you know—and he, who is always so sweet, made no resistance, but actually helped me over the difficulties, as he knows more anatomy than I do.

MAURICE. Did he seem to be dead?

HENRIETTE. No, he was alive.

MAURICE. How horrible! How could you bear to do it?

HENRIETTE. I didn't mind at all. That's what surprised me, because I'm pretty sensitive about other people's sufferings. That's true, isn't it, Adolphe?

ADOLPHE. Absolutely true. Specially where animals are concerned.

MAURICE. I, on the other hand, am rather indifferent to my own sufferings and those of others.

ADOLPHE. Now he's telling lies about himself. Isn't he, Madame Cathérine?

MME CATHÉRINE. Monsieur Maurice is kind to the point of folly. Just think, he nearly called in the police because I hadn't changed the goldfishes' water—those on the buffet there. Look at them! You'd think they could hear what I'm saying.

MAURICE. And here we sit, you see, white-washing ourselves into angels, when by and large any one of us is capable of committing some polite atrocity where glory, gold, or women are concerned. . . . So you are a sculptor, Mademoiselle Henriette?

HENRIETTE. Bit of a one. Good enough anyhow to do a bust. And to do one of you. That's been my dream for a long time, and I'm sure I could.

MAURICE. At your service. That dream at least can be realised at once.

HENRIETTE. But I don't want to visualise you until after to-night's success, when you first become what you really should be.

MAURICE. How certain you are of victory!

HENRIETTE. Yes. It's written in your face that you're going to win this battle, and you must be feeling that yourself.

MAURICE. Why so?

HENRIETTE. Because I feel it. You know, I wasn't well this morning, but now I'm fine again.

ADOLPHE *begins to look depressed.*

MAURICE, *embarrassed.* Listen, I have one theatre ticket left —but only one. It's at your disposal, Adolphe.

ADOLPHE. Thank you, old man, but I surrender it to Henriette.

HENRIETTE. Oh, but would that do?

ADOLPHE. Why not? And I never go to the theatre anyhow. I can't stand the heat.

HENRIETTE. But you will at least come and fetch me when the play's over?

ADOLPHE. If you insist. Or why not come back here with Maurice, where we shall all be waiting for him?

MAURICE. Surely you can take the trouble to come and meet us. I want you to. I beg you to do so. Look here, if you don't want to wait outside the theatre, there's the Auberge des Adrets. You can meet us there. Is that settled?

ADOLPHE. Wait a bit. You have a way of settling things to suit yourself, before one has time to consider.

MAURICE. What is there to consider? It's just a matter of escorting your lady or not.

ADOLPHE. You never know what may come out of such a simple matter. I have a sense of foreboding.

HENRIETTE. Tut, tut! You can't be spooky in broad daylight. *To* MAURICE. Whether he turns up or not, we can always come back here.

ADOLPHE *rises.*

ADOLPHE. Well, anyway, I must leave you now. I have a model coming. Goodbye. Good luck, Maurice! Tomorrow you will have got there. Goodbye, Henriette.

HENRIETTE. Do you really have to go?

ADOLPHE. Must.

MAURICE. Goodbye, then. See you later.

ADOLPHE *salutes* MME CATHÉRINE *and goes out.*

HENRIETTE. To think that we should meet at last!

MAURICE. Do you find that so remarkable?

HENRIETTE. It's as if it were meant to happen, though Adolphe has done his best to prevent it.

MAURICE. Has he?

HENRIETTE. Surely you noticed that.

MAURICE. I did notice it. So why should you mention it?

HENRIETTE. I had to.

MAURICE. Well, I don't have to tell you that I meant to escape through the kitchen just now so as to avoid meeting you, but was stopped by someone shutting the door in my face.

HENRIETTE. Why talk about that now?

MAURICE. Don't know.

MME CATHÉRINE *upsets a number of glasses and bottles.*
Don't upset yourself, Madame Cathérine, there's no danger.

HENRIETTE. Was that meant as a signal or a warning?

MAURICE. Probably both.

HENRIETTE. Am I a locomotive that I need signalmen?

MAURICE. And switchmen. The most dangerous part is the switch-over.

HENRIETTE. How wicked you can be!

MME CATHÉRINE. Monsieur Maurice is not wicked at all. Up to now, nobody could have been kinder or more loyal to those who belong to him or those he's under an obligation to.

MAURICE. Hush, hush, hush!

HENRIETTE, *to* MAURICE. How that old woman pokes her nose in!

MAURICE. We can go over to the boulevard if you like.

HENRIETTE. By all means. This is no place for me. I feel hatred clawing at me.

HENRIETTE *goes out.*

MAURICE *begins to follow her.*

MAURICE. Goodbye, Madame Cathérine.

MME CATHÉRINE. One moment. May I say a word, Monsieur Maurice?

MAURICE, *stopping unwillingly.* What is it?

MME CATHÉRINE. Don't do it! Don't do it!

MAURICE. What?

MME CATHÉRINE. Don't do it!

MAURICE. Have no fear. This lady is not my kind. She just interests me. Scarcely even that.

MME CATHÉRINE. Don't trust yourself!

MAURICE. Yes, I do trust myself. Goodbye.

MAURICE *goes out.*

ACT II

SCENE 1

SCENE: *The Auberge des Adrets the same night.*

A café in theatrical seventeenth-century style, with alcoves containing tables and chairs.

The walls hung with armour and weapons, the shelves along the panelling holding glasses, pitchers, etc.

On one side a fireplace.

MAURICE *and* HENRIETTE, *in evening dress, sit facing one another at a table, on which stand a bottle of champagne and three filled glasses. The third glass is on the far side of the table and a third chair is placed for the expected third person.*

MAURICE *puts his watch on the table.*

MAURICE. If he doesn't come in five minutes, he won't come at all. . . . Shall we drink meanwhile with his ghost?

He touches the third glass with his own.

HENRIETTE *does likewise.*

HENRIETTE. Your health, Adolphe!

MAURICE. He won't come.

HENRIETTE. He will.

MAURICE. He won't.

HENRIETTE. He will.

MAURICE. What an evening! What a wonderful day! I can't grasp it yet—that a new life has begun. Just imagine, the manager believes I can count on at least a hundred thousand francs. I shall buy a villa for twenty thousand—outside the city—and I shall still have eighty thousand left. I shan't be able to take it all in until tomorrow. I'm so tired, tired, tired. *Sinks back in his chair.* Have you ever had a real stroke of luck?

HENRIETTE. Never. What does it feel like?

MAURICE. Well, how shall I put it? I can't really express it. But what I'm chiefly thinking about is the chagrin of my enemies. It's unpleasant of me, but that's how it is.

HENRIETTE. What's the point of thinking about one's enemies?

MAURICE. The conqueror always counts the enemy's dead and wounded in order to gauge his victory.

HENRIETTE. Are you as bloodthirsty as that?

MAURICE. Not really. But when you have felt other people's heels trampling on your chest for years, it's very pleasant to shake the enemy off and breathe.

HENRIETTE. Don't you find it strange to be sitting here alone with me, an insignificant girl and a stranger to you? On a night like this, when by rights you should be showing yourself as the triumphant hero to all the people on the boulevards and in the big restaurants.

MAURICE. Well, it is a little odd, but I like it here, and your company is all I want.

HENRIETTE. You're not very gay, are you?

MAURICE. No, I'm feeling rather sad. I should like to shed a few tears.

HENRIETTE. But why?

MAURICE. Success recognising its own emptiness and anticipating disaster.

HENRIETTE. How sad, how truly sad! What more can you want?

MAURICE. The one thing that makes life worth living. . . .

HENRIETTE. Then . . . you no longer love her?

MAURICE. No, not in the way I understand love. Do you imagine she has read my play or wants to see it? Oh, she is so good, so self-sacrificing and considerate, but she would think it wrong to go out and celebrate like this tonight. You know, I did once treat her to champagne and, instead of being pleased, she picked up the wine list to see what it cost. And when she saw the price, she cried. Cried because Marion needed new stockings. . . . Beautiful if you like, very moving. But what pleasure can one have when that's the way things are? And I want some pleasure before I get any older. So far I have lived in privation, but now, now . . . life is beginning for me.

A clock strikes twelve.

Now a new day is beginning. A new era.

HENRIETTE. Adolphe's not coming.

MAURICE. No, he's not coming. And now it's too late to go to the Crémerie.

HENRIETTE. But they are expecting you.

MAURICE. Then they must expect. They made me promise to come and I take my promise back. . . . Do you want to go there?

HENRIETTE. Far from it.

MAURICE. Then will you give me the pleasure of your company?

HENRIETTE. Willingly. If you can put up with it.

MAURICE. Well, considering I've begged you for it! Strange that the victor's crown should be worthless if you can't lay it at some woman's feet. That everything is worthless if you haven't a woman. . . .

HENRIETTE. Surely you have no need to be without a woman? You!

MAURICE. A question.

HENRIETTE. Don't you know that at the moment of success and fame a man is irresistible?

MAURICE. No, I don't. I haven't had that experience.

HENRIETTE. You are an extraordinary person. At this moment, when you're the most envied man in Paris, you just sit here brooding. Perhaps you have a bad conscience because you've neglected the invitation to drink chicory coffee with the old woman in the milk shop.

During the following dialogue somebody in the adjacent room begins to play the finale of Beethoven's Piano Sonata in D major (Op. 31, No. 3). The final Allegretto is played softly at first, but growing louder and more passionate until it ends in complete abandon.

MAURICE. Yes, my conscience does prick me on that score, and even here I can sense their resentment, their wounded feelings, their justifiable indignation. My comrades in distress had the right to demand my presence tonight. The good Madame Cathérine had a special stake in my success, which was to have given a glimmer of hope to the poor fellows who haven't had any luck as yet. . . . And I have cheated them of their good faith in me. I can hear them swearing: "Maurice will come. He's a good chap. He doesn't look down on us and he won't break his word." Now I have broken my word and theirs. . . . Who can be playing here at this time of night?

HENRIETTE. Some nightbird like us, I suppose. . . . But look, you're not putting the case as it is. Don't forget Adolphe promised to meet us. We have waited and he has broken his promise. So you are not to blame.

MAURICE. Is that what you think? I believe you while you're talking, but when you stop, my conscience starts up again. . . . What have you got there?

HENRIETTE. Oh, it's only a laurel wreath. I meant to send it up on to the stage, but I didn't get the chance. Let me give it to you now. It's supposed to cool the heated brow.

She rises, places the wreath on his head, and kisses his forehead.

Hail, victor!

MAURICE. No, don't!

HENRIETTE, *kneeling.* Hail, King!

MAURICE, *rising and taking off the wreath.* Don't! It frightens me.

HENRIETTE. How timid you are! So timid you're even scared of good fortune. Who took away your self-esteem and turned you into a dwarf?

MAURICE. Dwarf? Yes, you're right. I don't work up in the clouds like a giant, crashing and booming, but forge my sword down in the silent heart of the mountain. You think my modesty shrinks from the victor's wreath. No, I despise it because it's too slight for me. You think I fear the ghost sitting there with the green eyes of jealousy, keeping a watch on my feelings—of whose strength you have no notion. Away with you, ghost!

He sweeps the third, untasted, glass of champagne off the table.

Away, you unwanted third! You absent one, who have lost your rights if you ever had any. You shunned the field of battle because you knew yourself already beaten. So, as I crush this glass beneath my foot, I will crush to pieces the image you set up for yourself in a little temple which shall never again be yours.

HENRIETTE. Bravo! That's how it will be. Bravo, my hero!

MAURICE. Now I have sacrificed my best friend, my most faithful supporter, on your altar, Astarte. Are you satisfied?

HENRIETTE. Astarte. That's a beautiful name and I shall keep it. You must be in love with me, Maurice.

MAURICE. Naturally . . . *Femme fatale,* who scents the victim and rouses man's passion, where have you come from and where will you lead me? When they spoke of you, I trembled. And when I saw you—in the doorway—your spirit flew to mine. When you went away, you were still there in my arms. I wanted to flee from you, but something stopped me, and tonight we are driven together like quarry in the hunter's net. Who is to blame? Your friend, who played pander for us.

HENRIETTE. Blame or no blame, what's that got to do with it? What does it mean? Adolphe is to blame because he didn't bring us together before. He is guilty of the crime of robbing us of two weeks' life of bliss, to which he had no right. I am jealous of him on your behalf; I hate him for cheating you of your true love; I should like to blot him out of the numbers of the living and his memory too, to obliterate him from the past and make him unmade, unborn.

MAURICE. Then we will bury him under our own memories. We will peg him down in the depths of the forest and pile stones over him so that he can never raise his head again. *Raising his glass.* Our fate is sealed. Woe betide us! What is to happen now?

HENRIETTE. Now a new era will begin. . . . What's in that packet?

MAURICE. I don't remember.

HENRIETTE *opens the packet and brings out a tie and a pair of gloves.*

HENRIETTE. What a frightful tie! It must have cost quite fifty centimes.

MAURICE *snatches the things from her.*

MAURICE. Don't touch those!

HENRIETTE. Are they from her?

MAURICE. Yes, they are.

HENRIETTE. Give them to me.

MAURICE. No! She's better than us, better than us all.

HENRIETTE. I don't believe it. She's just simpler and stingier. A woman who cries because there's champagne . . .

MAURICE. When there aren't any stockings for her child. Yes, she's good.

HENRIETTE. You bourgeois! You'll never be an artist. But I am an artist, and I shall make a bust of you with a shopkeeper's cap instead of a laurel wreath. . . . Is she called Jeanne?

MAURICE. Yes. How do you know?

HENRIETTE. That's what all housekeepers are called.

MAURICE. Henriette!

HENRIETTE *picks up the gloves and the tie and throws them into the fireplace.*

Weakly. Astarte! Now you're demanding the sacrifice of women. That you shall have. But if it's to be innocent children, then you must go.

HENRIETTE. Do you know what it is that binds you to me?

MAURICE. If I knew, I would tear myself away. But I believe it is your evil qualities which I need. I believe it is the vice in you which attracts me with the irresistible pleasure of the new. . . .

HENRIETTE. Haven't you ever committed a crime?

MAURICE. No, not a real one. Have you?

HENRIETTE. Yes.

MAURICE. Well? What was that like?

HENRIETTE. It outweighed doing any good deed, for that only puts you on a level with others. It outweighed performing

any feat, because that puts you above others and is rewarded. This crime put me outside, on the other side of
life and society and my fellow-beings. Since that time, I
have only been living a half life, a dream life, so reality no
longer has any meaning for me.

MAURICE. What did you do?

HENRIETTE. I won't tell you. You'd be afraid again.

MAURICE. Can you never be found out?

HENRIETTE. Never. But that doesn't stop me from often seeing
the five stones in the Place de Roquette, where the scaffold
used to stand. And that's why I never touch cards, for the
five of diamonds always comes up. . . .

MAURICE. Was it that kind of crime?

HENRIETTE. Yes, that kind.

MAURICE. That's pretty horrible, but it's interesting. Have you
never had a conscience?

HENRIETTE. Never. But if we might talk about something else,
I should be grateful.

MAURICE. What shall we talk about—love?

HENRIETTE. You don't talk about that until it's over.

MAURICE. Were you in love with Adolphe?

HENRIETTE. I don't know. The purity of his nature attracted
me like some beautiful forgotten memory of childhood, but
there was a great deal about his person that offended my
eye. It took me a long time to erase, change, and add to and
take from, so as to make a passable figure of him. When he
talked, I could tell he had learnt his views from you, and
they were often half understood and clumsily applied. So
you can imagine how poor the copy appears now that I can
see the original. That's why he was scared of letting us two
meet, and when it did happen, he knew at once his time
was up.

MAURICE. Poor Adolphe!

HENRIETTE. I'm sorry for him too. He must be suffering tor-
ments.

MAURICE. Hush! Someone's coming.

HENRIETTE. Suppose it is he?

MAURICE. That would be intolerable.

HENRIETTE. It isn't he, but if it had been, what do you think would have happened?

During the following dialogue the pianist in the adjacent room practises the D major Sonata, sometimes pianissimo, sometimes wildly fortissimo. At times there is silence: at others only bars 96–107 of the Finale are heard.

MAURICE. At first he would have been rather cross with you, because he had made a mistake about the café—looked for us in vain in the wrong place—but his arrogance would soon have given way to pleasure at seeing us—at seeing that we hadn't deceived him. And in his joy at finding he had wronged us by his suspicions, he would have loved us both, and so been delighted to find that we were such good friends. It had always been his dream—hm, this is him speaking now—his dream, that the three of us would make a trio and show the world a fine example of a friendship making no demands. "Yes, I trust you, Maurice, partly because you are my friend, partly because your affections are engaged elsewhere."

HENRIETTE. Bravo! Have you been in such a situation before that you are able to reproduce it so exactly? You know, Adolphe is just the kind that has to be a third, who can't enjoy his girl unless he has a friend along.

MAURICE. That is why I was called upon to entertain you. . . . Hush, there's someone outside! . . . It is he.

HENRIETTE. No, these are the hours when ghosts walk, you know, and when one hears so many things and sees them sometimes too. To be awake at night, when one should be sleeping, has the same charm for me as crime. One has set oneself above and beyond the laws of nature.

MAURICE. But the penalty is heavy. I am shivering or trembling, whichever it is.

HENRIETTE *takes her opera cloak and puts it round him.*

HENRIETTE. Have this round you. That will warm you.

MAURICE. It's beautiful. It's as if I were inside your skin, as if my vigil-worn body were recast in your form. I can feel it being moulded. But I am getting a new soul too, new thoughts, and here, my own breast is filling the curve which yours has left.

The music interrupts his thought.

What a monster to sit there all night practising the piano! I'm sick of it. I tell you what. We will drive out to the Bois de Boulogne and have breakfast in the Pavilion and watch the sun rise over the lake.

HENRIETTE. Good!

MAURICE. But first I must send a note home, so that my mail and the morning papers and the rest are sent out by messenger to the breakfast place. Listen, Henriette. Shall we invite Adolphe?

HENRIETTE. Yes, it's too crazy, but why not? The ass can surely be harnessed to the triumphal chariot. Let him come.

They rise.

MAURICE *removes the cloak.*

MAURICE. Then I'll ring.

HENRIETTE. Wait a moment!

She throws herself into his arms.

SCENE 2

SCENE: *The Bois de Boulogne. Dawn.*

A large, magnificently furnished room of a restaurant, with rugs and mirrors, chaise-longues and divans.

Back, French windows overlooking the water.

Centre, a table spread with flowers, bowls of fruit, decanters of wine, oyster platters, many kinds of wine glasses, and two lighted candelabra.

Right, a low table with newspapers and telegrams.

MAURICE *and* HENRIETTE *are sitting opposite one another at this table.*

The sun is rising.

MAURICE. There is no longer any doubt. The press says it is so, and these telegrams congratulate me on my success. This is a new life beginning, and my life is wedded to yours through this night, in which you alone have shared my hopes and my triumphs. It was from your hand I received my laurels and I feel everything has come to me from you.

HENRIETTE. What a wonderful night! Have we dreamt it or have we really lived it?

MAURICE, *rising*. And what a dawn for such a night! I feel as if it were the world's first day now being lighted by the rising sun. The earth has just been created and spun itself free of those white membranes now floating away. There lies the Garden of Eden in the rosy light of dawn, and here is the first pair of human beings. . . . Do you know, I am so happy I could weep to think that the whole of mankind is not as happy as I am. . . . Listen to that distant murmur, like waves on a pebbly beach, like the wind in the woods. Do you know what that is? It is Paris whispering my name. Do you see the smoke spiralling up to the sky in thousands and tens of thousands? That is Paris whispering my name. Those are my altar fires—or if they aren't, they shall be, for I will it to be so. At this very moment every telegraph in Europe is tapping out my name; the Oriental express is carrying the news to the Far East, into the rising sun, and the ocean liners to the furthest West . . . the earth is mine, and so it is beautiful. Now I wish for wings for both of us, so we could take flight far, far away, before anyone can spoil my happiness, before envy wakes me from my dream—because this probably is a dream.

HENRIETTE, *giving him her hand*. Feel! You are not dreaming.

MAURICE. It is not a dream, yet it has been one. You know, when as a penniless young man I used to walk down there in the woods and look up at this Pavilion, I saw it as an enchanted castle, and I always imagined myself up in this room with its balcony and its rich curtains—a place of pure bliss. To be here with a beloved woman, watching the sunrise with the candles still alight, was the most audacious dream of my youth. Now it has come true, and now I have no more to ask of life. . . . Would you like to die—now, with me?

HENRIETTE. No, you idiot! Now I want to begin to live.

MAURICE. To live is to suffer. Now comes reality. I hear his footsteps on the stairs. He is panting with anxiety; his heart is pounding with the dread of having lost the most precious thing of all. Believe me, Adolphe is under this roof. In one moment he will be standing here in the room.

HENRIETTE, *uneasily.* It was a stupid idea to invite him here, and I already regret it. . . . Well, at least we shall see if your forecast was right.

MAURICE. Of course, one can easily be mistaken about a person's feelings.

The HEAD WAITER *enters and hands him a card.*

Ask the gentleman to come in.

Exit the HEAD WAITER.

I am afraid we *shall* regret it.

HENRIETTE. Too late to think of that. Hush!

Enter ADOLPHE, *white and hollow-eyed.*

MAURICE, *trying to speak naturally.* So here you are! Wherever did you get to last night?

ADOLPHE. I went to join you at the Hôtel des Arrêts and waited a whole hour. . . .

MAURICE. But you went to the wrong place. We waited a couple of hours for you at the Auberge des Adrets and are still waiting, as you see.

ADOLPHE, *relieved.* Thank God!

HENRIETTE. Good morning, my dear. You are a gloomy bird, always expecting the worst. I suppose you imagined we were trying to avoid your company, and although you know we sent for you, you still think yourself *de trop*.

ADOLPHE. Accept my apologies. I was wrong, but the night was frightful.

They sit down. Embarrassed silence.

HENRIETTE, *to* ADOLPHE. Well, aren't you going to congratulate Maurice on his great success?

ADOLPHE. Oh, yes! You have had a real success—that envy itself can't deny. Everybody is at your feet. You make me feel quite small.

MAURICE. What nonsense! Henriette, pour Adolphe out a glass of wine.

ADOLPHE. Thank you, not for me. Nothing.

HENRIETTE, *to* ADOLPHE. What's the matter? Are you ill?

ADOLPHE. No, but I feel I may be.

HENRIETTE. Your eyes . . .

ADOLPHE. What about them?

MAURICE. How was it at the Crémerie last night? I suppose they're offended with me.

ADOLPHE. No one's offended with you, but your absence cast a gloom that was painful to see. But no one was offended, I assure you. Your understanding friends regarded you and your absence with sympathy and tolerance. Madame Cathérine herself took on your defence and proposed your health. We all rejoiced in your success as if it had been our own.

HENRIETTE. But what nice people! What good friends you have, Maurice!

MAURICE. Yes, better than I deserve.

HENRIETTE. No one has better friends than he deserves, and you are blessed in your friends. . . . Can't you feel how the very air is softened for you today by the stream of pure good wishes reaching you from a thousand hearts?

MAURICE *rises to conceal his emotion.*

ADOLPHE. From a thousand hearts which you have set free from the nightmare which had oppressed them all their lives. Human nature had been slandered and you have redeemed it, so people are grateful to you. Today they lift their heads again, saying: "See, we are better than our reputations!" And the thought makes them better.

HENRIETTE *tries to hide her emotion.*

Am I bothering you? Let me just warm myself for a moment in your sunshine, Maurice. Then I will go.

MAURICE. Why should you go when you have only just come?

ADOLPHE. Why? Because I have seen what I need never have seen, because I know now that my time is over. *Silence.* That you sent for me I take as a sign of consideration, an acknowledgement of what has happened, a candour less wounding than deceit. You know, Maurice, how well I think of human nature, and it's you who taught me to, Maurice. *Silence*. But, my friend, just now I went into the Church of Saint-Germain, and there I saw a woman and a child. I'm not sorry that you weren't there to see them, because what has happened cannot be changed; but if you had given them a thought or a word before you set them adrift on the open seas of the great city, then you might enjoy your good fortune in peace. And now I bid you goodbye.

HENRIETTE. Why are you going?

ADOLPHE. You ask that! Do you want me to tell you?

HENRIETTE. No, I don't.

ADOLPHE. Then goodbye.

Exit ADOLPHE.

MAURICE. The Fall. "And lo, they knew that they were naked."

HENRIETTE. How different this scene was from the one we imagined. He is better than we are.

MAURICE. I feel now everyone is better than we are.

HENRIETTE. Do you see? The sun has gone behind the clouds and the wood has lost its rosy tint.

MAURICE. I do see. And the blue water is black. Let us flee to where the sky is always clear and the trees are always green.

HENRIETTE. Yes, let us do that. But without farewells.

MAURICE. No, with farewells.

HENRIETTE. We should fly. You offered me wings, but your feet are of lead. I am not jealous; but if you go to say goodbye and find two pairs of arms about your neck, you will not be able to break away.

MAURICE. You are perfectly right, except that only one small pair of arms is needed to hold me.

HENRIETTE. It is the child that holds you then, not the woman.

MAURICE. It is the child.

HENRIETTE. The child! Another's child! And for that I am to suffer. Why should that child block the path, the path I must now take?

MAURICE. Why, indeed? Better if it had never existed.

HENRIETTE. Yes, but it does exist. Like a stone on the road, an immovable boulder which cannot fail to upset the carriage.

MAURICE. The triumphal chariot! The ass is driven to its death, but the boulder remains. Confound it!

Silence.

HENRIETTE. There's nothing to be done.

MAURICE. Yes. We must get married; then *our* child will make us forget the other one.

HENRIETTE. The other one would kill ours.

MAURICE. Kill? What a thing to say!

HENRIETTE, *changing her tone.* Your child will kill our love.

MAURICE. No, my dear. Our love will kill everything that stands in its way, but it will not be killed.

HENRIETTE *picks up a pack of cards from the mantelpiece.*

HENRIETTE. Look! The five of diamonds. The scaffold. Is it possible that our fates are predestined? That our thoughts are led as if through pipes, the way they must go, without our being able to stop them? No, I don't want to go that way! I don't want to! Do you realise I should go to the scaffold if my crime were discovered?

MAURICE. Tell me about your crime. This is the moment.

HENRIETTE. No, I should regret it afterwards, and you would loathe me. . . . No, no, no! *Pause.* Have you ever heard that one can hate a person to death? Well, my father came to be hated by my mother and his children, and he melted away like wax before a fire. Horrible! Let's talk about something else. . . . Above all, let's leave Paris. Here the air is poisoned; tomorrow your laurels will be withered, the triumph forgotten, and in a week all eyes will be on another victor. Away from here, to work for new victories! But first of all, Maurice, you must go and embrace your child and provide for its immediate future. The mother, you need not see.

MAURICE. Thank you. Your heart does you honour, and you are all the more dear to me when you show the kindness you sometimes hide.

HENRIETTE. And then go to the Crémerie and say goodbye to the old woman and your friends. Leave nothing behind you undone that might weigh on your mind on our journey.

MAURICE. I will do everything that should be done, and to-night we will meet at the railway station.

HENRIETTE. Agreed! And so, away from here, en route for the sunshine and the sea!

ACT III

SCENE 1

SCENE: *The Crémerie. Evening of the same day. The gas is lighted.*

MADAME CATHÉRINE *is sitting beside the buffet.*

ADOLPHE, *at a table.*

MME CATHÉRINE. Such is life, my dear Monsieur Adolphe. But you young people are always demanding too much and then coming here and moaning about it.

ADOLPHE. No, it's not like that. I don't reproach anyone and I am still as fond as ever of them both. But there is something that makes me rather sick. You see, I was so much attached to Maurice, yes, so much that I wanted him to have everything that would make him happy. But now I have lost him; that hurts me more than the loss of her. I have lost them both, and so my loneliness is doubly painful. But there is something else too which I'm not quite clear about.

MME CATHÉRINE. Don't brood so much. Work and find things to do. Do you ever go to church, for example?

ADOLPHE. What should I do there?

MME CATHÉRINE. Oh, there's so much to see! And then there's the music. That at least is not banal.

ADOLPHE. Possibly not. But I don't belong to the fold, because I'm not devout. You see, Madame Cathérine, faith is undoubtedly a gift, and one that so far I have not got.

MME CATHÉRINE. Wait then, till you do get it. . . . But what

is this tale I heard today? Is it true you have sold a picture
in London at a very high price and won the top award?

ADOLPHE. Yes, it's true.

MME CATHÉRINE. But good heavens! And you haven't said a
word about it?

ADOLPHE. I'm afraid of good fortune, and anyway it's almost
worthless to me at this moment. I'm afraid, in the way one
is of ghosts. It's bad luck to speak of having seen one.

MME CATHÉRINE. Well, you always were a strange fellow.

ADOLPHE. No, Madame, but I have seen so much bad luck follow on good, and I have seen how in misfortune one always
has true friends, and in success only false ones . . . You
asked me if I ever went to church and I didn't give you a
straight answer. I did go into Saint-Germain this very morning, without quite knowing why. It was as if I went to look
for someone to whom I could offer silent thanks—but I didn't
find anyone. Then I put a gold coin in the poor box—that's
all I got out of my churchgoing—and it was pretty banal.

MME CATHÉRINE. It was something at least. It was good to
think about the poor when you were in luck.

ADOLPHE. It was neither good nor bad; it was just something I
did because I couldn't help myself. But something else happened to me in the church too. I saw Maurice's friend
Jeanne and his child. Struck down, crushed by his triumphal chariot; it was as if they bore the whole weight of his
past misfortunes.

MME CATHÉRINE. Well, my child, how you come to terms with
your consciences, I don't know. But that a decent person, a
kindly, conscientious man like Monsieur Maurice, can throw
over a woman and child in the twinkling of an eye—explain
that to me.

ADOLPHE. I can't explain it, and he doesn't seem to understand
it himself. I saw them this morning and it all seemed to
them so natural, so right, that they couldn't imagine things
otherwise. It was as if they were enjoying the satisfaction
of having done some good deed or performed some sacred
duty. There are things we can't explain, Madame Cathérine,
and therefore it is not for us to judge. Besides, surely you

saw how it came about. Maurice felt the danger in the air. I had a premonition; I tried to prevent their meeting. It's really as if an intrigue had been woven by some invisible power, as if they had been driven by a trick into one another's arms. I'm certainly disqualified in this case, but I don't hesitate to pronounce the verdict: not guilty.

MME CATHÉRINE. Well now, look, to be able to forgive as you do, that's religion.

ADOLPHE. Good heavens! Am I religious without knowing it?

MME CATHÉRINE. But, you see, to *let* oneself be driven or tempted into evil like Monsieur Maurice, that's either weakness or wickedness. And if you feel your strength failing, then you pray for help, and you get it. But he didn't do that—he was too stuck-up. . . . Who's this coming? Oh, I think it's the Abbé.

ADOLPHE. What does he want here?

Enter the ABBÉ.

ABBÉ. Good evening, Madame. Good evening, Monsieur.

MME CATHÉRINE. What can I do for you, Monsieur l'Abbé?

ABBÉ. Has Monsieur Maurice, the author, been here today?

MME CATHÉRINE. No, not today. There's this play of his on at the theatre, and that is probably keeping him busy.

ABBÉ. I have . . . bad news to give him. Bad in many respects.

MME CATHÉRINE. Dare I ask what kind of . . . ?

ABBÉ. Yes, there is no secret about it. His daughter, by Jeanne, born out of wedlock, is dead.

MME CATHÉRINE. Dead!

ADOLPHE. Marion dead!

ABBÉ. Yes. She died suddenly this morning, without any previous illness.

MME CATHÉRINE. O God! Who can tell Thy ways?

ABBÉ. The mother's despair calls for Monsieur Maurice's presence, and we must try to find him. . . . And now a question—in confidence. Was Monsieur Maurice known to be fond of the child, or was he indifferent to her?

MME CATHÉRINE. Did he love his little Marion? Monsieur l'Abbé, we all know how he doted upon her.

ADOLPHE. There is no doubt of that, Monsieur l'Abbé.

ABBÉ. I am glad to hear it. As far as I am concerned, that doubt is dispelled.

MME CATHÉRINE. Has there been a doubt?

ABBÉ. Unfortunately, yes. An evil rumour has been running round the *Quartier* that he had abandoned the child and its mother in order to go off with a strange woman. In a few hours this rumour has developed into definite accusations, and the feeling against him has now reached such a pitch that his life is threatened, and he is being called a murderer.

MME CATHÉRINE. O God, what is all this? What is it?

ABBÉ. I will tell you my own view. I am convinced that the man is innocent of this charge, and the mother is as sure of this as I am. But Monsieur Maurice has appearances against him, and he will not find it easy to clear himself, when the police come to interrogate him.

MME CATHÉRINE. Have the police got hold of the matter?

ABBÉ. Yes, the police have to be prepared to protect him from these evil rumours and the people's anger. I believe the Commissaire is on his way here now.

MME CATHÉRINE, *to* ADOLPHE. You see what happens when a man can't tell the difference between good and evil and flirts with vice. The Lord punishes.

ADOLPHE. Then He is more merciless than man.

ABBÉ. What do you know about this matter?

ADOLPHE. Nothing much more, but I can see how it happened. . . .

ABBÉ. And understand it too?

ADOLPHE. Not yet perhaps.

ABBÉ. Let us look more closely at the matter. . . . Here is the Commissaire.

Enter the COMMISSAIRE.

COMMISSAIRE. Messieurs, Madame, I must trouble you for a moment with some enquiries about Monsieur Maurice Gérard, who, as you have probably heard, is the object of a hideous rumour, which, by the way, I don't myself believe.

MME CATHÉRINE. None of us believe it either.

COMMISSAIRE. That strengthens my own opinion; but for his own sake I must give him a chance to defend himself.

ABBÉ. That is good. And he will surely find justice, hard though it may be.

COMMISSAIRE. Appearances are terribly against him, and I have seen innocent people mount the scaffold before their innocence was discovered. Listen to what they say against him. The child, Marion, left alone by her mother, was secretly visited by the father, who seems to have chosen the hour when the child would be alone. A quarter of an hour after the visit the mother returned and found the child dead. This is a serious situation for the accused. . . . The postmortem shows no sign of violence nor any trace of poison, but the doctors affirm that there are newly discovered poisons which leave no trace. . . . To me this visit seems a coincidence, and I am well used to those. But worse was to come. Last night Monsieur Maurice was seen at the Auberge des Adrets with a strange lady. The conversation, according to the waiter, turned to crime. The Place de Roquette and the scaffold were mentioned. An unusual topic of conversation between lovers of good breeding and position. However this could have been, and we know from experience that people, who are short of sleep and have been drinking a good deal, tend to dig up the worst from the depths of their souls. More serious still is the evidence of the head waiter from the champagne breakfast in the Bois de Boulogne this morning. He states that he heard them wishing the life out of a child. The man appears to have said: "Better if it had never existed," to which the woman replied: "Yes, but it does exist." And later in the conversation came these words: "The other one would kill ours," to which the answer was: "Kill! What a thing to say!" and: "Our love will kill everything that stands in its way." And then: "The five of diamonds," "the scaffold," "the Place de Roquette." . . . All this, you see, is hard to explain away, and so finally is this foreign journey planned for tonight. These are serious matters.

ADOLPHE. He is lost.

MME CATHÉRINE. It is a horrifying story. What is one to believe?

ABBÉ. This is not the work of man. God have mercy on him!

ADOLPHE. He is caught in the net and will never get out.

MME CATHÉRINE. Why did he let himself get into it?

ADOLPHE. Are you beginning to suspect him, Madame Cathérine?

MME CATHÉRINE. Yes and no. I can no longer have any opinion in the matter. . . . Hasn't one seen angels turn into devils in the twinkling of an eye and then become angels again?

COMMISSAIRE. It's an extraordinary business. However, we must just wait and hear what he has to say. Nobody is condemned unheard. Good evening, Messieurs, good evening, Madame.

Exit the COMMISSAIRE.

ABBÉ. This is not the work of man.

ADOLPHE. It certainly looks like the work of demons for man's undoing.

ABBÉ. It is either retribution for hidden sins, or else a fearful test.

Enter JEANNE, *wearing mourning.*

JEANNE. Good evening. Excuse my asking, but has Monsieur Maurice been here?

MME CATHÉRINE. No, Madame. But he might come in at any moment. . . . Then you haven't seen him since . . .

JEANNE. Not since this morning.[1]

MME CATHÉRINE. Please accept my sympathy in your great sorrow.

JEANNE. Thank you, Madame. *To the* ABBÉ. Ah, you are here, Father!

ABBÉ. Yes, my child. I thought I might be of some help to you here. And it was fortunate, as I was able to have a few words with the Commissaire just now.

[1] NOTE. In the Swedish: "*yesterday* morning," which does not fit with Maurice's line in Act IV, Scene 1.

JEANNE. The Commissaire! He doesn't suspect Maurice too, does he?

ABBÉ. No, he does not, and nor do any of us here. But appearances are terribly against him.

JEANNE. You mean because of that conversation the waiter overheard . . . That means nothing to me. I've heard the same sort of things before when Maurice has had a few drinks. It's his habit then to speculate on crime and punishment. Besides, it seems to have been the woman he had with him who made the most dangerous remarks. I should like to look that woman in the eyes.

ADOLPHE. My dear Jeanne, however much wrong that woman may have unintentionally done you, she had no evil purpose, no evil purpose at all. She just followed the dictates of her heart. I know she is good and could look anyone straight in the eyes.

JEANNE. Your judgement in this matter is of great value to me, Adolphe, and I believe you. So there is no one I can blame for what has happened but myself. Yes, it is my heedlessness that is now being punished. *She weeps.*

ABBÉ. Do not reproach yourself unjustly. I know you, and how seriously you took your motherhood. That this responsibility was not sanctioned by the Church and Civil Law is not your fault. No, here we are facing something different.

ADOLPHE. What?

ABBÉ. Who can say?

Enter HENRIETTE *in travelling dress.*

ADOLPHE *rises resolutely and goes to meet her.*

ADOLPHE. You here?

HENRIETTE. Yes, where is Maurice?

ADOLPHE. Do you know . . . or don't you?

HENRIETTE. I know everything. Excuse me, Madame Cathérine, but I was all ready for the journey and had to come in here for a moment. *To* ADOLPHE. Who is that woman? . . . Ah!

HENRIETTE *and* JEANNE *stare at one another.*

EMILE *is seen in the doorway of the kitchen.*

To JEANNE. I ought to say something, but I don't know what, because whatever I say will sound crude or mocking. . . . But, Madame, if I ask you quite simply to believe that I share in your deep sorrow, as much as anyone closer to you does, then you must not repulse me. . . . You must not, for I deserve your pity, if not your forbearance.

HENRIETTE *holds out her hand to* JEANNE. JEANNE *gazes at her.*

JEANNE. I believe you now, but in another moment I shall not believe you.

JEANNE *takes* HENRIETTE'S *hand.*

HENRIETTE, *kissing her hand.* Thank you.

JEANNE *draws back her hand.*

JEANNE. No, don't. I don't deserve that. I don't deserve it.

ABBÉ. Forgive me, but while we are all gathered here, in harmony, so it seems, for the moment, won't you shed some light, Mademoiselle Henriette, on the uncertainty and darkness surrounding the main point of this accusation? I ask you, as among friends, to tell us what you meant by what you said about death and crime and the Place de Roquette. We are all convinced that these words had no connection with the death of the child, but it would relieve us to hear what that conversation meant. Will you tell us?

Pause.

HENRIETTE. I can't tell you. I can't.

ADOLPHE. Tell us, Henriette. Say the words that will bring peace to us all.

HENRIETTE. I can't. Don't ask me to do that.

ABBÉ. This is not the work of man.

HENRIETTE. To think that this moment had to come! And like this, like this! *To* JEANNE. Madame, I swear that I am not guilty of your child's death. Is that not enough?

JEANNE. It is enough for us, but not for justice.

HENRIETTE. Justice! If you knew how true your words were!

ABBÉ, *to* HENRIETTE. And if you understood what you said just now.

HENRIETTE. Do you understand it better than I?

ABBÉ. Yes.

HENRIETTE *gazes at the* ABBÉ.

Have no fear. For even if I guess your secret, I will not betray it. For that matter, human justice is not my concern. But divine grace is.

MAURICE *enters hastily, in travelling clothes. He does not look at the rest of the company in the foreground, but goes straight to the counter, where* MADAME CATHÉRINE *is sitting.*

MAURICE. Madame Cathérine, you are not angry with me for staying away? Anyway, I have come now to ask you to forgive me, before I start South at eight o'clock tonight.

MADAME CATHÉRINE *is too much taken aback to speak.*

Then you are angry with me. *Looks round.* What is all this? Is it a dream, or isn't it? . . . Yes, I see it is real, but it looks like a wax tableau. . . . There is Jeanne like a statue—all in black . . . And Henriette like a corpse . . . What does this mean?

Silence.

No one answers. . . . Then it means something terrible.

Silence.

But please *speak!* Adolphe, you are my friend, what is it? *Indicates* EMILE. And—there is a detective.

ADOLPHE, *coming forward.* You know nothing then?

MAURICE. Nothing. But I must know.

ADOLPHE. Well then . . . Marion is dead.

MAURICE. Marion—dead?

ADOLPHE. Yes, she died this morning.

MAURICE, *to* JEANNE. And that is why you are in mourning. Jeanne, Jeanne, who has done this to us?

JEANNE. He who holds life and death in His hand.

MAURICE. But I saw her well and rosy this very morning. How did it happen? Who did it? Somebody did this to us.

His eyes seek HENRIETTE.

ADOLPHE. Don't look for the guilty one here, for it is no one here. Unfortunately the police have turned their suspicions in a direction where there should be none.

MAURICE. Where is that?

ADOLPHE. Well . . . You must know that your reckless conversation last night and this morning has placed you in a light that is anything but favourable.

MAURICE. Were they listening to us? Let me think what it was that was said? . . . It's true . . . Yes, then I am lost.

ADOLPHE. But explain your thoughtless words. And we will believe you.

MAURICE. I can't. I will not. I shall be sent to prison, but that's nothing. Marion is dead! Dead! And I have killed her.

General consternation.

ADOLPHE. Think what you are saying! Weigh your words! Do you realise what you said?

MAURICE. What did I say?

ADOLPHE. You said that you had killed Marion.

MAURICE. Could anyone believe that I am a murderer and could kill my own child? Madame Cathérine, you who know me, tell me, do you believe it, do you believe it?

MME CATHÉRINE. I don't any longer know what to believe. What's in the heart the tongue will speak, and you have spoken evil words.

MAURICE. She does not believe me.

ADOLPHE. Well, but explain yourself. Explain what you meant by your love would kill everything that stood in its way.

MAURICE. I see. They know that too. Henriette, will you explain that?

HENRIETTE. I can't do that.

ABBÉ. Yes. There is something wrong behind all this, and you have lost our sympathy, my friends. Just now I would have sworn that you were innocent, but I cannot do that now.

MAURICE, *to* JEANNE. What you say means more to me than anything else.

JEANNE, *coldly*. First answer this question: who was it you cursed during that orgy out in the Bois?

MAURICE. Did I do that? Perhaps. Yes, yes, I am guilty, and at the same time guiltless. Let me go away from here, for I am ashamed, and my misdeeds are greater than I can forgive myself.

HENRIETTE, *to* ADOLPHE. Go with him or he will do himself some harm.

ADOLPHE. I?

HENRIETTE. Who else?

ADOLPHE, *without bitterness*. You were nearest. Hush! There's a carriage.

MME CATHÉRINE. It's the Commissaire. I have seen a great deal of life. But never would I have believed that success and fame were such brittle things.

MAURICE, *to* HENRIETTE. From the triumphal chariot to the police van.

JEANNE, *simply*. And the ass drawing it—who was that?

ADOLPHE. That was certainly me.

Enter the COMMISSAIRE, *with papers in his hand.*

COMMISSAIRE. A summons to appear at the Préfecture immediately, this evening, for Monsieur Maurice Gérard . . . and Mademoiselle Henriette Mauclerc. Present?

MAURICE *and* HENRIETTE. Yes.

MAURICE. Is this an arrest?

COMMISSAIRE. No, not yet. This is only a summons to attend in person.

MAURICE. And after that?

COMMISSAIRE. One does not know.

MAURICE and HENRIETTE *move towards the door.*

MAURICE. Goodbye to you all!

Everyone shows emotion.

The COMMISSAIRE, MAURICE, *and* HENRIETTE *go out.*

EMILE *enters and goes up to* JEANNE.

EMILE. Now, my dear sister, I will see you home.

JEANNE. And what do you think about all this?

EMILE. The man is innocent.

ABBÉ. Yes, but in my view it is and always will be despicable to break one's promise, and unpardonable where a woman and a child are concerned.

EMILE. I should certainly be inclined to feel the same as you now, as this concerns my sister, but I am unfortunately prevented from casting the first stone, because I have committed the same offence myself.

ABBÉ. Although I am innocent in this respect, I still cast no stones; but the act condemns itself and is punished by its consequences.

JEANNE. Pray for him! For them!

ABBÉ. No, that I shall not do, for it is presumptuous to wish to change the counsels of the Lord. And what has happened is surely not the work of man.

SCENE 2

SCENE: *The Auberge des Adrets. Evening of the following day.*

ADOLPHE *and* HENRIETTE *are sitting at the table where* MAURICE *and* HENRIETTE *sat in Act II, Scene 1.*

ADOLPHE *has a cup of coffee in front of him.* HENRIETTE, *nothing.*

ADOLPHE. You really believe he will come here?

HENRIETTE. Without any doubt. He was released this morning for lack of evidence, but he did not want to show himself outside until dusk.

ADOLPHE. Poor fellow. You know, life has seemed quite horrible to me since yesterday.

HENRIETTE. And what about me? I am afraid to live, scarcely dare breathe, scarcely dare think even, as I know someone is spying not only on my words but on my thoughts.

ADOLPHE. So you were here that night when I couldn't find you.

HENRIETTE. Yes, but don't speak of it. I could die of shame when I think of it. Adolphe, you are made of other and better stuff than he and I. . . .

ADOLPHE. No, no, no!

HENRIETTE. Yes, yes. And what persuaded me to stay? I was lazy; I was tired. His success bewitched me. I can't explain it. But if you had come, it would never have happened. . . . And today you are the great one and he the little, least of the least. Yesterday he had a hundred thousand francs, and today he is penniless, as his play has been withdrawn. He will never be cleared in public opinion, for it will condemn him for his infidelity as severely as if he were the murderer. Anyhow, the most considered opinion is that the child died from sorrow, so he *was* the cause of its death.

ADOLPHE. Henriette, you know my opinion, but I should like to be sure you are both completely innocent. Won't you tell me what your terrible words meant? It can't have been just idle chatter on such a festive occasion to talk so much of killing and the scaffold.

HENRIETTE. It wasn't idle chatter. It was something that had to be said and something I can't talk about. But I have no right to appear innocent in your eyes, for I am not innocent.

ADOLPHE. I don't understand.

HENRIETTE. Then let's talk about something else. . . . Has it ever occurred to you that there are many unpunished criminals at large, even among our intimate friends?

ADOLPHE, *uneasily*. How so? What do you mean?

HENRIETTE. Don't you think everyone at some time in his life does something that would be against the law if it were found out?

ADOLPHE. Yes, I think that is so, but no misdeed remains unpunished, at least by conscience.

He rises and unbuttons his coat.

And . . . nobody is a really good human being who has not erred. *Breathing heavily.* For to know how to forgive, one must have needed forgiveness oneself. . . . I once had a friend whom we called the Saint; he never spoke an ill word about anyone, forgave everything and everybody, and received insults with an extraordinary kind of satisfaction which we couldn't explain. At last, late in life, he told me his secret in a word: "I am a penitent."

He sits down. HENRIETTE *regards him silently, in surprise.* ADOLPHE *continues as if to himself.*

There are crimes not mentioned in the Criminal Code, and

they are the worst ones, for we have to punish them ourselves, and no judge is so severe as oneself.

Pause.

HENRIETTE. Well, this friend of yours, did he find peace?

ADOLPHE. After years of self-torture, he attained a certain degree of peace, but life never held any pleasure for him. He
dared not accept any mark of distinction and never felt he
deserved a kind word or well-earned praise. In a word, he
could never forgive himself.

HENRIETTE. Never? What had he done?

ADOLPHE. He wished the life out of his father, and when the
father suddenly died, the son imagined he had killed him.
These imaginings were taken as symptoms of sickness, and
he was put into a Home, from which after a while he
emerged cured—so they said. But he still had his sense of
guilt, and so he continued to punish himself for his evil
thoughts.

HENRIETTE. Are you sure an evil will cannot kill?

ADOLPHE. In a mystic way, you mean?

HENRIETTE. If you like. Let's call it mystic. In my family I am
sure that my mother, and we brothers and sisters, killed my
father with our hatred. You see, he had a terrible way of
systematically opposing all our likes and desires, and where
he found any real vocation he tried to uproot it. And so he
roused an opposition that became charged with hatred, and
in the end it grew so powerful that he pined away, was
neutralised, lost his will-power, and finally wished himself
dead.

ADOLPHE. And your conscience never reproached you?

HENRIETTE. No. For that matter, I don't know what conscience
is.

ADOLPHE. Don't you? Well, you will know soon. *Silence.* How
do you think Maurice will look when he walks in here? What
do you think he will say?

HENRIETTE. Do you know, yesterday, while we were waiting
for you, he and I tried to make the same sort of guesses
about you.

ADOLPHE. And?

HENRIETTE. We guessed completely wrong.

ADOLPHE. Can you tell me why you sent me that message?

HENRIETTE. Malice, recklessness, sheer cruelty.

ADOLPHE. Strange, the way you recognise your misdeeds but don't repent of them.

HENRIETTE. It's surely because I don't feel fully responsible for them. They are like the dirt left by all the things one handles during the day that one washes off at night. . . . But tell me something. Do you really think as highly of human nature as you profess to?

ADOLPHE. Well, we are a little better than our reputation—and a little worse.

HENRIETTE. That's not a direct answer.

ADOLPHE. No, it's not. But will you give me a direct answer when I ask you: do you still love Maurice?

HENRIETTE. I don't know until I see him. But at this moment I feel no longing for him, and I think I could live very well without him.

ADOLPHE. I think that's quite likely. But you are chained now to his fate. . . . Hush! Here he comes.

HENRIETTE. How everything repeats itself! Just the same situation and the same words as yesterday, when it was *you* who were expected.

MAURICE *enters, white as death, hollow-eyed, unshaven.*

MAURICE. Here I am, dear friends, if this be me. For last night in the cell has changed me into another person. *Gazes at* HENRIETTE *and* ADOLPHE.

ADOLPHE. Sit down and pull yourself together. Then we can talk things over.

MAURICE, *to* HENRIETTE. Perhaps I am *de trop*.

ADOLPHE. Don't be bitter towards us.

MAURICE. I have grown evil in these twenty-four hours, and so suspicious that I shall soon have to go my way alone. Anyhow, who wants to keep a murderer company?

HENRIETTE. Surely you have been cleared.

MAURICE, *picking up a newspaper*. By the police, yes, but not by the public. Here you see the murderer, Maurice Gérard,

once the playwright, and his mistress, Henriette Mauclerc . . .

HENRIETTE. Oh my mother! My brothers and sisters! Lord
Jesus, help us!

MAURICE. Do you see? I really do look like a murderer too.
And it's also hinted that I stole my play. So not a trace is
left of yesterday's conqueror. And in his place my rival,
Octave, appears on the playbill. And it is he who will collect
my hundred thousand francs. O Solon, Solon! Such is fortune, such is fame! You are lucky, Adolphe, not to have had
any success so far.

HENRIETTE. Oh, but don't you know Adolphe has had a great
success in London and won the top award?

MAURICE, *darkly*. No, I didn't know. Is that true, Adolphe?

ADOLPHE. Perfectly true, but I have refused the award.

HENRIETTE, *pointedly*. That I didn't know. Are you debarred
from accepting distinctions—like your friend?

ADOLPHE. My friend? *Embarrassed*. Oh yes, yes!

MAURICE. I'm glad of your success, but it makes a gulf between
us.

ADOLPHE. I expected that. I'm bound to be as lonely with my
success as you with your adversity. To think that one's good
fortune should hurt others. Life is appalling.

*During the following speech two men in civilian clothes
enter unnoticed and sit at a table in the background.*

MAURICE. You say that. And what am I to say? It's as if a
black veil had been pulled over my eyes and changed the
whole shape and colour of life. This room is like yesterday's
room, but it is quite different. I recognise you both, it is true,
but you have new faces. I'm searching for words, because
I don't know what to say to you. I ought to defend myself,
but I can't. And I almost miss my cell, which at least protected me from those curious glances which pierce right
through me. The murderer Maurice and his mistress. You
don't love me any more than I care for you. Today you are
ugly, clumsy, empty, repellent.

ADOLPHE. Come, come, pull yourself together! That you have
been discharged, cleared of all suspicion, is bound to appear

in some evening paper. And that will put an end to all the accusations. Your play is certain to be put on again, and at worst you can write a new one. Leave Paris for a year and let the whole thing be forgotten. You, who exonerated human nature, will be reinstated yourself.

MAURICE. Ha ha! Human nature! Ha ha!

ADOLPHE. Have you lost your faith in its goodness?

MAURICE. Yes. If I ever believed in it. Perhaps that was just a mood, a way of looking at things, a courtesy to wild beasts. If I, who was held to be among the better ones, can be so utterly base, how vile the others must be!

ADOLPHE. Now I'm going out to buy all the evening papers. Then we shall certainly have a basis for new points of view.

MAURICE, *turning.* Two detectives . . . That means I am released under surveillance, so as to give myself away by careless talk.

ADOLPHE. They aren't detectives. That's just your imagination. I recognise them both. *Begins to go.*

MAURICE. Don't leave me alone, Adolphe. I fear Henriette and I may come to open explanations.

ADOLPHE. Be reasonable, Maurice, and think of your future. Try to calm him, Henriette. I shall be back in a moment. *Exit* ADOLPHE.

HENRIETTE. Maurice, what do you think now about our guilt or guiltlessness?

MAURICE. I have not murdered. I only talked a lot of hot air when I was drunk. But it is your crime which walks again— and you have grafted it on to me.

HENRIETTE. Is that the tone you're taking? Was it not you who cursed your own child, who wished that it did not exist, and wanted to go away without farewells? And was it not I who begged you to go and see Marion and pay a visit to Madame Catherine's place?

MAURICE. Yes, you are right. Forgive me. You were more humane than I, and the guilt is all mine. Forgive me. But at the same time I am guiltless. Who has tied this net out of which I can never escape? Guilty and guiltless, guiltless and guilty. This is driving me mad. Look! They are sitting over there, listening. . . . And no waiter cares to serve us. I shall go and order a cup of tea. Do you want anything?

HENRIETTE. Nothing.

Exit MAURICE.

The FIRST DETECTIVE *approaches* HENRIETTE.

DETECTIVE. Let me look at your papers, young woman.[2]

HENRIETTE. Young woman! How dare you!

DETECTIVE. Dare? I'll teach you, you tart!

HENRIETTE. Whatever do you mean?

DETECTIVE. Prostitutes are under my supervision. Well, yesterday you were here with one man, today with another. That amounts to prostitution. And unescorted ladies are not served here. So come along. Follow me!

HENRIETTE. My escort will be back in a minute.

DETECTIVE. Nice kind of escort. Hardly a protection for a lady.

HENRIETTE. O God! My mother! My brothers and sisters! . . . Don't you realise that I'm of good family?

DETECTIVE. A fine one, I'm sure. But anyway, the evening papers have made you famous. Come along!

HENRIETTE. Where to? Where am I to go?

DETECTIVE. To the Bureau, of course. To get a little card; a license which obliges you to have free medical attention.

HENRIETTE. Lord Jesus Christ, this can't be true!

DETECTIVE, *taking her arm.* Not true, eh?

HENRIETTE, *falling on her knees.* Save me! Maurice, help!

DETECTIVE. Hold your tongue! Don't struggle, damn you!

Enter MAURICE, *followed by the* WAITER.

WAITER. Gentlemen of your kind are not served here. Pay and get out! And take your tart with you.

MAURICE *desperately searches his pocket-book.*

MAURICE. Henriette, pay for me and let's get away. I haven't a sou on me.

HENRIETTE *looks in her purse.*

[2] NOTE. In the original, the Detective uses the familiar second person to Henriette, which enrages her. "Young woman" is used as an equivalent insult.

WAITER. So it's the lady who pays for her "Alphonse." "Alphonse!" Do you know what that means?

HENRIETTE. My God! I haven't any money either. Why doesn't Adolphe come back?

DETECTIVE. What a damned pack of people! Get going! Leave something as security. Women like her usually have their fingers covered with rings.

MAURICE. Is it possible that we have sunk so low?

HENRIETTE *pulls off a ring and hands it to the* WAITER.

HENRIETTE. The Abbé was right. This is not the work of man.

MAURICE. No, it's the work of the devil. . . . But if we leave before Adolphe comes back, he will think that we have deceived him and slipped away.

HENRIETTE. That would be in keeping with the rest. Anyhow, it's the river for us now, isn't it?

MAURICE *takes* HENRIETTE's *hand as they go out.*

MAURICE. The river, yes!

ACT IV

SCENE 1

SCENE: *Beside the statue of Adam and Eve in the Luxembourg Gardens, late afternoon the following day.*
The wind is blowing in the trees and stirring leaves, straws, and bits of paper on the ground.

MAURICE *and* HENRIETTE *are seated on a bench.*

HENRIETTE. You don't want to die?

MAURICE. No, I daren't. I imagine myself freezing in the grave, with only a sheet over me and a few shavings underneath. Besides, it seems to me that I still have something left undone, although I don't know what it is.

HENRIETTE. I can guess what it is.

MAURICE. Tell me.

HENRIETTE. It is revenge. . . . You, like me, suspect Jeanne and Emile of having set those detectives on me yesterday. Only a woman could think up such a revenge on a rival.

MAURICE. Those were my thoughts. But you know my suspicions go even further. It's as if these last days of suffering have sharpened my wits. For instance, can you explain why the waiter at the Auberge des Adrets and the head waiter at the Pavilion were not called to give evidence at the hearing?

HENRIETTE. I hadn't thought of it before, but yes, I do know why. They had no evidence to give, because they had not listened to our conversation at all.

MAURICE. Then how did the Commissaire know what we had said?

HENRIETTE. He didn't know, but he figured it out. He guessed and guessed right. Perhaps he has had a similar case before.

MAURICE. Or else he knew from our looks what we had said. There certainly are people who can read the thoughts of others. He found it quite natural that we should call Adolphe, as he was the dupe, the ass. That appears to be the rule, with the slight exception that he is generally called the idiot. But as there was talk of a chariot, a triumphal chariot, ass came more readily to mind. It's simple to find the fourth factor when you know three.

HENRIETTE. To think that we let ourselves be so completely taken in!

MAURICE. That's due to thinking well of people. That's what one gets for it. But I may tell you that, behind this Commissaire, who, by the way, must be an unmitigated scoundrel, I suspect there is another.

HENRIETTE. You mean the Abbé, who was playing the part of private detective.

MAURICE. That's who I mean. That man has to hear so many confessions. And don't forget this—Adolphe told me himself he had been in Saint-Germain that morning. What did he do there? Told the tale, of course, and bewailed his fate. And then the Abbé added two and two together for the Commissaire.

HENRIETTE. Tell me something. Do you trust Adolphe?

MAURICE. I don't trust any human being any longer.

HENRIETTE. Not even Adolphe?

MAURICE. Him least of all. How can I trust an enemy, a man whose mistress I stole?

HENRIETTE. Well, as you said it first, I will give you a few details about our friend. You know he refused that award from London. Can you think of any reason?

MAURICE. No.

HENRIETTE. Well, he considers himself unworthy of it, and he has taken a penitential vow not to receive any distinctions.

MAURICE. Is that possible? Why, what has he done?

HENRIETTE. He has committed a crime which is not punishable by law. That's what he told me, in an indirect way.

MAURICE. He too! He, the best, the most perfect of men, who never speaks ill of anyone, and forgives everything.

HENRIETTE. Yes. So you see, we are no worse than others. Although we are hunted as if by devils night and day.

MAURICE. He too! Then human nature has not been slandered. . . . But if he was capable of *one* crime, then one may expect anything of him. Perhaps it was he who set the police on you yesterday. Now that I come to think of it, it was he who sneaked away from us, when he saw us in the newspaper, and he was lying when he insisted those fellows weren't police. One may expect anything of a lover who has been deceived.

HENRIETTE. Would he be so low? No, it's impossible. Impossible.

MAURICE. Why? As he is a scoundrel . . . What did you talk about yesterday before I came?

HENRIETTE. He spoke nothing but good of you.

MAURICE. You're lying.

HENRIETTE, *collecting herself and changing her tone.* Listen, there's still one person you haven't suspected at all—I don't know why. Have you considered Madame Cathérine's changing attitude about all this? In the end, didn't she say right out that she believed you capable of anything?

MAURICE. Yes, she certainly did say that—and that shows what kind of a person she is. Because to think so ill of another without good reason, you must be a complete scoundrel yourself.

HENRIETTE *stares at him. Silence.*

HENRIETTE. To think so ill of another, you must be a complete scoundrel yourself.

MAURICE. What do you mean?

HENRIETTE. What I said.

MAURICE. Do you mean that I . . . ?

HENRIETTE. Yes, that's what I do mean now. Listen. Did you meet anyone but Marion on your visit that morning?

MAURICE. Why do you ask?

HENRIETTE. Why do you think?

MAURICE. Well, as you appear to know it, yes, I met Jeanne too.

HENRIETTE. Then why did you lie to me?

MAURICE. I wanted to spare you.

HENRIETTE. And now you want me to believe someone who has lied to me. No, my dear, now I believe that you committed that murder.

MAURICE. Wait a minute! Now we have reached the point where my thoughts have been heading, but which I resisted for as long as possible. . . . It is remarkable how the thing that lies nearest is the last thing one sees, and what one does not want to believe, one does not believe. . . . Tell me something. Where did you go yesterday morning, after we parted in the Bois?

HENRIETTE. Why?

MAURICE. You were either at Adolphe's, which you couldn't have been, because he was giving a lesson, or you went—to—Marion.

HENRIETTE. Now I am convinced that you are the murderer.

MAURICE. And I that you are the murderess. Because you alone had an interest in the child being out of the way—the stone upsetting the carriage, as you so aptly put it.

HENRIETTE. That was your expression.

MAURICE. And the one who had the interest committed the crime.

HENRIETTE. Maurice, we have been running round and round this treadmill, scourging one another. Let us stop now or else we shall go quite mad.

MAURICE. You are that already.

HENRIETTE. Don't you think it is time for us to part, before we drive one another insane?

MAURICE. Yes, I do think so.

HENRIETTE, *rising*. Then, goodbye.

Two men in civilian clothes appear in the background.

HENRIETTE *turns back to* MAURICE.

There they are again.

MAURICE. The dark angels who will drive us from the garden.

HENRIETTE. And force us upon each other, as if we were welded together.

MAURICE. Or as if we were condemned to life-long marriage. Should we in fact marry? Share the same home, and be able to shut the door on the world and perhaps in the end find peace?

HENRIETTE. Shut ourselves in to torture one another to death; lock ourselves in, each with his ghost as marriage portion, you tormenting me with Adolphe's memory and I torturing you with Jeanne's—and Marion's.

MAURICE. Never mention Marion's name again! You know that she is being buried today—perhaps at this very moment.

HENRIETTE. And you are not there. What does that mean?

MAURICE. It means that both Jeanne and the police have warned me of the crowd's fury.

HENRIETTE. Coward too?

MAURICE. All the vices. How could you care for me?

HENRIETTE. Because two days ago you were a different person, worthy of being loved.

MAURICE. And now sunk to such depths.

HENRIETTE. Not that. But you are beginning to flaunt bad qualities which are not your own.

MAURICE. But yours.

HENRIETTE. Perhaps. For when you appear worse, I at once feel rather better.

MAURICE. It's like going about, passing on a certain kind of disease.

HENRIETTE. And you have become coarse too!

MAURICE. I notice that myself. I don't recognise myself since that night in gaol. They put in one person and let out another, through that gate that separates us from society. You know, now I feel I am the enemy of mankind. I should like to set fire to the earth and dry up the sea, for nothing less than a world conflagration can wipe out my dishonour.

HENRIETTE. I had a letter from my mother today. My mother is the widow of a major and has high-minded, old-fashioned ideas about honour and all that. Would you care to read the letter? No, you wouldn't! Do you realise I am an outcast? My respectable acquaintances won't have anything to do with me, and if I go about alone, the police will take me up. Do you understand now that we must marry?

MAURICE. We hate one another and yet we must marry. That is hell itself. But, Henriette, before we join our destinies, you must tell me your secret, so that we are more evenly matched.

HENRIETTE. Very well, I will tell you. I had a friend who got into trouble . . . you understand me? I wanted to help her, for her future was at stake. And as I was unskilled, she died.

MAURICE. That was a rash thing to do, but it was rather noble.

HENRIETTE. So you say now, but next time you are angry, you will reproach me with it.

MAURICE. No, I won't do that . . . but I cannot deny that this shakes my confidence. I'm afraid to be with you. Tell me —is her lover still alive and does he know you were responsible?

HENRIETTE. He was just as guilty.

MAURICE. Then suppose his conscience were to awake—that often does happen—and he felt obliged to denounce you. Then you would be lost.

HENRIETTE. I know that very well, and it is this constant dread which drives me to live so fast and furiously, so as not to have time to wake to full consciousness.

MAURICE. And now you want me to take my marriage portion of your dread. That is asking too much.

HENRIETTE. But since I have shared the dishonour of Maurice, the murderer . . .

MAURICE. Let's put an end to . . .

HENRIETTE. No, this is not the end yet, and I shall not loose my hold until I have seen right through you. For you shan't go round thinking yourself better than I am.

MAURICE. You want to fight me, do you? Very well, you shall.

HENRIETTE. For life and death.

A roll of drums in the distance.

MAURICE. The garden is to be closed. "Cursed is the ground for thy sake . . . thorns also and thistles shall it bring forth to thee."

HENRIETTE. "And the Lord said unto the woman . . ."

The park KEEPER, *in uniform, approaches.*

KEEPER, *courteously.* Monsieur, Madame, the garden must be closed.

SCENE 2

SCENE: *The Crémerie. The same evening.*

MADAME CATHÉRINE *at the counter, making entries in a book.*

ADOLPHE *and* HENRIETTE *at a table.*

ADOLPHE, *calmly, kindly.* But if for the hundredth time I swear that I did not sneak away, but on the contrary thought you had given me the slip, that ought to convince you.

HENRIETTE. But why did you fool me by saying they weren't police?

ADOLPHE. I didn't think they were myself, and I also said it to reassure you.

HENRIETTE. When you put it that way, I do believe you. And

now you must believe me too, when I reveal my innermost thoughts to you.

ADOLPHE. Go on.

HENRIETTE. But you mustn't make your usual retort about fancy and imagination.

ADOLPHE. You seem to have reason to fear I may.

HENRIETTE. I don't fear anything, but I know you and your scepticism. . . . Well then . . . but you mustn't tell anyone this. Promise me that.

ADOLPHE. I promise.

HENRIETTE. Well, you've got to take in, terrible though it is, that I have some proof that Maurice is guilty—or at least reasonable grounds for suspicion. . . .

ADOLPHE. What are you saying?

HENRIETTE. Listen. Then you can judge. When Maurice left me in the Bois, he said he was going to see Marion alone, while the mother was out. But now, afterwards, it has come out that he did meet the mother. So he was lying to me.

ADOLPHE. That's possible, and probably from the best of motives, but how can anyone conclude from that that he committed murder?

HENRIETTE. Can't you see? Don't you understand?

ADOLPHE. Not in the least.

HENRIETTE. Because you don't want to. Well, then I have no choice but to inform on him, and then we will see if he can establish an alibi.

ADOLPHE. Henriette, let me tell you the whole grim truth. You and he are both on the brink—of madness. You are in the grip of the demons of suspicion, and each of you is tearing the other to pieces with your sense of partial guilt. Let me see if my guess is right. Doesn't he also suspect you of murdering his child?

HENRIETTE. Yes, he's as insane as that.

ADOLPHE. You call his suspicions insane, but not your own.

HENRIETTE. Prove the contrary—or that I suspect him unjustly.

ADOLPHE. Yes, that is easily done. A further autopsy has proved that Marion died of a recognised disease—with a strange name I can't now remember.

HENRIETTE. Is that true?

ADOLPHE. The official report is in today's paper.

HENRIETTE. You can't go by that. It may have been falsified.

ADOLPHE. Henriette! Take care, or you may go over the edge without realising it. Above all, beware of making accusations which might land you in prison. Beware! *He puts his hand on her head.* Do you hate Maurice?

HENRIETTE. Beyond all bounds.

ADOLPHE. Where love turns to hatred, the love was already tainted.

HENRIETTE, *more calmly.* What shall I do? Tell me, you who alone understand me.

ADOLPHE. But you don't want any sermons.

HENRIETTE. Have you nothing else to offer me?

ADOLPHE. Nothing. But they have helped me.

HENRIETTE. Preach away then.

ADOLPHE. Try to turn your hatred against yourself. Lance your own boil, because that is the seat of *your* evil.

HENRIETTE. Explain yourself!

ADOLPHE. First, break with Maurice, so you haven't a chance to cultivate your consciences together. Put an end to your artistic career, for which your only vocation was a desire for the gay Bohemian life, as they call it. You see now how gay it is! Go home to your mother.

HENRIETTE. Never.

ADOLPHE. Somewhere else then.

HENRIETTE. Adolphe, I presume you know I have guessed your secret and realise why you wouldn't accept that award.

ADOLPHE. I suppose you understood that half-hinted story?

HENRIETTE. Well, yes. But what did you do to gain peace?

ADOLPHE. As I intimated. I grew conscious of my guilt, repented, resolved to atone, and lived the life of a penitent.

HENRIETTE. How can you repent when, like me, you haven't any conscience? Is repentance a grace one gets like faith?

ADOLPHE. Everything is grace, but one doesn't get it, you know, unless one seeks for it. . . . Seek!

HENRIETTE *is silent.*

And don't let the time go by. If you do, you may harden and go to pieces among those past helping.

HENRIETTE, *after a further silence.* Is conscience fear of punishment?

ADOLPHE. No, it is the hatred of our better natures for the misdeeds of our lower natures.

HENRIETTE. In that case, I have a conscience too.

ADOLPHE. Of course you have, but . . .

HENRIETTE. Tell me, Adolphe, are you what one means by religious?

ADOLPHE. Not in the least.

HENRIETTE. It's all so extraordinary. Whatever is religion?

ADOLPHE. I just don't know, and I don't believe anyone can tell you. It seems to me sometimes that it's a punishment, because no one gets religion who hasn't a bad conscience.

HENRIETTE. Yes, it is a punishment. . . . Now I know what I must do. . . . Goodbye, Adolphe.

ADOLPHE. Are you going away?

HENRIETTE. Yes, I am going away . . . To where you said. Goodbye, my friend. Goodbye, Madame Cathérine.

MME CATHÉRINE. Are you off in such a hurry?

HENRIETTE. Yes.

ADOLPHE. Would you like me to come with you?

HENRIETTE. That wouldn't do. I must go alone, as alone as I came in here one spring day, here where I didn't belong, believing that there was something called freedom, which doesn't exist. Goodbye.

Exit HENRIETTE.

MME CATHÉRINE. I hope that lady never comes back and I wish she had never come here at all.

ADOLPHE. Who knows if she had not some mission to fulfil here? And in any case, she deserves pity, boundless pity.

MME CATHÉRINE. I don't deny that, for we all deserve it. . . .

ADOLPHE. She has actually done less wrong than the rest of us. . . .

MME CATHÉRINE. Possible, but not probable.

ADOLPHE. You are always hard, Madame Cathérine. Tell me something. Haven't you ever done anything wrong?

MME CATHÉRINE, *startled.* Certainly, for I am a sinful human being. But anyone who has fallen through thin ice has the right and the duty to tell others not to go that way. And without being considered hard or uncharitable. Didn't I say to Monsieur Maurice, when that same lady came in here: "Take care! Don't go there!" But he went and so he fell in. Like a naughty, self-willed child. And whoever behaves in that way gets a thrashing like a disobedient boy.

ADOLPHE. Well, hasn't he had his thrashing?

MME CATHÉRINE. Yes, but it doesn't seem to have been enough, for he's still going round pitying himself.

ADOLPHE. That is a very popular interpretation of this complicated matter.

MME CATHÉRINE. Bosh! You do nothing but philosophise about your vices, and while you're at it, the police come and solve the riddle. Now leave me in peace to do my accounts.

ADOLPHE. Here is Maurice.

MME CATHÉRINE. Yes, God bless him!

MAURICE *enters, very flushed, and sits down beside* ADOLPHE.

MAURICE. Good evening.

MADAME CATHÉRINE *nods and goes on adding.*

ADOLPHE. How are things with you?

MAURICE. Well, beginning to straighten out now.

ADOLPHE *hands him a newspaper, which he does not take.*

ADOLPHE. So you have seen the paper?

MAURICE. No, I don't read the papers any more. There's nothing in them but infamy.

ADOLPHE. Well, but you had better read this before . . .

MAURICE. No, I won't. It's only lies. But now you shall hear a new view. . . . Have you guessed who committed the murder?

ADOLPHE. No one! No one!

MAURICE. Do you know where Henriette was during that quarter of an hour when the child was alone? Well, she was *there*. And it is she who did it.

ADOLPHE. You are crazy, man!

MAURICE. Not I, but Henriette is crazy, for she suspects me and has threatened to inform on me.

ADOLPHE. Henriette was here just now and used the same words as you. You are both crazy, for it has now been established by a second autopsy that the child died from a recognised disease, the name of which escapes me.

MAURICE. That's not true.

ADOLPHE. That's what she said too. But the official report is there in the paper.

MAURICE. Official report? Then it's been falsified.

ADOLPHE. She said that too. You have the same mental sickness, the two of you. But I managed to make her see her lunacy.

MAURICE. Where has she gone?

ADOLPHE. She has gone far away—to begin a new life.

MAURICE. Mm, mm! . . . Did you go to the funeral?

ADOLPHE. Yes, I was there.

MAURICE. Well?

ADOLPHE. Well, Jeanne was calm and had no hard word to say about you.

MAURICE. She is a good woman.

ADOLPHE. Then why did you throw her over?

MAURICE. I was crazy, quite beyond myself, and then we drank champagne . . .

ADOLPHE. Do you understand now why she cried when you drank champagne?

MAURICE. Yes, I understand now. . . . And because I do, I have already written and asked her to forgive me. . . . Do you think she will forgive me?

ADOLPHE. I am sure she will, for she hasn't it in her to hate anyone.

MAURICE. Do you think she will really forgive, so that she will want to come back to me?

ADOLPHE. I don't know about that. You have given such proof of your infidelity that she can hardly trust her fate to you any longer.

MAURICE. Yes, but I can feel that her affection for me has not gone. I know she will come back.

ADOLPHE. How do you know that? What makes you believe it? Didn't you suspect her and that decent brother of hers of revenging themselves by setting the police on Henriette as a prostitute?

MAURICE. I don't think that any longer. Although Emile is a queer customer.

MME CATHÉRINE. Now look here, what are you saying about Monsieur Emile? Of course, he is only a workman, but if only everyone was as correct as he is! There's no flaw in him, and he has understanding and tact . . .

Enter EMILE.

EMILE. Monsieur Gérard?

MAURICE. Here I am.

EMILE. Excuse me, but I have something private to say to you.

MAURICE. Please say it. We are all friends here.

The ABBÉ *enters and seats himself.*

EMILE *glances at him.*

EMILE. Perhaps after all . . .

MAURICE. It makes no difference. The Abbé is a friend too, although he and I hold different opinions.

EMILE. You know who I am, Monsieur Gérard? My sister has only asked me to give you this package as an answer to your letter.

MAURICE *takes the package and opens it.*

Now I only have to add, as I am, as it were, my sister's guardian, that on her behalf and on my own, I acknowledge you, Monsieur Gérard, free of all obligations, now that the natural bond between you no longer exists.

MAURICE. But you must have a grudge against me.

EMILE. Must I? No, I don't see why. On the other hand, I should like to have a declaration from you, Monsieur Gérard, here in the presence of your friends, that you don't think me or my sister so low that we could have put the police on Mademoiselle Henriette.

MAURICE. I wish to take back what I said and offer you my apologies, if you will accept them.

EMILE. They are accepted. I wish you all a good evening.

ALL. Good evening.

Exit EMILE.

MAURICE. The tie and the gloves which Jeanne gave me for the opening night of my play, and which I let Henriette throw into the fireplace. Who snatched them back? Everything is dug up; everything repeats itself. . . . And when she gave them to me in the cemetery, she said I was to look fine and handsome, so that others would like me too. . . . She stayed at home herself. . . . This hurt her too deeply, and well it might. I should not be in the company of decent people. Oh, have I done this? Scoffed at a gift from a kind heart, scorned a sacrifice to my own good. This I threw away for—a laurel wreath, which is lying on the rubbish heap, and a bust which should stand in the pillory. . . . Monsieur l'Abbé, now I put myself in your hands.

ABBÉ. Welcome!

MAURICE. Say the word I need.

ABBÉ. Do you mean me to contradict your self-accusations and inform you that you have done nothing wrong?

MAURICE. Say the right word!

ABBÉ. With your permission then, I must say that I have found your behaviour as abominable as you have found it yourself.

MAURICE. What shall I do? What shall I do to get free of all this?

ABBÉ. You know as well as I do.

MAURICE. No, I only know that I am lost, that my life is ruined, my career closed, my reputation in this world lost for ever.

ABBÉ. And so you are looking for a new existence in another, better world, in which you are beginning to believe?

MAURICE. That is so.

ABBÉ. You have been living for the flesh and now you wish to live for the spirit. Are you sure then that this world no longer holds any attractions for you?

MAURICE. None. Honour—an illusion; gold—dry leaves; women —intoxicants . . . Let me hide behind your consecrated walls and forget this appalling dream, which has taken two days and lasted two eternities.

ABBÉ. Very well. But this is not the place to go into the matter more closely. Let us arrange to meet in Saint-Germain this evening at nine o'clock. I am going, as it happens, to preach to the penitentiaries of Saint-Lazare, and that can be your first step on the hard road of penance.

MAURICE. Penance?

ABBÉ. Yes, did you not wish . . . ?

MAURICE. Yes, yes!

ABBÉ. After that we have a vigil from midnight until two o'clock.

MAURICE. That will be good.

ABBÉ. Give me your hand, so that you will not look back.

MAURICE, *rising and giving him his hand.* Here is my hand with all my heart.

The SERVING GIRL *enters from the kitchen.*

GIRL. There is a telephone call for Monsieur Maurice.

MAURICE. Who from?

GIRL. From the theatre.

MAURICE *tries to break away from the* ABBÉ, *but he holds him fast.*

ABBÉ, *to the* GIRL. Ask what it is about.

GIRL. Well, they want to know if Monsieur Maurice will be at the performance tonight.

ABBÉ, *to* MAURICE, *who is still trying to get free.* No, I will not let go.

MAURICE, *to the* GIRL. What performance is it?

ADOLPHE. Why don't you read the paper?

MME CATHÉRINE *and* ABBÉ. He hasn't read the paper!

MAURICE. It's all lies and slander. *To the* GIRL. Tell them at the theatre that I am engaged tonight. I am going to church. *The* GIRL *goes out to the kitchen.*

ADOLPHE. As you won't read the paper, I had better tell you that the theatre is putting on your play again, now that you are exonerated. And your literary friends have arranged to pay a tribute to you tonight—on the stage with the curtain up—a tribute to your uncontested talent.

MAURICE. It's not true.

ALL. It is true.

MAURICE, *after a silence.* I don't deserve this.

ABBÉ. Good!

ADOLPHE. And there's more still, Maurice.

MAURICE, *hiding his face in his hands.* More!

MME CATHÉRINE. A hundred thousand francs. You see how they have come back to you. And the villa outside the city. Everything is coming back, except Mademoiselle Henriette.

ABBÉ, *smiling.* You should take it all a little more seriously, Madame Cathérine.

MME CATHÉRINE. No, but you see I can't, I can't keep serious any longer.

She puts her handkerchief to her face and bursts out laughing.

ADOLPHE. Well, Maurice, it's eight o'clock at the theatre.

ABBÉ. But it's nine o'clock at the church.

ADOLPHE. Maurice!

MME CATHÉRINE. Monsieur Maurice, we must hear the end now.

MAURICE *puts his head on his arms on the table.*

ADOLPHE. Free him, Monsieur l'Abbé!

ABBÉ. It is not for me to set free or to bind. He must do that himself.

MAURICE, *rising.* Very well, I shall go with the Abbé.

ABBÉ. No, my young friend. I have nothing to give you but

a scolding, which you can give yourself. And you have a responsibility to yourself and your good reputation. That you have come through this so quickly is to me a sign that you suffered your punishment as intensely as if it had lasted an eternity. And when Providence has granted you absolution, there is nothing for me to add.

MAURICE. Why was I punished so severely when I was guiltless?

ABBÉ. Severely? Only two days. And guiltless you were not, for we are responsible for our thoughts, our words, and our desires. You murdered in your mind when you wished the life out of your child.

MAURICE. You are right. . . . But my decision is made. Tonight I will meet you at the church to have a reckoning with myself about all this—but tomorrow I shall go to the theatre.

MME CATHÉRINE. A good solution, Monsieur Maurice.

ADOLPHE. Yes, that's the solution. Phew!

ABBÉ. Yes, that is it.

THE DANCE OF DEATH

A Drama in Two Parts

FOREWORD

After *Crime and Crime* Strindberg wrote a number of historical dramas in which Shakespeare's influence is apparent. Then came *Easter*, his tender play of redemption, but even before his marriage to Harriet Bosse, the wheel had turned and Strindberg was once more plunged into icy gloom. Memories racked him and the old poisoned streams of hatred and suspicion demanded further violent expression. He decided to write a *Dance Macabre*, using Saint-Saëns' music; then, finding that the hated Ibsen had forestalled him by introducing this music in *John Gabriel Borkman*, Strindberg took the march, *Entry of the Boyars*, as theme tune for his new play, called by turn *Dance Macabre*, *Fight with Death*, *Death in the Dance*, *The Vampire*, and finally *The Dance of Death*.

Strindberg was uncertain at first whether to make his leading character a pilot captain, a retired professor, or a doctor, but finally chose a superannuated Captain of Artillery, O.C. of an island fortress. In this grim stone tower, which had once been a prison, Strindberg concentrated his sense of life's malevolence. Again, as in *The Father*, the theme of the play is married misery, and Edgar, the larger-than-life Captain, destroys the peace of all who are in contact with him, as he staggers from one death throe to the next.

The immediate model for Edgar was the son of a Swedish Battery Commander who had fought on the Danish side in the Prusso-Danish war of 1864; but the Captain in the *Dance of Death* is a highly composite character. Not only is he a caricature of a friend of Strindberg's who, as a Customs Inspector, became such an insufferable bully that in the end he had no one left to talk to, but also of several other of Strindberg's former associates, whom he now regarded as enemies— and of course the character also contains a great deal of Strindberg himself. The Captain's behaviour is in the highest degree extraordinary and his defence is Strindberg's own:

> Life is so strange. So against me, so
> vindictive that I became vindictive too . . .

In Kurt, the Quarantine Officer, returned after fifteen years
abroad, divorced and robbed of his children, Strindberg depicted another of his selves, sensuous, well-meaning, weak.
Even the use of the telegraph apparatus in the play derives
from Strindberg's own experience, for he was once apprenticed
to the telegraph service and learnt to send out weather reports.

Alice, the Captain's wife, is painted with the venom that
memories of his love-hatred for Siri von Essen, his first actress
wife, always roused in Strindberg, yet in *The Dance of Death*
he does not, in his usual way, lay the chief responsibility for
the disastrous marriage on the woman. It is interesting to consider what may have been in Strindberg's mind as he depicted
this bizarre couple. We know that at some point he had discovered from his horoscope, cast at his request by a friend,
that the hour of his birth was dominated by Saturn and Venus,
the most incompatible of planets. He may well have had this
planetary conflict in mind while he was creating Edgar and
his wife, Alice, in whom the saturnine evil and rancour run
parallel with an unresolved passion whose traces influence
even their most desperate moments. Another influence in the
depiction of this marriage "not made in heaven" may well
have been Swedenborg's *De coelo et inferno,* for at this period
Strindberg was deeply affected by his work.

By and large, with its battering cynical dialogue, its silent
nightmare action, and the pounding of the *Entry of the Boyars,*
Part One of *The Dance of Death* is a masterpiece of horror,
a caricature of tragedy.[1]

In Part Two, Strindberg for the first time created adolescent
characters. There are children in *The Father* and in *Easter,*
but here in Judith and Allan, the Captain's daughter and the
Quarantine Officer's son, are young adults in the turmoil of
first love. It is probable that the fact that Strindberg had spent
the summer of 1899 out in his beloved Baltic skerries, with
several young nephews and nieces and one of his daughters by

---

[1] How startlingly modern this play is, comparable with today's off-
beat theatre, with, for instance, certain of Eugène Ionesco's gro-
tesque and wildly funny tragedies.

his first marriage, had something to do with this. While maintaining the horrific atmosphere of the play, these young characters are amusingly but tenderly drawn. As Judith's mother, Alice, comments: "To think that flowers can grow out of filth!"

Part One of *The Dance of Death,* being in itself a full-length play, is usually presented alone, while Part Two, which is shorter and could not stand by itself, is seldom seen. But undoubtedly the two parts were intended to be played together as one play. Strindberg's compact scenes and terse dialogue are, of course, difficult to cut, but surely a skilled director could make a single play—even if a long one—out of the two parts.[2]

E. S.

I am indebted to Dr. O. Wieselgren for giving me permission to include, in the above Foreword, material from his programme note to the August 1959 production of *The Dance of Death* in Stockholm.

[2] And would not a Ionesco touch aid the production?

CHARACTERS: PART ONE

EDGAR, *Captain in the Garrison Artillery*
ALICE, *his wife, formerly an actress*
KURT, *Quarantine Officer*
JENNY, *a maid*
AN OLD WOMAN
A SENTRY (*non-speaking*)

The whole action takes place inside a fortress on an island off the coast of Sweden in the nineties.

SCENE: *The living-room in the round, grey stone fortress.*

Centre back is the old main entrance to the fortress: a double stone archway inset with glass doors. Beyond is a beach with gun emplacements and the sea.

In the walls on each side are smaller doors leading to other rooms. The one on the left also leads out of doors.

On either side of the big doorway are windows, in one of which are pots of flowers and in the other a cage of birds.

On the right is a cottage piano; below it a sewing-table and two armchairs.

On the left, towards the centre, is a writing-table equipped with telegraphic apparatus; below this family photographs are ranged on a whatnot. Nearby is a couch and against the wall a sideboard and a round porcelain stove.

Further left, beside the door, is a stand hung with accoutrements: swords and so forth. A mercurial barometer hangs on the wall. Near this is a bureau.

A lamp hangs from the ceiling. Over the piano is a portrait of a woman in theatrical costume between two large, beribboned laurel wreaths.

PART ONE

ACT I

SCENE 1

It is a warm autumn evening. The glass doors are open, and an artilleryman on sentry duty is seen down by the shore battery. He is wearing a busby with brush. Now and then his sword glitters in the red light of the setting sun. The sea is dark and still.

THE CAPTAIN is sitting in the armchair on the left of the sewing-table, fingering a cigar which has gone out. He is in undress uniform, the worse for wear, with riding-boots and spurs. He looks tired and bored.

ALICE is sitting in the armchair on the right, doing nothing. She looks tired but expectant.

THE CAPTAIN. Won't you play something for me?

ALICE, *indifferently but not crossly.* What shall I play?

THE CAPTAIN. What you like.

ALICE. You don't like my repertoire.

THE CAPTAIN. Nor you mine.

ALICE, *ambiguously.* Do you want the doors left open?

THE CAPTAIN. As you wish.

ALICE. Let's leave them then. *Pause.* Why aren't you smoking?

THE CAPTAIN. I can't stand strong tobacco any longer.

ALICE, *more kindly.* Smoke something milder then. As you say, it's your only joy.

THE CAPTAIN. Joy? Whatever's that?

ALICE. Don't ask me. I know no more of it than you. . . . Won't you have your whisky now?

THE CAPTAIN. I'll wait a little. . . . What's for supper?

ALICE. How should I know? Ask Kristin.

THE CAPTAIN. Oughtn't mackerel to be in soon? It *is* autumn now.

ALICE. Yes, it *is* autumn.

THE CAPTAIN. Outside and in. But, in spite of the cold that autumn brings, outside and in, a broiled mackerel with a slice of lemon and a glass of white burgundy is not to be despised.

ALICE. How eloquent you've become!

THE CAPTAIN. Have we any burgundy in the wine cellar?

ALICE. I'm unaware that we've had a wine cellar for the past five years.

THE CAPTAIN. You never are aware. However, we must get in a supply for our silver wedding.

ALICE. Do you really mean to celebrate that?

THE CAPTAIN. Naturally.

ALICE. It would be more natural to hide our misery, our twenty-five years of misery . . .

THE CAPTAIN. Misery there has been, my dear Alice, but pleasure too now and then. And one must make use of the short time left, for then comes the end.

ALICE. Is it the end? If only it were!

THE CAPTAIN. It *is* the end. Just enough left to wheel out on a barrow and put on a garden plot.

ALICE. All this fuss for a garden plot.

THE CAPTAIN. Well, that's how it is. It's not my doing.

ALICE. All this fuss! *Pause.* Have you had the mail?

THE CAPTAIN. Yes.

ALICE. Did the butcher's bill come?

THE CAPTAIN. Yes.

ALICE. How much was it?

THE CAPTAIN *takes a paper from his pocket and puts on his glasses, but immediately takes them off again.*

THE CAPTAIN. Look for yourself. I can't make it out.

ALICE. What's wrong with your eyes?

THE CAPTAIN. Don't know.

ALICE. Old age.

THE CAPTAIN. What nonsense! Me?

ALICE. Well, not me!

THE CAPTAIN. Hm.

ALICE, *looking at the bill.* Can you pay it?

THE CAPTAIN. Yes, but not at the moment.

ALICE. Later on, of course. In a year, when you've retired on
a small pension, and it's too late. Later on, when you get ill
again and . . .

THE CAPTAIN. Ill? I've never been ill. Just a little out of sorts
once. I shall live for another twenty years.

ALICE. That's not what the doctor thought.

THE CAPTAIN. Doctor!

ALICE. Well, who else could have a sound opinion about an
illness?

THE CAPTAIN. I haven't any illness, never have had, and never
shall have. I shall just drop down dead like an old soldier.

ALICE. Talking of the doctor, you know he's having a party
this evening.

THE CAPTAIN, *irritated.* Well, what of it? We haven't been invited because we don't mix with the doctor's family, and we
don't mix with 'em because we don't want to, because I
despise them. They're scum.

ALICE. You say that about everyone.

THE CAPTAIN. Everyone is scum.

ALICE. Except you.

THE CAPTAIN. Yes. I've behaved decently whatever's come
about. So I am not scum.

Pause.

ALICE. Do you want to play cards?

THE CAPTAIN. Might as well.

ALICE *takes a pack of cards from the drawer of the sewing-
table and begins to shuffle.*

ALICE. Just think of them having the band at the doctor's—for a private party!

THE CAPTAIN, *angrily*. That's because he sucks up to the Colonel in town. Sucks up, see? If you can do that . . . !

ALICE, *dealing*. Gerda and I were friends once, but she cheated me.

THE CAPTAIN. They're all cheats, the whole pack of them! . . . What's that card? What's trumps?

ALICE. Put your glasses on.

THE CAPTAIN. They're no use. . . . Well? Well?

ALICE. Spades are trumps.

THE CAPTAIN, *disappointed*. Spades?

ALICE, *playing*. Yes, that may be. In any case, we're written off by the new officers' wives.

THE CAPTAIN, *playing and taking the trick*. What's that matter? We don't give any parties, so it won't be noticed. I can get on alone—I always have.

ALICE. So can I. But the children—the children are growing up without any companions.

THE CAPTAIN. They'll have to find those for themselves in the town. . . . That was my trick. Any trumps left?

ALICE. Yes, one. That was mine.

THE CAPTAIN. Six and eight, that makes me fifteen.

ALICE. Fourteen! Fourteen!

THE CAPTAIN. Six and eight makes me fourteen . . . I seem to have forgotten how to count. And two makes sixteen . . . *Yawns*. Your deal.

ALICE. You're tired.

THE CAPTAIN, *dealing*. Not a bit.

ALICE, *listening*. One can hear the music even here. *Pause*. Do you think Kurt has been invited?

THE CAPTAIN. He arrived in the morning, so I daresay he's had time to unpack his dress suit, even if not to call on us.

ALICE. Quarantine Officer. Will there be quarantine here?

THE CAPTAIN. Yes.

ALICE. After all, he is my cousin—my name was the same as his once.

THE CAPTAIN. No great honour in that.

ALICE, *sharply.* Look here! You leave my family alone, and I'll leave yours!

THE CAPTAIN. Now, now! Don't let's start that again.

ALICE. Is the Quarantine Officer a doctor?

THE CAPTAIN. No. He's just a kind of clerk in the civil administration. Kurt has never got anywhere.

ALICE. He was a poor creature . . .

THE CAPTAIN. Who cost me money . . . And to leave his wife and children like that was scandalous.

ALICE. Don't be too harsh, Edgar!

THE CAPTAIN. Yes, that's what it was. And what's he been doing since, and in America? Eh? I can't say I'm aching for his company here. Although he was a nice lad and I used to enjoy arguing with him.

ALICE. Because he always gave in.

THE CAPTAIN, *haughtily.* Whether he gave in or not, he was at least somebody one could talk to. Here on the island there isn't one person who understands what I say. It's a community of nitwits.

ALICE. It's odd, isn't it, that Kurt should turn up just in time for our silver wedding? Whether it's celebrated or not.

THE CAPTAIN. Why is it odd? Oh yes, of course, it was he who brought us together and got you married, so they said.

ALICE. Didn't he?

THE CAPTAIN. Of course he did. It was all his idea . . . the merits of which I leave you to judge.

ALICE. A frivolous notion . . .

THE CAPTAIN. For which we've had to pay, not he.

ALICE. Yes. Just think if I were still on the stage. All my friends are stars now.

THE CAPTAIN, *rising.* Yes, yes, yes! Now I'll have my grog. *Goes to the cupboard and mixes a drink, which he takes standing.*

There ought to be a rail here to put one's foot on. Then one could imagine oneself in Copenhagen at the American Bar.

ALICE. We must have a rail made, just to remind us of Copenhagen. Those really were the best times we had.

THE CAPTAIN, *taking a long drink.* Yes. Do you remember Nimb's *navarin aux pommes? Smacks his lips.*

ALICE. No, but I remember the Tivoli concerts.

THE CAPTAIN. You have such exclusive tastes.

ALICE. You ought to be glad to have a wife with taste.

THE CAPTAIN. On occasions . . .

ALICE. When you want to boast about her.

THE CAPTAIN, *drinking.* They must be dancing at the doctor's. I can hear the bass tubas' three-four time—boom—boom—boom.

ALICE. I can hear the whole tune of the *Alcazar Waltz.* . . . Though the last time I waltzed wasn't yesterday.

THE CAPTAIN. Could you do it still?

ALICE. Still?

THE CAPTAIN. Ye-es. You're a bit past dancing, same as I am.

ALICE. I'm ten years younger than you.

THE CAPTAIN. Then we're the same age—for the lady always has to be ten years younger.

ALICE. How dare you! You're an old man, and I'm in my prime.

THE CAPTAIN. Oh, I know you can be perfectly charming—to others—when you choose.

ALICE. Shall we have the lamps lighted now?

THE CAPTAIN. If you like.

ALICE. Then ring.

THE CAPTAIN *goes slowly to the writing-table and rings a bell.*

Enter JENNY, *right.*

THE CAPTAIN. Will you please light the lamp, Jenny.

ALICE, *sharply.* Light the hanging lamp!

JENNY, *impudently.* Yes, milady!

JENNY *lights the lamp while* THE CAPTAIN *watches her.*

ALICE, *curtly.* Have you cleaned the chimney properly?

JENNY. It will do.

ALICE. That's not the way to answer.

THE CAPTAIN. Now, now . . .

ALICE, *to* JENNY. Go away! I'll light the lamp myself. That's best.

JENNY, *going.* I think so too.

ALICE, *rising.* Go away!

JENNY, *turning.* I wonder what you'd say if I did go, ma'am.

> ALICE *does not reply.*

> *Exit* JENNY.

> THE CAPTAIN *comes forward and lights the lamp.*

ALICE, *uneasily.* Do you think she will leave?

THE CAPTAIN. Wouldn't surprise me. Then we'd be ditched.

ALICE. It's your fault. You spoil them.

THE CAPTAIN. Rubbish! Look how polite they always are to me.

ALICE. Because you cringe to them. Just as you cringe to all your inferiors. Although you're a despot, at bottom you're a slave.

THE CAPTAIN. Come, come!

ALICE. Yes, you cringe to your men and your non-commissioned officers, but you can't get on with your equals and superiors.

THE CAPTAIN. Ouf!

ALICE. Just like all tyrants! . . . Do you think she'll leave?

THE CAPTAIN. Yes, unless you go and say something nice to her.

ALICE. Me?

THE CAPTAIN. If I go, you'll say I'm flirting with the maids.

ALICE. To think, if she does leave, I'll have to do all that housework like last time, and ruin my hands.

THE CAPTAIN. And what's worse, if Jenny goes, Kristin will go too, and we'll never get another servant on the island. The mate of the steamboat will scare away anyone who comes to apply for the place, and should he forget, then my bombardiers will do it.

ALICE. Yes, your bombardiers, whom I have to feed in my kitchen because you don't dare show them the door.

THE CAPTAIN. No, or they'd go at the end of their service—and then we'd have to close down the gun-shop.

ALICE. That would ruin us!

THE CAPTAIN. Which is why the Officers' Corps intends to request His Majesty for a maintenance grant . . .

ALICE. Who for?

THE CAPTAIN. The bombardiers.

ALICE, *laughing.* You're quite crazy!

THE CAPTAIN. Yes, let's have a little laughter. We may need it.

ALICE. I shall soon have forgotten how to laugh.

THE CAPTAIN, *lighting a cigar.* One must never forget that. It's boring enough as it is.

ALICE. It's certainly not amusing. . . . Do you want to go on playing?

THE CAPTAIN. No, it exhausts me.
   Pause.

ALICE. You know, considering he's my cousin, it does annoy me that the new Quarantine Officer should make his first visit here to people who are not our friends.

THE CAPTAIN. Not worth a thought.

ALICE. Well, but did you see in the paper—in the list of arrivals—it said he was of independent means? He must have come into some money.

THE CAPTAIN. Independent means! Aha! A rich relation! Certainly the first in this family.

ALICE. In your family, yes. There have been many in mine.

THE CAPTAIN. If he has any money, he's sure to be stuck-up. But I'll keep him in check, and he won't get a chance of seeing my cards.
   The telegraph apparatus begins to tap out a message.
   THE CAPTAIN *rises.*

ALICE. Who is it?

THE CAPTAIN, *not moving.* Quiet a moment, please!

ALICE. Well, go and see!

THE CAPTAIN. I can hear. I can hear what they're saying. . . . It's the children.

He goes to the apparatus and taps out a reply.

The apparatus taps for a while and he replies again.

ALICE. Well?

THE CAPTAIN. Wait a minute! . . . *Gives the ending signal.* It was the children. They were at the guardhouse in the town. Judith is off colour again and staying away from school.

ALICE. *Again?* What else did they say?

THE CAPTAIN. Money, of course.

ALICE. Why should Judith be in such a hurry? If she took her exam next year that would be time enough.

THE CAPTAIN. Tell her so and see what effect it has.

ALICE. You ought to tell her.

THE CAPTAIN. Haven't I done so times without number? You know very well children do as they please.

ALICE. In *this* household at any rate.

THE CAPTAIN *yawns.*

Must you yawn in your wife's face?

THE CAPTAIN. What do you suggest I should do? . . . Don't you realise we go through the same rigmarole every day? When you repeated your old dig just now: "In *this* household at any rate," my cue was to retort: "The household isn't just *my* affair." But as I've already said this five hundred times, now I yawn instead. And my yawn can be taken to mean that I can't be bothered to answer, or: "You're perfectly right, my angel," or: "Let's shut up!"

ALICE. You're in good form this evening.

THE CAPTAIN. Isn't it nearly time for supper?

ALICE. Do you know they have ordered supper from the Grand Hotel for the doctor's party?

THE CAPTAIN. Really? Then they will be having woodcock. *Smacks his lips.* You know, woodcock is the best bird there is, but to roast it in pork fat is barbarous.

ALICE. Oh, must we talk about food?

THE CAPTAIN. About wine then? I wonder what the barbarians are drinking with their woodcock.

ALICE. Shall I play for you?

THE CAPTAIN, *seating himself at the writing-table.* The last re-
source! Yes, if you keep off your funeral marches and dirges
—which sound all too appropriate. I always find myself in-
toning: "See how unhappy I am, miaow, miaow!" Or: "See
what a dreadful husband I have! Pom, pom, pom! Oh, if
only he would die! Joyful roll of drums! Fanfares! End the
Alcazar Waltz! The *Champagne Galop!*" Apropos champagne, surely there are two bottles left. Shall we get them
up and pretend we have guests?

ALICE. No, we won't. They're mine. They were sent to me.

THE CAPTAIN. You're always economical.

ALICE. And you're always stingy—anyhow to your wife.

THE CAPTAIN. Then I don't know what to suggest. . . . Shall
I dance for you?

ALICE. No, thank you. Your dancing days are over.

THE CAPTAIN. You ought to ask some woman here to stay with
you.

ALICE. Thanks. You ought to ask some man to stay with you.

THE CAPTAIN. Thanks. That was tried—to our mutual dissatis-
faction. But what was interesting in the experiment was how
happy we were as soon as we had a stranger in the house
—to begin with.

ALICE. And then!

THE CAPTAIN. Oh, don't talk about it!

There is a knock on the door, left.

ALICE. Who can that be at this hour?

THE CAPTAIN. Jenny doesn't usually knock.

ALICE. Go and open it and don't call "come in"—that sounds
like a workshop.

THE CAPTAIN, *going to the door.* You don't like workshops.

The knocking is repeated.

ALICE. Open it, do!

THE CAPTAIN *opens it and takes the visiting card which is
handed to him.*

THE CAPTAIN. It's Kristin. . . . *To the unseen* KRISTIN. Has
Jenny gone? *Her reply is inaudible. To* ALICE. Jenny has
gone.

ALICE. So I'm to be the maid again.

THE CAPTAIN. And I the man.

ALICE. Can't we have one of the garrison to help in the kitchen?

THE CAPTAIN. Not these days.

ALICE. But surely it wasn't Jenny who sent in that card?

THE CAPTAIN *puts on his glasses and looks at the card, then hands it to* ALICE.

THE CAPTAIN. You read it. I can't.

ALICE, *looking at the card.* Kurt! It's Kurt. Go and bring him in.

THE CAPTAIN, *going out, left.* Kurt! Well, that is nice!

ALICE *arranges her hair and seems to come to life.*

THE CAPTAIN *and* KURT *enter, left.*

Here he is, the blackguard! Welcome, old man! *Pats him on the back.*

ALICE. Welcome to my home, Kurt!

KURT. Thank you. . . . It's a long time since we saw one another.

THE CAPTAIN. What is it? Fifteen years. And we've grown old.

ALICE. Oh, Kurt looks just as he was to me!

THE CAPTAIN. Sit down, sit down! Now first of all your programme. Any engagement this evening?

KURT. I've been invited to the doctor's, but I haven't promised to go.

ALICE. Then stay with your relatives.

KURT. That would be the natural thing to do, but on the other hand, the doctor is my chief, and there'd be unpleasantness later.

THE CAPTAIN. Nonsense! I've never been afraid of my chiefs.

KURT. Afraid or not, there'd be unpleasantness just the same.

THE CAPTAIN. Here on the island, I'm master. Stick behind me and no one will dare get at you.

ALICE. Be quiet, Edgar! *Takes* KURT's *hand.* Never mind about masters and chiefs—you stay here with us. It's only right and proper.

KURT. So be it. Specially as I find myself welcome here.

THE CAPTAIN. Why shouldn't you be welcome? We haven't any quarrel with you.

KURT *cannot hide a certain embarrassment.*

Why should we have? You were a bit reckless, but you were young, and I've forgotten it. I don't bear grudges.

ALICE *looks vexed.*

All three sit at the sewing-table.

ALICE. Well, have you been round the world?

KURT. Yes, and now I've landed up with you . . .

THE CAPTAIN. Whom you married off twenty-five years ago.

KURT. Hardly that . . . but let it go. It's nice to see that you've stuck together for twenty-five years.

THE CAPTAIN. Yes, we've rubbed along. Sometimes it's been a bit touch and go, but as you say, we've stuck it out. And Alice has had nothing to complain of. Plenty of everything, oodles of money . . . Perhaps you don't know I'm a famous writer—writer of textbooks.

KURT. Yes, I remember when our ways parted you had just brought out a shooting manual that was doing well. Is it still used in the military schools?

THE CAPTAIN. It is still there and still number one, although they've tried to throw it out for an inferior one . . . which of course is used now, though it's utterly worthless.

Embarrassing silence.

KURT. You've been abroad, I hear.

ALICE. Yes, just imagine. We've been to Copenhagen five times.

THE CAPTAIN. Yes. You see, when I took Alice away from the theatre . . .

ALICE. Took me?

THE CAPTAIN. Yes, I took you, as a wife should be taken . . .

ALICE. You're talking very big.

THE CAPTAIN. But afterwards I was always having it thrown at me that I'd ruined her brilliant career. . . . Hm! So I had to make amends by promising to take my wife to Copenhagen. And I've kept my promise faithfully. Five times we've been there. *Holds up the fingers of his left hand.* Five. Have you been to Copenhagen?

KURT, *smiling.* No, I've been chiefly in America.

THE CAPTAIN. America? Pretty low place, what?

KURT, *taken aback.* It's not Copenhagen.

ALICE. Have you . . . heard at all . . . from your children?

KURT. No.

ALICE. Forgive me, my dear, but it was rather heartless to leave them like that.

KURT. I didn't leave them. The Court gave their mother custody.

THE CAPTAIN. We won't talk about that now. Seems to me you were lucky to get out of that mess.

KURT, *to* ALICE. Are your children well?

ALICE. Yes, thank you. They're at school in the town—they'll be grown up soon.

THE CAPTAIN. Yes, they're bright youngsters. The boy has a brilliant mind. Brilliant. He'll be on the General Staff.

ALICE. If they'll have him.

THE CAPTAIN. Have him? The makings of a Minister of War.

KURT. To change the subject . . . There's to be this Quarantine Station here—for plague, cholera, and so forth—and the doctor, as you know, will be my chief. What sort of man is he?

THE CAPTAIN. Man? He's not a man. He's a brainless scoundrel.

KURT, *to* ALICE. How very unpleasant for me!

ALICE. It's not as bad as Edgar says, but I must admit he doesn't appeal to me.

THE CAPTAIN. He's a scoundrel. And so are the rest of them— the Customs Officer, the Postmaster, the telephone girl, the chemist, the pilot—the what-do-they-call-him, the Alderman —scoundrels, the whole pack of them.

KURT. Are you on bad terms with the whole lot?

THE CAPTAIN. The whole lot.

ALICE. Yes, it's true, you can't have anything to do with those people.

THE CAPTAIN. It's as if all the tyrants in the country had been interned on this island.

ALICE, *ironically*. How true!

THE CAPTAIN, *good-humouredly*. Hm. Is that a dig at me? I'm no tyrant, not in my own home at any rate.

ALICE. You be careful!

THE CAPTAIN, *to* KURT. You mustn't believe a word she says. I'm a very good husband and my old woman's the best wife in the world.

ALICE. Would you like a drink, Kurt?

KURT. No thanks, not at the moment.

THE CAPTAIN. You haven't become a . . . ?

KURT. Rather moderate, that's all.

THE CAPTAIN. American?

KURT. Yes.

THE CAPTAIN. I say be immoderate—or leave it alone. A man should be able to hold his liquor.

KURT. To return to our neighbours on the island—my position will bring me into contact with everyone. And it won't be plain sailing, because, however little one wants to, one's bound to become involved in other people's intrigues.

ALICE. Go on then, but you'll always come back to us, because your true friends are here.

KURT. Isn't it frightful to sit here alone surrounded by enemies?

ALICE. It's not pleasant.

THE CAPTAIN. It's not frightful at all. All my life I've had enemies and they've helped rather than harmed me. And when my time comes to die, I shall be able to say: "I owe nobody anything and I've never had anything as a gift. Everything I've got I've had to fight for."

ALICE. Yes, Edgar's path has not been strewn with roses.

THE CAPTAIN. With thorns and stones—flints. But there's your own strength. Do you know what I mean?

KURT, *simply*. Yes, I learnt the limits of mine ten years ago.

THE CAPTAIN. Then you're a milksop.

ALICE. Edgar!

THE CAPTAIN. Well, he is a milksop if he can't rely on his own strength. True, when the mechanism's done for, nothing's left but a barrowful to tip out on a garden plot. But as long as the mechanism's intact, the thing is to kick and fight for all your worth, with both hands and both feet. That's my philosophy.

KURT, *smiling*. You're amusing to listen to.

THE CAPTAIN. But don't you believe it?

KURT. No, I don't believe it.

THE CAPTAIN. Well, anyhow it's true.

During the above scene the wind has risen, and now one of the glass doors slams.

THE CAPTAIN, *rising*. A gale's getting up. I felt it coming.

He shuts the doors and taps the barometer.

ALICE, *to* KURT. You'll stay to supper, won't you?

KURT. Thank you.

ALICE. It will be very simple. Our maid's just left.

KURT. I'm sure it will be fine.

ALICE. You're so easy to please, my dear Kurt.

THE CAPTAIN, *at the barometer*. You should just see how the barometer's falling. I felt it in my bones.

ALICE, *aside to* KURT. He's all on edge.

THE CAPTAIN. It's time we had supper.

ALICE, *rising*. I'm just going to see to it. You two stay here and talk philosophy. *To* KURT, *aside*. But don't contradict him or he'll lose his temper. And don't ask him why he isn't a Major.

KURT *nods assent.* ALICE *goes towards the door, right.*

THE CAPTAIN *sits down at the sewing-table with* KURT.

THE CAPTAIN. See we have something good, old girl!

ALICE. You would have if you gave me some money.

THE CAPTAIN. Always money!

Exit ALICE.

To KURT. Money, money, money! All day long I run round with a purse, till I begin to think I am a purse. Do you know what I mean?

KURT. Surely. With this difference . . . I thought I was a pocket-book.

THE CAPTAIN. Ha! So you know the type—those ladies! Ha! And you picked a proper one.

KURT, *evenly*. All that can be forgotten now.

THE CAPTAIN, *ironically*. A perfect jewel that one. Whereas I —in spite of everything—at least got myself a good woman. For she is honest, in spite of everything.

KURT, *smiling amiably*. In spite of everything!

THE CAPTAIN. Don't laugh.

KURT, *as before*. In spite of everything!

THE CAPTAIN. Yes, she's been a faithful wife . . . a good mother, exceptionally good, but . . . *Glances at the door, right* . . . she has the devil of a temper. There have been times, you know, when I've cursed you for saddling me with her.

KURT, *affably*. But I never did. Listen, my dear fellow . . .

THE CAPTAIN. Damn it, man! You talk a lot of rubbish and forget anything that's unpleasant to remember. . . . Don't get me wrong. You see, I'm used to commanding and blustering, but you know me and won't take offence.

KURT. Of course not. But I didn't saddle you with a wife. On the contrary . . .

THE CAPTAIN, *not allowing his flow to be interrupted*. Don't you think life's an extraordinary business anyway?

KURT. It surely is.

THE CAPTAIN. As for growing old, it's not nice but it's interesting. Of course, I'm not old, but age is beginning to make itself felt. Your acquaintances die off and you grow lonely.

KURT. The man who has a wife to grow old with is fortunate.

THE CAPTAIN. Fortunate? Yes, that is fortunate, for one's children leave one too. You should never have left yours.

KURT. But I didn't. They were taken from me.

THE CAPTAIN. Now you mustn't take offence when I say that.

KURT. But it wasn't so.

THE CAPTAIN. Well, how it happened has been forgotten. But you *are* alone.

KURT. My dear fellow, one gets used to anything.

THE CAPTAIN. Could one . . . could one really get used to being entirely alone?

KURT. Just look at me.

THE CAPTAIN. What have you achieved these fifteen years?

KURT. What a question! These fifteen years.

THE CAPTAIN. They say you've come into some money and are rich.

KURT. I'm not rich . . .

THE CAPTAIN. I wasn't thinking of borrowing.

KURT. If you were, I'm ready . . .

THE CAPTAIN. Thank you so much, but I have my own debit and credit account. You see . . . *Glances at the door, right* . . . in this household there must be no shortage of anything. The day I hadn't any money, off she'd go.

KURT. Oh no!

THE CAPTAIN. Oh yes! I know it. Believe it or not, she's always on the look-out for the times when I do happen to be out of funds, just for the pleasure of proving to me that I don't support my family.

KURT. But I thought you said you had a big income.

THE CAPTAIN. Certainly I have a big income . . . but it isn't enough.

KURT. Then it's not big in the ordinary sense.

THE CAPTAIN. Life is extraordinary, and so are we.

The telegraph begins tapping.

KURT. What's that?

THE CAPTAIN. Only the time signal.

KURT. Haven't you got a telephone?

THE CAPTAIN. Yes, in the kitchen. But we use the telegraph, because the telephone girls repeat everything we say.

KURT. Social life out here must be grim.

THE CAPTAIN. Yes, it's perfectly abominable. The whole of life is abominable. And you, who believe in a sequel, do you think there'll be peace afterwards?

KURT. There's bound to be storm and stress there too.

THE CAPTAIN. There too—if there is a there. Then rather annihilation.

KURT. How do you know annihilation would come without pain?

THE CAPTAIN. I shall drop down dead, without pain.

KURT. I see. You know that, do you?

THE CAPTAIN. Yes, I know it.

KURT. You aren't satisfied with your existence, are you?

THE CAPTAIN, *sighing.* Satisfied? The day I die I shall be satisfied.

KURT. You can't know that. . . . Now, tell me, what are you two up to in this house? What's going on here? The very walls smell of poison—one feels sick the moment one comes in. I'd rather be off, if I hadn't promised Alice to stay. There's a corpse under the floor . . . and such hatred that one can scarcely breathe.

THE CAPTAIN *collapses in his chair and stares vacantly.*

What's wrong with you? Edgar!

THE CAPTAIN *does not move.* KURT *slaps him on the back.* Edgar!

THE CAPTAIN, *coming to.* Did you say something? *Looking round.* Oh, it's you! I thought it was Alice. . . . Now . . . *Relapses into apathy again.*

KURT. This is terrible. *Goes over and opens the door, right.* Alice!

ALICE *enters, wearing an apron.*

ALICE. What's the matter?

KURT. I don't know. Look at him!

ALICE, *calmly.* He does sometimes lose his senses like this. I'll play—that will bring him round. *Goes towards the piano.*

KURT. No, don't, don't! Let me try. Can he hear? Can he see?

ALICE. At this moment he can neither hear nor see.

KURT. Yet you can speak so calmly. Alice, what are you two up to in this house?

ALICE. Ask that man there.

KURT. That man! Why he's your husband!

ALICE. To me he's a stranger, as much of a stranger as twenty-
five years ago. I know nothing about this man except that
he . . .

KURT. Stop! He may hear you.

ALICE. He can hear nothing now.

A bugle call is heard.

THE CAPTAIN *springs to his feet and seizes his sword and cap.*

THE CAPTAIN. Excuse me. I must just inspect the posts.

Exit THE CAPTAIN *through the centre doorway.*

KURT. What's the matter with him?

ALICE. I don't know.

KURT. Is he out of his mind?

ALICE. I don't know.

KURT. Does he drink?

ALICE. There's more boasting about it than drinking.

KURT. Sit down and talk. Calmly and truthfully now.

ALICE, *sitting.* What am I to say? That I've been in this tower
a lifetime, imprisoned, guarded by a man I've always hated,
and now hate so utterly that the day he died, I'd laugh
aloud.

KURT. Why haven't you separated?

ALICE. Question! Twice we broke off our engagement, and
since then not a day has passed in which we haven't tried
to separate. But we are welded together—we can't escape.
Once we *did* separate—in our own home—for five years. Now
only death can separate us. We know it, so we wait for him
as the deliverer.

KURT. Why are you so alone?

ALICE. Because he has isolated me. First he uprooted my
brothers and sisters from the house—"uprooted" is his own
word for it—and after that my girlhood's friends . . . and
the rest.

KURT. But what about *his* relatives? Did you uproot them?

ALICE. Yes. For they were sapping my very life by robbing
me of my honour and good name. In the end, my only contact with the world and other human beings was through

this telegraph—for the telephone is spied on by the girls. I taught myself how to telegraph, but this he doesn't know. You mustn't tell him or he would kill me.

KURT. Horrible! Horrible! But why does he blame me for your marriage? Let me tell you what really happened. When we were young, Edgar was my friend. He fell in love with you at first sight and came and asked me to act as go-between. I at once refused and, my dear Alice, as I knew you had a cruel and domineering streak in your nature, I warned him. Then, when he insisted, I sent him to ask your brother to plead for him.

ALICE. I believe what you say, but having deceived himself all these years, you'll never get the idea out of his head.

KURT. Very well, let him blame me if that makes him feel better.

ALICE. That's asking too much.

KURT. I'm used to it. . . . But what does hurt is his unjust accusation that I deserted my children.

ALICE. That's how he is. He says what he chooses and believes it. But he seems to like you—chiefly, I suppose, because you don't contradict him. . . . Please try not to get tired of us. . . . I think you've come at a fortunate moment for us, that your coming is an act of providence. . . . Kurt, you mustn't get tired of us! Because we really are the most unhappy people in the whole world. *Weeps.*

KURT. *One* marriage I have seen at close quarters, and that was horrible. But this is almost worse.

ALICE. Do you think so?

KURT. Yes.

ALICE. Whose fault is it?

KURT. Alice, the moment you stop asking whose fault it is, you'll have a sense of relief. Try just to accept it as a fact, as a trial that must be borne.

ALICE. I can't. It's too much. *Rises.* It's hopeless.

KURT. You poor things! Do you know why you hate one another?

ALICE. No, it's a quite unreasoning hatred. It has no cause, no object, but also no end. And why do you think he fears death most? He's afraid I shall marry again.

KURT. Then he loves you.

ALICE. Maybe. But that doesn't stop him from hating me.

KURT, *as if to himself.* That's known as *love-hatred,* and comes from the lowest depths. . . . Does he like you to play to him?

ALICE. Yes, but only hideous tunes—like that revolting *Entry of the Boyars.* When he hears that, he goes quite crazy and has to dance.

KURT. Dance?

ALICE. Yes. He's really very funny sometimes.

KURT. Another thing—forgive my asking. Where are the children?

ALICE. Perhaps you don't know that two of them are dead?

KURT. You've been through that too?

ALICE. What haven't I been through?

KURT. But the two others?

ALICE. In the town. They couldn't stay at home. He set them against me. . . .

KURT. And you against him.

ALICE. Yes, naturally. Then it came to taking sides, canvassing, bribery . . . So, in order not to destroy the children, we parted from them. What should have been a bond drove us apart; the blessing of a home became its curse. . . . Yes, sometimes I think our stock is cursed.

KURT. Since the Fall, yes, that's so.

ALICE, *with a venomous glance, sharply.* What fall?

KURT. Adam and Eve's.

ALICE. Oh, I thought you meant something else!

Embarrassed silence.

ALICE *wrings her hands.*

Kurt! My cousin, my girlhood's friend, I have not always treated you as I should. But now I am punished and you have your revenge.

KURT. Not revenge. There's no revenge about it. Hush!

ALICE. Do you remember one Sunday, when you were engaged? I had invited you to dinner . . .

KURT. Hush!

ALICE. I must speak. Have pity on me. . . . When you came, we were out—you had to go away again.

KURT. You had been asked out yourselves. It's not worth talking about.

ALICE. Kurt, when I asked you to supper just now, I thought there was something in the larder. *Hides her face in her hands.* But there's nothing, not even a bit of bread. . . . *Cries.*

KURT. Poor, poor Alice!

ALICE. And when *he* comes in and wants something to eat and there isn't anything, he'll fly into a rage. You've never seen him in a rage. . . . O God, I'm so humiliated!

KURT. Let me go out and put that right.

ALICE. There's nothing to be got on the island.

KURT. Not for my sake, but for his and yours, I must think of something, something . . . When he comes in, we must make a joke of it. I'll suggest we have a drink, and meanwhile I'll think of something. . . . Get him into a good humour, play to him—play any rubbish he likes. . . . Sit at the piano and be ready.

ALICE. Look at my hands! Are they fit to play? I have to polish the brass and wipe the glasses, do the fires and the rooms . . .

KURT. But you have two servants.

ALICE. We have to say so, because he's an officer . . . but the servants keep on leaving, so sometimes we have none, more times than not. . . . How shall I get out of this—this supper business? Oh, if only the house would catch fire!

KURT. Hush, Alice, hush!

ALICE. Or the sea rise and sweep us away!

KURT. No, no, no, I won't listen to you!

ALICE. What will he say? What will he say? Don't go, Kurt, don't leave me!

KURT. No, my poor friend, I won't go.

ALICE. But when you do go . . .

KURT. Has he ever struck you?

ALICE. Struck me? Oh no, he knows that then I would leave him. One must have some pride.

Outside is heard: Halt! Who goes there? Pass, friend!

KURT, *rising.* Is that him?

ALICE, *nervously.* Yes, it's him.

Pause.

KURT. What on earth shall we do?

ALICE. I don't know, I don't know.

Enter THE CAPTAIN, *back.*

THE CAPTAIN, *gaily.* There we are! Now I'm free. . . . Well, has she got in all her complaints? Wretched life hers, what?

KURT. How's the weather out there?

THE CAPTAIN. Half a gale. *Sets one of the doors ajar. Facetiously.* Sir Bluebeard and the maiden in the tower, and outside the sentry marching with sword drawn, keeping watch over the beautiful maiden . . . And then come the brothers, but the sentry's on guard. Look at him! One, two! He's a fine sentry. Look at him! Meli-tam-tam-ta, meli-ta-lia-lay! Shall we do the sword dance? Kurt ought to see that.

KURT. No, have the *Entry of the Boyars.*

THE CAPTAIN. You know that, do you? Alice, in the kitchen apron, come and play! Come on, I say!

ALICE *goes unwillingly to the piano.*

He pinches her arm.

Been slandering me, haven't you?

ALICE. I?

KURT *turns away.* ALICE *strikes up the* Entry of the Boyars.

THE CAPTAIN *does a kind of Hungarian dance behind the writing-table, knocking with his spurs. Then he sinks to the floor, unobserved by* KURT, *or* ALICE, *who plays the piece to the end.*

Without turning round. Shall we have it again?

Silence.

ALICE *turns and sees* THE CAPTAIN *lying unconscious on the floor behind the writing-table.*

Lord Jesus!

ALICE *stands with her arms crossed over her breast and gives a sigh as of thankfulness and relief.*

KURT *turns and hurries to* THE CAPTAIN.

KURT. What is it? What is it?

ALICE, *in a state of great tension.* Is he dead?

KURT. I don't know. Help me!

ALICE, *without moving.* I can't touch him. . . . Is he dead?

KURT. No. He's alive.

ALICE *sighs.*

KURT *helps* THE CAPTAIN *up into a chair.*

THE CAPTAIN. What happened?

Silence.

What happened?

KURT. You just fell down.

THE CAPTAIN. Was there any . . . ?

KURT. You fell on to the floor. How do you feel now?

THE CAPTAIN. Feel? Nothing at all. I don't know anything about it. Why do you stand there gaping?

KURT. You are ill.

THE CAPTAIN. Fiddlesticks! Go on playing, Alice. . . . Ah! Now it's coming on again. *Clasps his head.*

ALICE. You see, you are ill.

THE CAPTAIN. Don't scream! It's only giddiness.

KURT. We must have the doctor. I'll go and telephone.

THE CAPTAIN. I won't have the doctor.

KURT. You must. We must call him for our own sakes, or we'll be held responsible.

THE CAPTAIN. I'll throw him out if he comes. I'll shoot him . . . Ah, here it is again! *Clasps his head.*

KURT, *going to the door, right.* I'll go and telephone right away.

Exit KURT.

ALICE *takes off her apron.*

THE CAPTAIN. Will you give me a glass of water?

ALICE. I suppose I must.

She gives him a glass of water.

THE CAPTAIN. How amiable!

ALICE. Are you ill?

THE CAPTAIN. Excuse me for not being well.

ALICE. Are you going to look after yourself then?

THE CAPTAIN. You don't seem to want to do it.

ALICE. You can be sure of that.

THE CAPTAIN. The time has come that you have waited for so long.

ALICE. Yes, and which you believed would never come.

THE CAPTAIN. Don't be angry with me.

Enter KURT, *right.*

KURT. That's the limit!

ALICE. What did he say?

KURT. He rang off, without a word.

ALICE, *to* THE CAPTAIN. This is what comes of your monstrous arrogance.

THE CAPTAIN. I think I'm getting worse. . . . Try and get a doctor from the town.

ALICE, *going to the writing-table.* I shall have to telegraph then.

THE CAPTAIN, *half rising, amazed.* Can—you—telegraph?

ALICE, *telegraphing.* Yes, I can.

THE CAPTAIN. Well! Go on then. What deceit! *To* KURT. Come and sit by me.

KURT *does so.*

Take my hand. I seem to be slipping down. Can you understand? Down somehow. It's queer.

KURT. Have you had attacks like this before?

THE CAPTAIN. Never.

KURT. While you're waiting for the answer from the town, I'm going over to have a talk with the doctor. Has he attended you before?

THE CAPTAIN. That he has.

KURT. Then he knows your constitution. *Goes to the door, left.*

ALICE. There'll be an answer here in a moment. It's kind of you, Kurt. But come back quickly.

KURT. As quickly as I can.

Exit KURT.

THE CAPTAIN. He is kind, Kurt. And so changed.

ALICE. Yes, for the better. But it's bad luck on him to be mixed up in our misery just now.

THE CAPTAIN. Good luck for us, though. I wonder how things really are with him. Did you notice he wouldn't talk about his personal affairs?

ALICE. I noticed it, but then I don't think anyone asked him to.

THE CAPTAIN. Think of his life. And ours. I wonder if everyone's life is like this.

ALICE. Perhaps, though they don't talk about it, as we do.

THE CAPTAIN. I've sometimes thought misery attracts misery, and the happy shun unhappiness. That's why we see nothing but misery.

ALICE. Have you ever known any happy people?

THE CAPTAIN. Let me think . . . No. Yes, the Ekmarks.

ALICE. What did you say? She had that operation last year.

THE CAPTAIN. That's true. Well, then I don't know . . . Yes, the von Kraffts.

ALICE. Yes, that whole family lived idyllically for half a century. Well-off, respected, good children, suitable marriages. Then that cousin went and committed a crime—prison and all the rest of it—and that was the end of their peace. The family name was disgraced in all the newspapers. . . . The Krafft murder made it impossible for that highly esteemed family to show their faces. The children had to be taken away from school. Good God!

THE CAPTAIN. I wonder what's the matter with me.

ALICE. What do you think?

THE CAPTAIN. Heart, or head. It's as if my soul is trying to escape and dissolve in smoke.

ALICE. Have you any appetite?

THE CAPTAIN. Yes. What about supper?

ALICE, *walking about, uneasily.* I'll ask Jenny.

THE CAPTAIN. But she's gone.

ALICE. Yes, yes, of course.

THE CAPTAIN. Ring for Kristin, so I can have some fresh water.

    ALICE *rings.*

ALICE. Supposing . . . *Rings again.* She doesn't hear.

THE CAPTAIN. Go and see. Supposing she has gone too.

    ALICE *opens the door, left.*

ALICE. What's this? Her trunk in the passage, packed.

THE CAPTAIN. Then she has gone.

ALICE. This is hell!

    Bursts into tears, falls on her knees, and puts her head on a chair, sobbing.

THE CAPTAIN. And everything at once! Of course Kurt would come and find us in this mess. If there's one humiliation left, let it come now, at once.

ALICE. Oh, do you know what I think? Kurt's gone and won't come back.

THE CAPTAIN. I can quite believe it of him.

ALICE. Yes, we are under a curse.

THE CAPTAIN. What on earth do you mean?

ALICE. Don't you see how everyone avoids us?

THE CAPTAIN. I snap my fingers at them.

    The telegraph begins tapping.

    Here's the answer. Quiet! Let me listen . . . No one has time . . . Excuses . . .

    The tapping ceases.

ALICE. That's what you get for snapping your fingers at your doctors . . . and not paying their fees.

THE CAPTAIN. It's not that.

ALICE. Even when you could, you wouldn't pay them, because you despised their work, just as you despised mine and everybody else's work. . . . They won't come. And the telephone's cut off, because you didn't consider that worth anything either. Nothing's worth anything except your guns and cannons.

THE CAPTAIN. Don't stand there chattering!

ALICE. The wheel is come full circle . . .

THE CAPTAIN. Old wives' tales!

ALICE. You'll see. . . . Do you know we owe Kristin six months' wages?

THE CAPTAIN. Well, she has stolen that much.

ALICE. But I've had to borrow from her too.

THE CAPTAIN. I can believe it of you.

ALICE. How ungrateful you are! You know I lent the money for the children's journey.

THE CAPTAIN. Kurt's made a pretty comeback. Rotter like the rest of them. And coward. Didn't dare say he'd had enough and it was more amusing at the doctor's ball. Suppose he expected a poor supper here. . . . Just like the wretch.

KURT *enters hastily, left.*

KURT. Well, my dear Edgar, this is how it is. The doctor has a thorough knowledge of your heart. . . .

THE CAPTAIN. Heart?

KURT. Yes, for a long time you have had a calcified heart . . .

THE CAPTAIN. Stony heart?

KURT. And . . .

THE CAPTAIN. Is it dangerous?

KURT. Yes, that's to say . . .

THE CAPTAIN. It is dangerous.

KURT. Yes.

THE CAPTAIN. Fatal?

KURT. You must take great care. First of all, cigars—away with them!

THE CAPTAIN *throws away his cigar.*

Then whisky—away with it! . . . And then to bed.

THE CAPTAIN, *alarmed.* No, *that* I won't do. Not bed. That means the end. That means never getting up again. I'll spend the night on the couch. What else did he say?

KURT. He was very friendly and will come at once if you call him.

THE CAPTAIN. Friendly, was he, the hypocrite? I won't see him. Am I allowed to eat?

KURT. Not tonight. And the next few days only milk.

THE CAPTAIN. Milk? I can't stand it.

KURT. You'll have to learn to.

THE CAPTAIN. No, I'm too old to learn. *Clasps his head.* Ah, here it is again!

He remains sitting, staring into space.

ALICE, *to* KURT. What did the doctor say?

KURT. That he *might* die.

ALICE. God be praised!

KURT. Take care, Alice! Take care! . . . And now go and get a pillow and a blanket. I'm going to put him to bed on the couch and spend the night in that chair.

ALICE. And I?

KURT. You go to bed. The sight of you seems to make him worse.

ALICE. Command! I'll obey, for you mean well by us both.

KURT. Both, mark that! I don't take sides.

Exit ALICE, *left.*

KURT *picks up the water carafe. Exit, right.*

The gale outside is heard. Then the glass doors blow open and an OLD WOMAN *of poor and unpleasing appearance peers in.* THE CAPTAIN *comes to, sits up, and looks about him.*

THE CAPTAIN. So they've deserted me, the rotters! *Catches sight of the* OLD WOMAN *and is startled.* Who is it? What do you want?

OLD WOMAN. I just wanted to shut the door, kind sir.

THE CAPTAIN. Why did you? Why?

OLD WOMAN. Because it blew open just as I was passing.

THE CAPTAIN. You meant to steal.

OLD WOMAN. There's not much to take, according to Kristin.

THE CAPTAIN. Kristin!

OLD WOMAN. Good night, sir. Sleep well.

She goes out, shutting the door.

ALICE *enters, left, with pillows and a blanket.*

THE CAPTAIN. Who was that at the door? Was there anybody?

ALICE. Yes, it was old Maja from the poorhouse going by.

THE CAPTAIN. Are you sure?

ALICE. Are you scared?

THE CAPTAIN. Scared? I? No, no!

ALICE. As you don't want to go to bed, lie down here now.

THE CAPTAIN *lies down on the couch.*

THE CAPTAIN. Yes, I'll lie down here.

As ALICE *puts the blanket over him he tries to take her hand, but she draws it away.*

KURT *enters with the water carafe.*

Don't leave me, Kurt!

KURT. I'm staying with you all night. Alice is going to bed.

THE CAPTAIN. Good night then, Alice.

ALICE. Good night, Kurt.

Exit ALICE, *left.*

KURT *draws up a chair and sits down beside the couch.*

KURT. Don't you want to take your boots off?

THE CAPTAIN. No! A soldier must always be equipped.

KURT. Are you expecting a battle then?

THE CAPTAIN. Perhaps. *Sits up.* Kurt, you're the only person I can confide in. Listen to me. If I die tonight . . . look after my children.

KURT. I'll do that.

THE CAPTAIN. Thank you. I trust you.

KURT. Tell me why you trust me?

THE CAPTAIN. We haven't been friends—I don't believe in friendship—and our two families were born enemies and have always been at war. . . .

KURT. And yet you trust me?

THE CAPTAIN. Yes—I don't know why. *Silence.* Do you think I'm going to die?

KURT. You, like everyone else. No exception is made for you.

THE CAPTAIN. You're bitter, aren't you?

KURT. Yes. . . . Are you afraid of dying? The wheelbarrow and the garden plot.

THE CAPTAIN. Think if that were not the end!

KURT. Many people do think it's not.

THE CAPTAIN. And then?

KURT. Utter astonishment, I imagine.

THE CAPTAIN. But one knows nothing for certain.

KURT. No, that's just it. So one has to be ready for anything.

THE CAPTAIN. You're not so childish as to believe in hell, are you?

KURT. Don't you believe in it—you who are right in it?

THE CAPTAIN. Only metaphorically.

KURT. You've described your hell so realistically that metaphors, however poetic, are out of the picture.
  Silence.

THE CAPTAIN. If you knew what agonies I'm suffering.

KURT. Physical?

THE CAPTAIN. No, not physical.

KURT. Then they must be spiritual. There's no third alternative.
  Pause.

THE CAPTAIN, *raising himself up.* I don't want to die!

KURT. A little while ago you wanted annihilation.

THE CAPTAIN. Yes, if it's painless.

KURT. But we know it's not.

THE CAPTAIN. Is this annihilation?

KURT. The beginning of it.

THE CAPTAIN. Good night.

KURT. Good night.

SCENE 2

SCENE: *The same.*

The lamp is going out. Through the windows and the glass panes of the doors a cloudy morning is seen. The sea is rough.

The SENTRY *is at his post as before.*

THE CAPTAIN *is lying on the couch asleep.*

KURT *is in the chair beside him, pale and vigil-worn.*

ALICE *enters, left.*

ALICE. Is he asleep?

KURT. Yes, since what should have been sunrise.

ALICE. How was the night?

KURT. He slept from time to time, but he would talk so much.

ALICE. What about?

KURT. He kept on arguing about religion like a schoolboy, yet claimed to have solved the riddle of the universe. Finally, towards dawn, he discovered the immortality of the soul.

ALICE. To his own honour.

KURT. Exactly. He really is the most arrogant person I have ever met. "*I am;* therefore God exists."

ALICE. Now you see. . . . Look at those boots! He'd have trampled the earth flat with them if he could. He's trampled other people's fields and gardens with them and other people's toes—and my skull. . . . Killer bear, you've got your bullet now!

KURT. He would be comic if he were not tragic, and there's a touch of greatness in his pettiness. Can't you say one good word for him?

ALICE, *sitting down.* Yes, so long as he doesn't hear it. One word of encouragement sends him mad with pride.

KURT. He can't hear anything. He has had morphia.

ALICE. He was brought up in a poor home with many brothers and sisters, and early on had to support his family by giving lessons, as his father was a waster—or worse. It's pretty hard for a young man to have to forego all the pleasures of youth and slave for a pack of ungrateful children whom he hasn't brought into the world. When I was a little girl I used to see Edgar as a young man; he had no overcoat in winter—in freezing weather—but his little sisters had duffel-coats. That was fine and I admired him, though his ugliness made me shudder. He is extraordinarily ugly, isn't he?

KURT. Yes, and his ugliness can be pretty sinister. I noticed that, specially when we weren't on good terms. And when he wasn't actually present, his image swelled and took on frightful shapes and sizes, so that he literally haunted me.

ALICE. Then think of me! . . . But his years as a young officer were certainly a martyrdom, although now and then he got help from somebody rich. He never will admit that—he's taken everything he could get as a tribute that was his due —without a word of thanks.

KURT. We were to speak well of him.

ALICE. After he's dead. Ah well, I don't remember any more!

KURT. Do you think he's vindictive?

ALICE. Yes—and yet he can be so kind and sentimental. As an enemy, he's simply terrible.

KURT. Why hasn't he been promoted?

ALICE. You ought to know that for yourself. They don't want a man over them who was a tyrant when he was under them. But you mustn't let on you know about that. He says himself he didn't want to be a Major. . . . Did he mention the children at all?

KURT. Yes, he misses Judith.

ALICE. I can well believe it. Oh! Do you know what Judith is? His own image, whom he has trained to bait me. Just think, she, my own daughter, raised her hand against me!

KURT. No, that's going too far!

ALICE. Hush! He's moving. . . . Supposing he heard! . . . He's cunning too.

KURT. He's just waking up.

ALICE. Doesn't he look like an ogre? I'm frightened of him. *Silence.*

THE CAPTAIN *stirs, wakes, sits up, and looks about.*

THE CAPTAIN. It's morning. At last!

KURT. How do you feel now?

THE CAPTAIN. Bad.

KURT. Do you want the doctor?

THE CAPTAIN. No. I want to see Judith. My child.

KURT. Wouldn't it be wise to get your affairs in order before —I mean, in case—anything should happen?

THE CAPTAIN. What do you mean? What should happen?

KURT. What happens to us all.

THE CAPTAIN. Oh rot! I shan't die as easily as that, you may be sure. Don't rejoice prematurely, Alice!

KURT. Think of your children. Make your Will, so that at least your wife can keep the furniture.

THE CAPTAIN. Is she to inherit it while I'm still alive?

KURT. No, but if anything does happen, she oughtn't to be thrown out into the street. The person who has looked after these things for twenty-five years and polished and dusted them ought to have the right to keep them. Shall I send for the lawyer?

THE CAPTAIN. No.

KURT. You're a hard man, harder than I thought.

THE CAPTAIN. Here it comes again!

He falls back, unconscious, on the couch.

ALICE, *moving, right.* There's someone in the kitchen. I must go.

KURT. Yes, go. There's nothing much to do here.

Exit ALICE, *right.*

THE CAPTAIN, *regaining consciousness.* Well, Kurt, how do you mean to run this Quarantine Station?

KURT. It will work out.

THE CAPTAIN. But I'm Commandant on the island, so you'll have to deal with me. Don't forget that.

KURT. Have you ever seen a Quarantine Station?

THE CAPTAIN. Have I? Yes, before you were born. And I'll give you a piece of advice. Don't put the disinfecting chambers too near the shore.

KURT. I thought they ought to be near the water.

THE CAPTAIN. That shows how much you know about your business. Why, water's the element of the bacilli, their life element.

KURT. But salt water's essential for washing away impurities.

THE CAPTAIN. Idiot! . . . Now, as soon as you've settled in, you must bring your children here.

KURT. Do you think they'll let themselves be brought?

THE CAPTAIN. Of course, if you're anything of a man. It would make a good impression on the neighbourhood to see you doing your duty in that respect too.

KURT. I've always done my duty in that respect.

THE CAPTAIN, *raising his voice.* It's in that respect you've failed most.

KURT. Haven't I told you that . . . ?

THE CAPTAIN, *going straight on.* Because one doesn't desert one's children in that way.

KURT. How you do go on!

THE CAPTAIN. As a relative of yours, an elder relative, I feel it's my place to tell you the truth, even if it's bitter. . . . And you mustn't take it amiss.

KURT. Are you hungry?

THE CAPTAIN. Yes, I am.

KURT. Would you like something light?

THE CAPTAIN. No, something substantial.

KURT. That would be the end of you.

THE CAPTAIN. Isn't it enough to be ill without starving too?

KURT. That's how it is.

THE CAPTAIN. And not to drink and not to smoke. Such a life's scarcely worth living.

KURT. Death requires sacrifices—or else he comes at once.

ALICE *enters with some flowers, telegrams, and letters.*

ALICE. These are for you.

She throws the flowers on the writing-table.

THE CAPTAIN, *flattered.* For me! Let me see them.

ALICE, *giving him the telegrams and letters.* Oh, they're only from the band and the bombardiers!

THE CAPTAIN. You're jealous.

ALICE. Oh no! If they were laurel wreaths it would be a different matter, but you could never get those.

THE CAPTAIN. Hm! Here's a wire from the Colonel. Read it, Kurt. The Colonel's a gentleman anyhow, though he's a bit of an ass. . . . This one's from—what does it say? It's from Judith. Please wire her to come by the next boat. . . . And this . . . So, one's not without friends after all, and it's good of them to think of a sick man, a deserving man, better than his rank, without fear and without reproach.

ALICE. I don't understand. Are they congratulating you for being ill?

THE CAPTAIN. Hyena!

ALICE, *to* KURT. Yes, we had a doctor here who was so much hated that when he left the island they gave a banquet not *for* him, but *after* him.

THE CAPTAIN. Put the flowers in vases. . . . I'm certainly not credulous, and people are scum, but this simple homage—by God, it's genuine! It can't be anything but genuine.

ALICE. Fool!

KURT, *reading the telegram.* Judith says she can't come because the boat's held up by the storm.

THE CAPTAIN. Is that all?

KURT. No—there's a bit more.

THE CAPTAIN. Out with it!

KURT. Well, she begs Papa not to drink so much.

THE CAPTAIN. What impertinence! There's children for you! There's my own beloved daughter—my Judith, my idol!

ALICE. And image.

THE CAPTAIN. There's life for you and its greatest blessings! Devil take it!

ALICE. Now you're reaping what you sowed. You set her against her mother; now she's turning against her father. Tell me there isn't a God!

THE CAPTAIN, *to* KURT. What does the Colonel say?

KURT. He grants you leave of absence—nothing more.

THE CAPTAIN. Leave of absence? I haven't asked for it.

ALICE. No, but I have.

THE CAPTAIN. I don't accept it.

ALICE. Arrangements have already been made.

THE CAPTAIN. I don't accept that.

ALICE. You see, Kurt, for this man no laws exist; he doesn't recognise any rules or regulations. He's above everything— everybody; the universe is created for his private use; the sun and the moon revolve to carry his praises to the stars. Such is my husband! The insignificant Captain who could never become a Major, whose pompousness makes him a laughing-stock to everyone, while he imagines he is feared! This poor creature who's afraid of the dark and puts his faith in barometers, and all this adds up to what a curtain —a barrowful of manure, and that not of the best quality!

THE CAPTAIN *has been fanning himself complacently with a bunch of flowers and not listening to* ALICE.

THE CAPTAIN. Have you asked Kurt to breakfast?

ALICE. No.

THE CAPTAIN. Then go at once and prepare two steaks, two really good Châteaubriands!

ALICE. Two?

THE CAPTAIN. I'm going to have one.

ALICE. But there are three of us.

THE CAPTAIN. Are you going to have some? Well, get three then.

ALICE. Where am I to get them? Last night you asked Kurt to supper and there wasn't a crust of bread in the house. Kurt has had to keep watch all night on an empty stomach, and he's had no coffee because there isn't any, and our credit's finished.

THE CAPTAIN. She's angry with me for not dying yesterday.

ALICE. No, for not dying twenty-five years ago—for not dying before I was born.

THE CAPTAIN, *to* KURT. Listen to her! This is the result of your match-making, my dear Kurt. Our marriage wasn't made in heaven, that's certain.

ALICE *and* KURT *look at each other meaningly.*

THE CAPTAIN *rises and goes towards the door, left.*

However, say what you will, I'm going on duty now.

He puts on an old-fashioned Artillery helmet, fastens on his sword, and puts on his cape.

ALICE *and* KURT *try to stop him, but in vain.*

Out of my way! *Exit.*

ALICE. Yes, go! You always do go; you always turn your back when the battle gets too hot for you and leave your wife to cover up your retreat. Boozer, boaster, liar! Curses on you!

KURT. This is a bottomless pit.

ALICE. And you don't know it all yet.

KURT. Is there more to come?

ALICE. But I'm ashamed . . .

KURT. Where has he gone now? And how has he got the strength?

ALICE. You may well ask. Well, he has gone down to the bombardiers to thank them for the flowers—and then he'll eat and drink with them and slander his fellow-officers. If you knew how many times he's been threatened with dismissal! Only consideration for his family has kept him his post. And he imagines it's fear of his superiority. And those poor officers' wives who have taken pains on our behalf, he hates and abuses.

KURT. I must confess that I applied for this post in order to get some peace out here by the sea. . . . I knew nothing of your circumstances.

ALICE. Poor Kurt! . . . How will you get something to eat?

KURT. Oh, I'll go to the doctor's. But what about you? Please let me arrange something for you.

ALICE. So long as he doesn't get to know of it—if he did he'd kill me.

KURT, *looking out of the window.* Look, there he is out in the storm on the rampart!

ALICE. He is to be pitied—for being like this.

KURT. You are both to be pitied. What can be done?

ALICE. I don't know. . . . A batch of bills came too, which he didn't see.

KURT. It can be an advantage sometimes not to see.

ALICE, *at the window.* He has opened his cape and is letting the wind blow on to his breast. So he wants to die!

KURT. I don't think he wants to, for, just now, when he felt his own life ebbing away, he held on fast to mine and began to busy himself with my affairs, as if he wanted to get inside me and live my life.

ALICE. That *is* his vampire nature—to seize hold of other people's fates, to suck interest from the lives of others, to order and arrange for others, because his own life is absolutely without interest. So remember, Kurt, never let him into your family life, never allow him to know your friends, for he'll take them from you and make them his own. . . . He's a real wizard at that. If he met your children, you'd soon find they were *his* nearest and dearest, and he'd tell them what to do and bring them up to suit his own ideas, and above all *against* yours.

KURT. Alice, it wasn't he who took my children away from me —at the time I was divorced?

ALICE. Since it's all over now—yes, it was he.

KURT. I suspected it, but never knew. It was he.

ALICE. When, putting your entire trust in my husband, you sent him as a mediator to your wife, he started an affair with her, and put her up to how she could get the children.

KURT. O God! O God in heaven!

ALICE. There you have another side of him.

Silence.

KURT. Do you know, last night, when he thought he was dying . . . he made me promise to look after his children.

ALICE. But surely you won't revenge yourself on my children?

KURT. By keeping my promise? Yes, I shall look after your children.

ALICE. That is really the greatest revenge you could take, for there's nothing he loathes so much as magnanimity.

KURT. So I can consider myself revenged—without taking any revenge.

ALICE. I love the justice of revenge. It delights me to see how evil gets punished.

KURT. You still feel like that?

ALICE. Yes, and always shall. The day I forgave or loved an enemy I should be a hypocrite.

KURT. Alice, it can be a duty not to say everything, not to see everything. That's known as tolerance—a thing we all need.

ALICE. I don't. My life is open and clear, and I have always been above board.

KURT. That's saying a lot.

ALICE. But it's not saying enough. What haven't I gone through for no fault of my own, for this man whom I have never loved?

KURT. Why did you marry?

ALICE. Ask yourself! . . . Because he took me, seduced me. I don't know. And then I wanted to better myself.

KURT. So you abandoned your art.

ALICE. Which was despised. But, you see, he cheated me. He promised me a good life—a beautiful home—and there was nothing but debts. . . . The only gold was on his uniform, and that wasn't gold either. He cheated me.

KURT. Wait a bit. When a young man falls in love, he sees ahead the fulfilment of all his hopes. He must be forgiven if these hopes aren't always realised. I have the same deceit on my own conscience, without considering myself a cheat. . . . What are you looking at out there?

ALICE. I was looking to see if he had fallen.

KURT. Has he fallen?

ALICE. Unfortunately not. He always cheats me.

KURT. Well, I shall go and see the doctor and the District Attorney.

ALICE, *seating herself by a window.* Go, my dear Kurt. I shall sit here and wait. I have learnt how to wait.

ACT II

SCENE 1

Two days later.

SCENE: *The same, by daylight. The sentry is marching by the battery as before.*

ALICE *is sitting in the armchair, right. Her hair is now grey. There is a knock on the door, left, and* KURT *enters.*

KURT. Good morning, Alice.

ALICE. Good morning, my dear. Sit down.

KURT, *sitting in the armchair, left.* The steamer's just coming in.

ALICE. Then I know what we're in for—if he's on it.

KURT. He is. I saw the glitter of his helmet. . . . I wonder what he's been doing in town.

ALICE. I can tell you. As he was in parade dress, he was seeing the Colonel, and as he took his best gloves, he was paying calls.

KURT. Did you notice how quiet he was yesterday? Since he's stopped drinking he's been a different person—calm, reserved, considerate . . .

ALICE. I know. If that man had always kept sober he would have been a power to reckon with. Perhaps it's lucky for people that he has made himself ridiculous and impotent with his whisky.

KURT. The spirit of the bottle has chastened him. . . . But have you noticed that since death has set his mark on him, he has a kind of lofty dignity? It's possible that these new thoughts of immortality have given him a new view of life.

ALICE. You're deceiving yourself. He's up to no good. And don't believe a word he says, because he lies deliberately and knows the art of intrigue better than anybody.

KURT, *gazing at* ALICE. Alice, what's this? In these two nights your hair has turned grey.

ALICE. No, my dear, it has been like that for a long time. I have simply stopped darkening it, as my husband is as good as dead. Twenty-five years in a fortress—did you know this was a prison in olden times?

KURT. Prison! The walls look like it.

ALICE. So does my complexion. Even the children had the pallor of prison here.

KURT. I find it hard to imagine small children prattling within these walls.

ALICE. Nor did they prattle much. And the two who died perished from lack of light.

KURT. What do you think's going to happen now?

ALICE. A determined attack on *us*. I saw a familiar gleam in his eye when you read out that telegram from Judith. It should, of course, have been for her, but she, as you know, always gets off scot free, so his hatred descended on you.

KURT. What does he mean to do to me, do you think?

ALICE. Hard to say, but he's very clever—or lucky—in nosing out other people's secrets. You must have noticed yesterday how he seemed to be living in your Quarantine Station; how he was sucking an interest in life from your existence and eating your children alive? Man-eater, you see—I know him. His own life is ebbing or has already ebbed.

KURT. I have that impression too—that he is already on the other side. His face seems phosphorescent, as if he's begun to decompose—and his eyes flicker like will-o'-the-wisps over graves and swamps. . . . Here he comes! Tell me, have you thought of the possibility of him being jealous?

ALICE. No, he's too conceited for that. "Show me the man I would need to be jealous of!" That's what he says.

KURT. So much the better. Even his faults have their merits. Well, in any case, shall I go and meet him?

ALICE. No. Be ungracious or else he'll think you're insincere. And when he starts lying, pretend to believe him. I'm so good at translating his lies and can always get at the truth with my dictionary. . . . I feel something terrible is going to happen—but, Kurt, don't lose your self-control! My one advantage in the long struggle has been that I was always sober and therefore had my wits about me. He always resorted to his whisky. . . . Now we shall see!

Enter THE CAPTAIN, *left, in parade dress, helmet, cape, and white gloves. Calm, dignified, but pale and hollow-eyed.*

He stumbles forward and sits down, right, still in his helmet and cape, at a distance from KURT *and* ALICE.

During the following dialogue THE CAPTAIN *holds his sword between his knees.*

THE CAPTAIN. Good morning. I apologise for sitting down like this, but I'm rather tired.

ALICE *and* KURT. Good morning.

ALICE. How are you?

THE CAPTAIN. Fine. Just a little tired.

ALICE. What news from town?

THE CAPTAIN. This and that. Among other things, I went to the doctor, and he said it was nothing and I could live another twenty years, if I looked after myself.

ALICE, *to* KURT, *aside.* Now he's lying. *To* THE CAPTAIN. That was very good news, my dear.

THE CAPTAIN. That it was.

Silence, during which THE CAPTAIN *looks at* ALICE *and* KURT *expectantly.*

ALICE, *to* KURT. Don't say anything. Let him talk first, then he'll show his hand.

THE CAPTAIN, *to* ALICE. Did you speak?

ALICE. No, I didn't.

THE CAPTAIN, *slowly.* Listen, Kurt . . .

ALICE, *to* KURT. You see, now it's coming.

THE CAPTAIN. I . . . I was in town, as you know.

KURT *nods assent.*

W-well, I made the acquaintance—among others—of a young cadet . . . *Hesitates* . . . in the Artillery.

Pause, during which KURT *appears uneasy.*

As . . . we are short of cadets here, I arranged with the Colonel that he should come over. . . . That ought to please you, particularly when I tell you that this cadet . . . was . . . your own son.

ALICE, *to* KURT. The vampire! You see!

KURT. In the ordinary way that would please a father, but in my circumstances it is merely painful.

THE CAPTAIN. I don't understand.

KURT. You don't need to. It's enough that I don't want this.

THE CAPTAIN. Really. Is that how you feel? Then you had better know that the young man has been ordered to report here, and from that moment he takes his orders from me.

KURT. Then I shall make him apply to be transferred to another regiment.

THE CAPTAIN. You can't do that, as you have no rights over your son.

KURT. No rights?

THE CAPTAIN. No, the Court assigned those to the mother.

KURT. Then I will get in touch with his mother.

THE CAPTAIN. There's no need to do that.

KURT. No need?

THE CAPTAIN. No, because I've already done it. Ha!

KURT *rises, but subsides again.*

ALICE, *to* KURT. Now he *must* die!

KURT. He really is a man-eater.

THE CAPTAIN. So much for *that*. . . . Did you two say something?

ALICE. No. Is anything wrong with your hearing?

THE CAPTAIN. Yes, slightly. . . . But if you'll come nearer, I'll tell you something in confidence.

ALICE. That's not necessary. And a witness may be an advantage to both parties.

THE CAPTAIN. You're right there. It's always good to have a witness. But first of all, have you got the Will ready?

ALICE, *handing him a document.* The solicitor drew it up himself.

THE CAPTAIN. In your favour. Good.

He reads the document and tears it carefully into strips, which he throws on the floor.

So much for that. Ha!

ALICE, *to* KURT. Did you ever see such a man?

KURT. He isn't a man.

THE CAPTAIN. Now, Alice, I have this to say to you.

ALICE, *uneasily.* Well, go on.

THE CAPTAIN, *calmly, as before.* On account of your long-expressed desire to put an end to this miserable life in an unfortunate union; on account of the lack of affection with which you have treated your husband and children; and on account of your neglect of your household duties, during my visit to town today, I filed a petition for divorce at the County Court.

ALICE. Indeed? On what grounds?

THE CAPTAIN, *calmly, as before.* Apart from the grounds already mentioned, on purely personal ones. In fact, now that it has been established that I may live for another twenty years, I have it in mind to exchange this unfortunate union for one that suits me better. I intend to unite my destiny with that of a woman who will bring into the home, not only devotion to her husband, but youth and, let it be said, a little beauty.

ALICE *takes off her wedding ring and throws it at* THE CAPTAIN.

ALICE. Here you are!

THE CAPTAIN *picks up the ring and puts it in his waistcoat pocket.*

THE CAPTAIN. She has thrown away her ring. Will the witness kindly mark that!

ALICE, *agitated.* So you mean to throw me out and put another woman in my house?

THE CAPTAIN. Maybe.

ALICE. Then we'll have some plain speaking now. Kurt, my cousin, this man is guilty of attempting to murder his wife.

KURT. To murder?

ALICE. Yes, he pushed me into the water.

THE CAPTAIN. There were no witnesses.

ALICE. That's a lie. Judith saw it.

THE CAPTAIN. What's that matter?

ALICE. She can give evidence.

THE CAPTAIN. No, she can't. She says she saw nothing.

ALICE. You've taught the child to lie.

THE CAPTAIN. I had no need to—you had taught her already.

ALICE. Did you see Judith?

THE CAPTAIN. Yes.

ALICE. O God! O God!

THE CAPTAIN. The fortress has surrendered. The enemy is granted ten minutes for evacuation under safe-conduct. *Puts his watch on the table.* Ten minutes by the watch on the table.

    THE CAPTAIN *remains standing with his hand on his heart.*

    ALICE *goes up to him and seizes his arm.*

ALICE. What is it?

THE CAPTAIN. I don't know.

ALICE. Do you want something? A drink?

THE CAPTAIN. Whisky? No, I don't want to die. See? *Straightens up.* Don't touch me! *Draws his sword.* Ten minutes, or the garrison will be cut down. *Exit, back.*

KURT. What is this man?

ALICE. He's a fiend, not a man.

KURT. What does he want with my son?

ALICE. He wants him as a hostage, so that he can be your master. He wants to isolate you from the island authorities. . . . You know that people call this island "Little Hell."

KURT. No, I didn't know. . . . Alice, you are the first woman who has aroused my pity. All the others seemed to me to deserve what they got.

ALICE. Don't desert me now! Don't leave me! He beats me— he has beaten me for twenty-five years—in front of the children too. . . . He has pushed me into the sea.

KURT. After this revelation, I am utterly against him. I came here without ill-feeling, putting out of my mind his former humiliations and slanders. I forgave him, even when you told me that it was he who had separated me from my children—because he was sick and dying. But now that he wants to rob me of my son, he must die—he or I!

ALICE. Well said! No surrender of the fortress. Rather blow it up and him with it, even if we must perish too. I have the gunpowder ready.

KURT. When I came here I bore no malice, and when I felt myself infected by your hatred, I made up my mind to go away. But now I feel impelled to hate this man—as I have hated evil itself. . . . What is to be done?

ALICE. He has taught me the tactics. Rouse his enemies and seek allies.

KURT. To think of him getting in touch with my wife! Why didn't those two meet a generation ago? Then there would have been battles enough to shake the earth.

ALICE. But now these kindred spirits have met—and they must be separated. I think I know his vulnerable point—I have long suspected it.

KURT. Who is his surest enemy on the island?

ALICE. The Quartermaster.

KURT. Is he an honest fellow?

ALICE. Yes, he is. And he knows what I—I know too. He knows what the Sergeant-Major and the Captain have been up to.

KURT. What they've been up to? Do you mean . . . ?

ALICE. Embezzlement.

KURT. That's really shocking. No, I won't have anything to do with that.

ALICE. Aha! So you can't aim a blow at an enemy.

KURT. I could once, but I can't now.

ALICE. Why not?

KURT. Because I have discovered that retribution comes in any case.

ALICE. While you're waiting for it, your son will be taken from you. Look at my grey hair . . . yes, and feel how thick it still is! . . . He means to get married—so I am free—to do the same. I am free! And in ten minutes' time he will be

down below, under arrest. *Stamping on the floor.* Down below! And I shall dance on his head. I shall dance the *Entry
of the Boyars.* . . .

She dances a few steps with her hands on her hips.

Ha, ha, ha, ha! And I shall play the piano so he hears.
Bangs on the keys. Ah! The tower is opening its gates, and
the guard with the drawn sword will not be guarding me
any more—but him! Meli-tam-ta, meli-ta-lia-lay! Him, him,
him will he guard.

KURT *watches her, fascinated.*

KURT. Alice! Are you a devil too?

ALICE *jumps on a chair and pulls down the laurel wreaths.*

ALICE. These I will take with me when I make my exit. The
laurels of triumph and waving ribbons. A little bit dusty,
but eternally green—like my youth. . . . I'm not old, Kurt!

KURT, *with shining eyes.* You're a devil!

ALICE. In Little Hell. Look, now I must make myself beautiful.
Takes down her hair. In two minutes I shall dress, and in
another two go to the Quartermaster. And then, up goes
the fortress, sky-high!

KURT, *as before.* You're a devil.

ALICE. You always said that, even when we were children. Do
you remember when we were children and got engaged? Ah!
You were shy, of course.

KURT, *seriously.* Alice!

ALICE. Yes, you were, and it suited you. You know, there are
bold women who like shy men, and . . . it seems there are
shy men who like bold women. . . . You did like me rather
in those days, didn't you?

KURT. I don't know where I am!

ALICE. With an actress whose manners are free, but who is all
the same a very fine woman. Yes, yes! But now I'm free,
free, free! Turn your back while I change my blouse.

She unbuttons her blouse.

KURT *rushes forward, takes her in his arms, and lifts her up.
He bites her neck and she screams.*

Then KURT *throws* ALICE *down onto the couch and rushes out, left.*

SCENE 2

SCENE: *The same, in the evening.*

The SENTRY *by the battery continues to be seen through the windows of the centre doorway.*

The laurel wreaths are hanging on the arm of a chair. The centre lamp is lighted. Soft music.

THE CAPTAIN, *pale and hollow-eyed, with grizzled hair, in his shabby undress uniform and riding-boots, is sitting at the writing-table, playing patience. He is wearing spectacles.*

The interval music continues after the curtain rises, until the next character appears.

THE CAPTAIN *lays out his patience, but now and then gives a start or looks up and listens anxiously.*

Apparently he can't get the patience out; he grows impatient and sweeps the cards together. Then he goes to the left window, opens it, and throws the pack out. The window remains open, grinding on its hooks.

He goes to the sideboard, is alarmed by the noise made by the window, and turns to see what it is. He takes out three dark, square whisky bottles, examines them, then throws them out of the window.

Next he takes some cigar boxes, sniffs inside one, and throws them out of the window.

After this he removes his spectacles, wipes them, and tests how well he can see with them. Then he throws these too out of the window.

Now he stumbles about among the furniture, as if he can't see properly, and lights the six-candled candelabra on the bureau. Catching sight of the laurel wreaths, he picks them up and goes towards the window, but turns back. He takes the cover off the piano and carefully wraps the wreaths in it, fastening the corners with pins from the writing-table, then lays the bundle on a chair.

He goes to the piano, bangs the keys with his fists, slams the lid, locks it, and throws the key out of the window. Then he lights the piano candles.

He goes to the whatnot, takes his wife's photograph, looks at it, and tears it up, throwing the pieces on to the floor. The window grinds on its hooks and he is again alarmed.

When he has calmed down once more, he takes the portraits of his son and daughter, kisses them, and puts them in his breast pocket. The rest of the portraits he sweeps down with his elbow and kicks into a heap.

Then he sits down wearily at the writing-table and clutches his heart; lights the candle on the table and sighs; then stares in front of him as if seeing dreadful visions.

He rises, goes to the bureau, opens the flap, and takes out a bundle of letters tied up with blue ribbon, which he throws into the stove. He closes the bureau.

The telegraph taps once and then stops.

THE CAPTAIN *shrinks back in mortal terror and remains standing with his hand to his heart, listening. When he hears nothing further from the telegraph, he turns, listening, towards the door, left. Then he goes over and opens it, steps out, and returns carrying a cat and stroking its back.*

THE CAPTAIN *goes out, right, with the cat.*

The music stops.

ALICE *comes in from the back. She is in outdoor clothes, with darkened hair, and wears a hat and gloves. She looks round, surprised to see so many lights.*

KURT *comes in left, obviously nervous.*

ALICE. It looks like Christmas Eve in here!

KURT. Well?

ALICE, *holding out her hand for him to kiss.* Thank me!

KURT *reluctantly kisses her hand.*

Six witnesses, four of them firm as rock. The charge has been laid and the reply is coming here—by telegraph—right into the fortress.

KURT. I see.

ALICE. Say thank you, not "I see."

KURT. Why has he lighted so many candles?

ALICE. Because he's afraid of the dark, of course. . . . Look at that telegraph-key. It looks like the handle of a coffee-grinder, doesn't it? I grind, I grind, and the beans crack—like when teeth are drawn out.

KURT. What has he been doing to the room?

ALICE. It looks as if he means to move. And move he shall—down below!

KURT. Alice, don't talk like that! I find it revolting. He was the friend of my youth and did me many a kindness when I was in difficulties. . . . He is to be pitied.

ALICE. Then what about me, who have done nothing wrong and have had to sacrifice my career to this monster?

KURT. What about that career? Was it so brilliant?

ALICE, *furiously.* What on earth do you mean? Don't you know who I am, what I was?

KURT. Now, now!

ALICE. Are you beginning too—already?

KURT. Already?

ALICE flings her arms round KURT's neck and kisses him.

KURT takes hold of her arms and bites her neck. She screams.

ALICE. You bit me!

KURT, *beside himself.* Yes, I want to bite your throat and suck your blood like a lynx. You have roused the wild beast in me, which for years I've been trying to kill by self-denial and penance. I came here thinking myself rather better than you two, but now I am the vilest of the three. Now that I have seen you—in the full horror of your nakedness—now that passion has distorted my vision, I know the full force of evil. Ugliness has become beauty and goodness is growing ugly and feeble. . . . Come to me! I will suffocate you—with a kiss.

He embraces her.

ALICE, *showing him her ring finger.* Look at the mark of the fetter you have broken! I was a slave and now am free.

KURT. But I shall bind you.

ALICE. You?

KURT. I!

ALICE. I thought at one moment you were . . .

KURT. Pious?

ALICE. Yes, you talked about the Fall.

KURT. Did I?

ALICE. And I thought you had come here to preach.

KURT. Did you? In an hour we shall be in town. Then you shall see what I am.

ALICE. We'll go to the theatre tonight and let everyone see us. The shame will be his if I run away. You realise that, don't you?

KURT. I'm beginning to realise it. Prison is not enough.

ALICE. No, it's not enough. There must be shame too.

KURT. A queer world! You commit a shameful act, and he has to bear the shame.

ALICE. As the world is so stupid.

KURT. It's as if these prison walls had soaked in all the evil of the criminals, and one only had to breathe here to catch it. You were thinking about the theatre and supper, I suppose. I was thinking about my son.

ALICE *strikes him across the mouth with her glove.*

ALICE. Prig!

KURT *raises his hand to box her ears.*

ALICE *shrinks back.*

Tout beau!

KURT. Forgive me!

ALICE. On your knees then!

KURT *falls on his knees.*

On your face!

KURT *touches the floor with his forehead.*

Kiss my foot!

KURT *kisses her foot.*

And never do that again! Get up!

KURT, *rising.* What have I come to? Where am I?

ALICE. You know where.

KURT, *looking round in horror.* I almost think I'm . . .

THE CAPTAIN *enters, right, leaning on a stick and looking wretched.*

THE CAPTAIN. May I talk to you, Kurt? Alone.

ALICE. About the safe-conduct?

THE CAPTAIN, *sitting at the sewing-table.* Will you be so kind as to stay here with me for a moment, Kurt? And, Alice, will you grant us one moment's . . . peace?

ALICE. What is it now then? New signals. *To* KURT. Do sit down.

KURT *unwillingly sits at the sewing-table.*

And listen to the words of age and wisdom. . . . If a telegram comes, let me know.

Exit ALICE, *left.*

THE CAPTAIN, *after a pause, with dignity.* Do you understand a human destiny like mine—like hers and mine?

KURT. No, as little as I understand my own.

THE CAPTAIN. Then what is the meaning of this mess?

KURT. In my better moments I have thought that the meaning was just that we should not understand, and yet submit.

THE CAPTAIN. Submit! Without some fixed point outside myself, I can't submit.

KURT. Obviously not. But as a mathematician, you should be able to find that unknown point from the data given you.

THE CAPTAIN. I have searched for it—but I haven't found it.

KURT. Then you've made some mistake in your calculations. Begin again.

THE CAPTAIN. I will begin again. Tell me, how did you come to be so resigned?

KURT. I'm not any longer. Don't overrate me.

THE CAPTAIN. You may have observed that my practice of the art of living has been—elimination. That's to say, to cancel out and pass on. Early in life I made myself a sack into which I stuffed my humiliations, and when it was full I chucked it into the sea. I don't believe any human being has suffered so many humiliations as I have. But when I cancelled them out and passed on, they ceased to exist.

KURT. I have noticed how you have created your own life in your imagination, and created your own environment.

THE CAPTAIN. How could I have borne life if I hadn't? How could I have endured?

Presses his hand to his heart.

KURT. How are you feeling?

THE CAPTAIN. Bad.

Pause, after which he speaks in an old man's quavering voice, his lower jaw sagging.

But there comes a moment when the ability to create in imagination, as you call it, fails. And then reality stands out in all its nakedness. . . . That's terrible. You see, my dear friend . . . *Controls himself and speaks in his ordinary voice.* Forgive me. When I was in town just now and saw the doctor . . . *His voice breaks again* . . . he said that I was done for . . . *In his ordinary voice* . . . and that I couldn't live for long.

KURT. He said *that?*

THE CAPTAIN. Yes, he said that.

KURT. Then it wasn't true.

THE CAPTAIN. What wasn't? Oh, I see—no, it wasn't true.

Pause.

KURT. Wasn't the other thing true either?

THE CAPTAIN. What, my dear fellow?

KURT. About my son being sent here as a cadet.

THE CAPTAIN. I haven't heard a word about that.

KURT. You know your ability to cancel out your own misdeeds is unparalleled.

THE CAPTAIN. My dear fellow, I don't know what you're talking about.

KURT. Then you *are* done for.

THE CAPTAIN. Yes, there's not much of me left.

KURT. Look here, perhaps you didn't really file a petition for that divorce which would bring your wife into such disgrace.

THE CAPTAIN. Divorce? No, heard nothing of that.

KURT, *rising.* Then you admit you were lying.

THE CAPTAIN. You use such strong language, my dear man. We all need to have allowances made for us.

KURT. You have found that out, have you?

THE CAPTAIN, *firmly, in a clear voice.* Yes, I have found that out. . . . So, forgive me, Kurt! Forgive the whole business!

KURT. Well said. But I have nothing to forgive you. And I'm not now the man you believe me to be—and am quite unworthy to receive your confidences.

THE CAPTAIN, *in a clear voice.* Life has been so strange. So against me, so vindictive . . . and people were so vindictive that I became vindictive too. . . .

KURT *walks about uneasily and looks at the telegraph apparatus.*

What are you looking at?

KURT. Can one switch off a telegraph receiver?

THE CAPTAIN. Hardly.

KURT, *with increasing anxiety.* Who is this Sergeant-Major Östberg?

THE CAPTAIN. An honest enough fellow. Looks after his own interests, of course.

KURT. And what about the Quartermaster?

THE CAPTAIN. He's got his knife into me all right, but I've nothing against him.

KURT *looks out of the window and sees a moving lantern.*

KURT. Why have they got a lantern out on the battery?

THE CAPTAIN. Is there a lantern there?

KURT. Yes, and people moving around.

THE CAPTAIN. It's probably what we call a fatigue-party.

KURT. What's that?

THE CAPTAIN. A few men and a bombardier. Probably some poor fellow's going to be locked up.

KURT. Oh!

Pause.

THE CAPTAIN. Now that you know Alice, what do you think of her?

KURT. I can't tell you . . . I don't understand people at all.

She is as much an enigma to me as you are—as I am myself. The fact is, I'm getting to the age when wisdom admits: "I know nothing, I understand nothing . . ." But when I see an action, I want to know its motive. . . . Why did you push her into the water?

THE CAPTAIN. I don't know. It just seemed perfectly natural to me when I saw her on the jetty that she should go in.

KURT. Didn't you feel any remorse?

THE CAPTAIN. Never.

KURT. That's extraordinary.

THE CAPTAIN. Yes, it certainly is. So extraordinary that I can't believe it was I who behaved in such a caddish way.

KURT. Didn't it occur to you that she'd take her revenge?

THE CAPTAIN. She certainly has—fully—and I find that equally natural.

KURT. How have you arrived so quickly at this cynical resignation?

THE CAPTAIN. Since looking death in the eyes, life has presented itself from another angle. . . . Listen! If you had to judge between Alice and me, which of us would you say was in the right?

KURT. Neither. But I'm desperately sorry for you both, perhaps a little more for you.

THE CAPTAIN. Give me your hand, Kurt.

KURT *gives* THE CAPTAIN *his hand and puts the other on his shoulder.*

KURT. Old friend!

ALICE *enters left, carrying a parasol.*

ALICE. Dear me, what intimacy! Ah, there's friendship for you! . . . Hasn't the telegram come?

KURT, *coldly.* No.

ALICE. I have no patience with this delay. And when I've no patience I speed things up. . . . Watch now, Kurt, I'm going to fire the last bullet at him—and then he'll fall. . . . First, I load—I know the rifle-manual, you see—that famous rifle-manual which never sold five thousand copies . . . Then I take aim . . . *Aims with her parasol* . . . fire! How is the new wife? The young, the lovely, the unknown? You don't know. But I know how my lover is.

She throws her arms round KURT's *neck and kisses him. He pushes her away.*

He's quite well, but he's still shy. . . . *To* THE CAPTAIN. You poor wretch, whom I have never loved, you who were too conceited to be jealous, you couldn't see how I've been leading you by the nose.

THE CAPTAIN *draws his sword and rushes at her, but only succeeds in striking the furniture.*

Help! Help!

KURT *does not move.*

THE CAPTAIN *falls with the sword in his hand.*

THE CAPTAIN. Judith! Avenge me!

ALICE. Hurrah! He's dead.

KURT *moves towards the door, back.*

THE CAPTAIN, *rising.* Not yet.

He sheathes his sword and goes to sit in the armchair by the sewing-table.

Judith! Judith!

ALICE, *going to* KURT. I'm coming now—with you.

KURT *pushes her away so that she falls to her knees.*

KURT. Go to the hell from which you came! Goodbye for ever.

Turns towards the door.

THE CAPTAIN. Don't leave me, Kurt, she'll kill me!

ALICE. Kurt! Don't desert me! Don't desert us!

KURT. Goodbye.

Exit KURT.

ALICE, *with a complete change of mood.* What a wretch! There's a friend for you!

THE CAPTAIN, *gently.* Forgive me, Alice, and come over here. Come quickly!

ALICE, *going to him.* I've never met such a wretch and such a hypocrite in all my life. . . . You are a man; I will say that for you.

THE CAPTAIN. Alice, listen . . . I can't live much longer.

ALICE. What?

THE CAPTAIN. The doctor said so.

ALICE. Then all that other talk wasn't true.

THE CAPTAIN. No.

ALICE, *distraught.* Oh, what have I done?

THE CAPTAIN. It can all be put right.

ALICE. This can't be put right.

THE CAPTAIN. There's nothing that can't be put right, so long as one cancels it out and passes on.

ALICE. But the telegram! The telegram!

THE CAPTAIN. What telegram?

ALICE *falls on her knees beside* THE CAPTAIN.

ALICE. Are we doomed? Must this happen? I've destroyed myself, destroyed us both! Oh, why did you pretend to have done all that? And why did that man come and tempt me? . . . We are lost! Everything could have been put right; everything could have been forgiven in the bigness of your heart.

THE CAPTAIN. What is there that can't be forgiven? What haven't I forgiven you?

ALICE. That's true . . . but this can't be put right.

THE CAPTAIN. I can't guess this one, although I know your devilish powers of invention.

ALICE. Oh, if I could only get out of this! If I could only get out of this, I'd take such care of you! Edgar, I would love you.

THE CAPTAIN. Just listen to that! Wherever am I?

ALICE. Do you realise no one can help us? No one on earth.

THE CAPTAIN. Who else then?

ALICE, *looking him in the eyes.* I don't know. . . . Oh, what is to become of the children—with their name dishonoured?

THE CAPTAIN. Have you dishonoured their name?

ALICE. Not I! Not I! . . . Now they'll have to leave school. And when they go out into the world, they'll be as lonely

as us, and as spiteful as us. . . . Then you didn't meet
Judith either? I realise that now.

THE CAPTAIN. No. But cancel that out.

The telegraph taps.

ALICE *jumps up.*

ALICE, *screaming.* Now we are done for! Don't listen to it!

THE CAPTAIN, *calmly.* I won't listen to it, dear child. Calm
yourself.

ALICE *stands by the telegraph and gets on her toes so as to
see out of the window.*

ALICE. Don't listen! Don't listen!

THE CAPTAIN, *putting his hands over his ears.* I'm stopping
my ears, Lisa, my child.

ALICE *kneels with her arms outstretched.*

ALICE. God help us—the fatigue-party is coming!

She moves her lips as if in silent prayer.

*The telegraph taps for a little longer, until a long strip of
paper has appeared. Then there is silence again.*

ALICE *rises, tears off the strip of paper, and reads it to herself. Then she raises her eyes to heaven, goes over and kisses*
THE CAPTAIN *on the forehead.*

It is over. It was nothing.

*She sits down in the other chair, takes out her handkerchief,
and bursts into tears.*

THE CAPTAIN. What are all these secrets?

ALICE. Don't ask me. It's over now.

THE CAPTAIN. Just as you please, my child.

ALICE. You wouldn't have said that three days ago. What's
happened to you?

THE CAPTAIN. Well, my dear, when I had that first attack, I
passed over for a while to the other side of the grave. What
I saw I have forgotten, but the effect has lasted.

ALICE. What effect?

THE CAPTAIN. The hope of something better.

ALICE. Something better?

THE CAPTAIN. Yes. I never really have believed that this could be life itself. This is death—or worse.

ALICE. And we . . . ?

THE CAPTAIN. Were destined to torment one another, so it seems.

ALICE. Haven't we tormented one another enough?

THE CAPTAIN. I should think so. What havoc we have played too! *Looks about.* Shall we put the place in order? And clean up?

ALICE, *rising.* Yes, if it's possible.

THE CAPTAIN, *rising and looking round the room.* It can't be done in one day, that's certain.

ALICE. In two, then. Many days.

THE CAPTAIN. Let's hope so.

Pause.

THE CAPTAIN *sits down again.*

So you didn't get free this time. But you didn't get me locked up either.

ALICE *looks surprised.*

Yes, I knew you wanted to put me in prison, but I cancel that out. . . . You have probably done worse things than that.

ALICE *is speechless.*

And I was not guilty of that embezzlement.

ALICE. And now I am to be your nurse?

THE CAPTAIN. If you will.

ALICE. What else is there for me to do?

THE CAPTAIN. I don't know.

ALICE *slumps down in despair.*

ALICE. These are surely the everlasting fires! Is there no end?

THE CAPTAIN. Yes, but we must have patience. Perhaps when death comes, life begins.

ALICE. Ah, if that were so . . . !

Pause.

THE CAPTAIN. You think Kurt was a hypocrite, do you?

ALICE. Yes, I certainly do.

THE CAPTAIN. I don't. But everyone who comes near us grows evil and goes his way. . . . Kurt was weak and evil is strong.

Pause.

How insipid life is now! One used to fight; now one only shakes one's fists. . . . I feel pretty sure that in three months' time we shall be having our silver wedding—with Kurt as best man, and the doctor and Gerda among the guests. The Quartermaster will propose the toast and the Sergeant-Major lead the cheering. And if I know the Colonel, he will invite himself. . . .

ALICE *giggles.*

Makes you laugh, eh? But do you remember Adolf's silver wedding—that fellow in the Rifles? The bride had to wear the ring on her right hand, because in a moment of tenderness the bridegroom had chopped off her left ring-finger with a bill-hook.

ALICE *holds her handkerchief to her face to stifle her laughter.*

Are you crying? No, you're laughing, surely. Yes, child, that's how it is for us—part laughter and part tears. Which it should be, don't ask me! The other day I read in the paper that a man who had been divorced seven times and had married again seven times, finally eloped in his ninety-ninth year and remarried his first wife. There's love for you! Whether life is serious or just trivial, I haven't a clue. It can be its most painful when it's comic, and its most agreeable and peaceful when it's serious. . . . But if you finally decide to take yourself seriously, someone comes and makes a fool of you. Kurt, for example. . . . Do you want a silver wedding?

ALICE *is silent.*

Do say yes. . . . They'll laugh at us, but what does that matter? We'll laugh with them—or else be serious—just as we choose.

ALICE. Yes—very well.

THE CAPTAIN, *seriously.* So silver wedding it is. . . . *Rises.* Cancel out and pass on! So—let us pass on!

CHARACTERS: PART TWO

EDGAR

ALICE

KURT

ALLAN, *Kurt's son*

JUDITH, *Edgar's daughter*

THE LIEUTENANT

The whole action takes place in a house on the island. The following summer.

SCENE: *An oval drawing-room in white and gold.*

In the back wall French windows, through which are seen a terrace with a stone balustrade and light-blue faïence pots of petunias and scarlet geraniums. This terrace is a public promenade. In the background is seen the shore battery with an artilleryman on sentry duty. Beyond, the open sea.

Inside the drawing-room: on the left a gilded sofa, table, and chairs; on the right a fireplace, a grand piano, and a writing-table.

Downstage an American easy chair.

Beside the writing-table is a small table with a copper standard lamp fixed to it.

On the walls are several old oil paintings.

PART TWO

ACT I

SCENE 1

A warm summer morning. The French windows open.

ALLAN *is sitting at the writing-table, making calculations.*

JUDITH *comes in through the French windows, wearing a short-skirted summer dress, her hair in a plait. In one hand she carries her hat, in the other a tennis-racquet. She stops in the entrance.*

ALLAN *rises, serious and courteous.*

JUDITH, *seriously but amiably.* Why don't you come and play tennis?

ALLAN, *shyly, fighting his emotion.* I'm so busy . . .

JUDITH. Didn't you see I left my bicycle *facing* the oak, not with its *back* to the oak?

ALLAN. Yes, I did.

JUDITH. Well, what does that mean?

ALLAN. It means . . . that you want me to come and play tennis. . . . But my work . . . I have some problems to solve . . . and your father is a pretty strict master.

JUDITH. Do you like him?

ALLAN. Yes, I do. He takes such an interest in all his pupils.

JUDITH. He takes an interest in everyone and everything. . . . Are you coming?

ALLAN. You know very well I want to—but I mustn't.

JUDITH. I'll ask Papa to give you leave.

ALLAN. Don't do that. There'd only be a fuss.

JUDITH. I can manage him, you know. What I want, he wants.

ALLAN. That must be because you're so hard—yes!

JUDITH. You ought to be too.

ALLAN. I'm not of the wolf breed.

JUDITH. Then you must be a sheep.

ALLAN. Rather that.

JUDITH. Tell me why you won't come and play tennis.

ALLAN. You know why.

JUDITH. Tell me all the same. The Lieutenant . . .

ALLAN. Yes, you don't care a pin about me, but you don't enjoy being with the Lieutenant unless I'm there too, so you can watch me being tortured.

JUDITH. Am I so cruel? I didn't know that.

ALLAN. You know it now.

JUDITH. Then I'll have to reform, because I don't want to be cruel. I don't want to be bad—in your eyes.

ALLAN. You're just saying that so as to get the upper hand of me. I'm your slave already, but you're not satisfied with that. The slave has to be tortured and thrown to the wild beasts. . . . You've already got the other one in your clutches, so what do you want with me then? Let me go my way and you go yours.

JUDITH. Are you turning me out?

ALLAN *does not answer.*

All right, I'll go. Being cousins, we're bound to meet now and then, but I won't bother you.

ALLAN *sits at the table and goes on with his calculations.*

JUDITH, *instead of going, gradually approaches him.*

Don't worry—I'm just going. I only wanted to see what the Quarantine Officer's quarters were like. . . . *Looks round.* White and gold! . . . And a grand piano—a Bechstein! Ho! We're still in the fortress tower, although Papa's been pensioned off—the tower where Mamma has lived for twenty-five years. . . . And we're only there as a favour too. But your people are rich. . . .

ALLAN, *calmly.* We aren't rich.

JUDITH. So you say, but you're always very well turned out. Though, as a matter of fact, whatever you wear suits you. . . . Do you hear what I'm saying? *Comes closer.*

ALLAN, *resigned.* I hear.

JUDITH. How can you hear while you're adding up, or whatever it is you're doing?

ALLAN. I don't hear with my eyes.

JUDITH. Your eyes . . . By the way, have you ever looked at them in a mirror?

ALLAN. Get along with you!

JUDITH. You despise me, don't you?

ALLAN. My dear girl, I'm not thinking about you at all.

JUDITH, *coming right up to the table.* Archimedes doing his sums, while the soldier comes and cuts him down.

She stirs his papers with her racquet.

ALLAN. Don't touch my papers!

JUDITH. That's what Archimedes said too. . . . You're imagining things, you know. You think I can't live without you.

ALLAN. Why can't you leave me in peace?

JUDITH. Be polite, and I'll help you with your exam.

ALLAN. You?

JUDITH. Yes. I know the examiners.

ALLAN, *severely.* What of it?

JUDITH. Don't you realise one has to be on good terms with one's instructors?

ALLAN. You mean your father and the Lieutenant.

JUDITH. And the Colonel.

ALLAN. You mean that under your protection I shouldn't have to work.

JUDITH. You are a bad translator.

ALLAN. Of a bad original.

JUDITH. You ought to be ashamed.

ALLAN. I am—of your behaviour and my own. I'm ashamed of having listened to you. Why don't you go away?

JUDITH. Because I know you value my company. . . . Yes, your way always leads under my window. You always have something that takes you to town by the same boat as me. You can't go out sailing without having me to man the foresail.

ALLAN, *bashfully*. That's not the way for a young girl to talk.

JUDITH. Do you think I'm a child?

ALLAN. Sometimes you're a good child and sometimes a wicked woman. You seem to have chosen me as your sheep.

JUDITH. You are a sheep. That's why I'm going to protect you.

ALLAN, *rising*. The wolf makes a jolly bad shepherd. . . . You want to eat me—that's the truth of the matter. You want to pledge your pretty eyes so as to redeem my head for yourself.

JUDITH. Oh, have you looked at my eyes? I didn't think you were as bold as that.

ALLAN *gathers up his papers and starts to go out, right.*

JUDITH *stands in front of the door.*

ALLAN. Get out of my way, or . . .

JUDITH. Or?

ALLAN. If only you were a boy, I'd . . . But you're just a girl.

JUDITH. So what?

ALLAN. If you had a spark of pride, you'd have gone—so you can consider yourself thrown out.

JUDITH. I'll pay you out for this.

ALLAN. I'm sure of that.

JUDITH, *as she goes, furiously*. I'll—pay—you—out!

Exit JUDITH, *back.*

Enter KURT, *left.*

KURT. Where are you off to, Allan?

ALLAN. Oh, is that you?

KURT. Who made such a violent exit that it made the bushes shake?

ALLAN. That was Judith.

KURT. She is rather violent, but a nice girl.

ALLAN. When a girl is ill-natured and crude, she's always called a nice girl.

KURT. You shouldn't be so intolerant, Allan. Don't you like your relatives?

ALLAN. I like Uncle Edgar.

KURT. Yes, he has many good points. And your other instructors? The Lieutenant, for example.

ALLAN. He's so moody. Sometimes I think he has a down on me.

KURT. Nonsense! You're always thinking things about people. Don't brood. Just do your own job properly and leave other people to do theirs.

ALLAN. Yes, I do, but . . . I don't get any peace. They drag one in—just like the cuttle-fish down by the jetty. . . . They don't bite, but they stir up an eddy that sucks one in.

KURT, *kindly.* I think you're a bit given to melancholy. Don't you like being here with me? Is there something you miss?

ALLAN. I've never had such a good time but . . . There is something here that chokes me.

KURT. Here, by the sea? Don't you like the sea?

ALLAN. Yes, the open sea. But on this shore there's nothing but goose-grass, cuttle-fish, jellyfish, and stingers, or whatever they're called.

KURT. You shouldn't stay indoors so much. Go out and play tennis.

ALLAN. That doesn't amuse me.

KURT. You're angry with Judith, aren't you?

ALLAN. Judith?

KURT. You're so critical of people. You shouldn't be. It makes one lonely.

ALLAN. I'm not critical, but . . . I feel as if I'm at the bottom of a wood-pile waiting my turn to be put on the fire. I'm weighed down, weighed down by all that's on top of me. . . .

KURT. Wait till your turn comes. The pile's diminishing.

ALLAN. Yes, but so slowly, oh so slowly! While I lie there rotting.

KURT. It's not easy to be young. And yet people envy you.

ALLAN. Do they? Would you like to change places with me?

KURT. No, thank you.

ALLAN. Do you know what's hardest of all? To hold one's tongue when one's elders are talking rot. When I know I know more about a subject than they do, and yet have to keep my mouth shut. . . . Oh, I beg your pardon! I wasn't counting you as one of the elders.

KURT. But why not?

ALLAN. Perhaps because we have really only just got to know one another.

KURT. And in the process you've formed a different opinion of me.

ALLAN. Yes.

KURT. I suppose during the years we were apart you didn't always feel very kindly towards me?

ALLAN. No.

KURT. Did you ever see a picture of me?

ALLAN. Only one—and that was most unflattering.

KURT. And old?

ALLAN. Yes.

KURT. Ten years ago my hair turned grey in a single night. Now it has changed back of its own accord. Let's talk about something else. . . . Ah, here comes your aunt, my cousin! What do you think of her?

ALLAN. I'd rather not say.

KURT. Then I won't ask.

Enter ALICE *in a light summer dress, carrying a parasol.*

ALICE. Good morning, Kurt.

Her look indicates that ALLAN *is to go.*

KURT, *to* ALLAN. You had better go.

ALLAN *goes out, right.*

ALICE *sits on the sofa, left, with* KURT *on a chair beside her.*

ALICE, *confused.* He's coming in a moment, so you needn't feel embarrassed.

KURT. Why should I?

ALICE. With your strict principles . . .

KURT. In regard to myself, yes.

ALICE. Yes . . . well . . . I forgot myself once, when I saw you as the liberator, but you kept your presence of mind . . . and so we have a right to forget—what never was.

KURT. Forget it then.

ALICE. However—I don't think *he* has forgotten.

KURT. Do you mean that night he fell down with a heart attack, and you rejoiced too soon, thinking he was dead?

ALICE. Yes. Since then he's been quite himself again, but when he stopped drinking he learnt to hold his tongue, and now he's terrifying. He's up to something I can't grasp.

KURT. Alice, your husband is a good-natured ass who does me endless favours.

ALICE. Beware of his favours! I know them.

KURT. Oh, really . . . !

ALICE. So he's hoodwinked you too. Don't you see the danger? Aren't you aware of the traps?

KURT. No.

ALICE. Then you're doomed to destruction.

KURT. Heaven preserve us!

ALICE. You see! Here am I, watching ruin creeping up on you like a cat. . . . I point it out, but you can't see it.

KURT. Allan, with his unbiased view, can't see it either. For that matter, he doesn't see anything but Judith, and surely that's a guarantee of good relations.

ALICE. Do you know Judith?

KURT. A coquettish little thing in pigtails and rather too short skirts.

ALICE. Quite. But I saw her in a long skirt the other day—and then she was a young lady—not so young either, with her hair up.

KURT. She is slightly precocious, I admit.

ALICE. And she's playing with Allan.

KURT. No harm in that, so long as it is play.

ALICE. I see—that's permitted. . . . Edgar will be here in a moment. He will sit in the easy chair—he has such a passion for it he could steal it.

KURT. He shall have it.

ALICE. Let him sit over there, and we'll stay here. And while he's talking about trivial matters, I'll interpret for you.

KURT. Oh, you're too cautious, too cautious, dear Alice! What could I have to fear, so long as I run the Quarantine Station efficiently and behave properly otherwise?

ALICE. You pin your faith in justice and honour and all that.

KURT. Yes—experience has taught me to. Once I pinned my faith in just the opposite. . . . That cost me dear.

ALICE. Here he comes!

KURT. I've never seen you frightened before.

ALICE. My courage was only unawareness of the danger.

KURT. The danger? You'll begin to frighten me soon.

ALICE. Oh, if only I could! . . . Here he is!

Enter THE CAPTAIN, *back, wearing a buttoned-up black morning coat and officer's cap, and carrying a silver-crooked cane. He greets them with a nod, crosses the room, and sits in the easy chair.*

To KURT. Let him speak first.

THE CAPTAIN. This is a superb chair you have, my dear Kurt. Really superb.

KURT. You shall have it as a present, if you will accept it.

THE CAPTAIN. I didn't mean that.

KURT. But that's what I mean. Just think of all I've had from you.

THE CAPTAIN, *volubly*. What rot! . . . And sitting here, I get a view of the whole island, of all the walks—I can see all the people on their verandahs, all the ships at sea—coming in and going out . . . You certainly have hit on the best bit of this island, which is by no means one of the Isles of the Blest. Is it, Alice? . . . Yes, it's known as Little Hell, and here Kurt has built himself a Paradise. Without Eve, of course, for when she came that was the end of Paradise.

By the way, did you know this was once a royal hunting lodge?

KURT. So I have heard.

THE CAPTAIN. You live royally, but shame to say, you have me to thank for it.

ALICE, *to* KURT. You see? Now he wants to get you in his clutches.

KURT. I have so much to thank you for.

THE CAPTAIN. Oh nonsense! Listen, did you get those cases of wine?

KURT. Yes.

THE CAPTAIN. And you're satisfied?

KURT. More than satisfied. Please give your wine merchant my compliments and tell him so.

THE CAPTAIN. He always provides first-class stuff.

ALICE, *to* KURT. At second-class prices—and you have to pay the difference.

THE CAPTAIN. What did you say, Alice?

ALICE. I? Nothing.

THE CAPTAIN. Yes. When this Quarantine Station was established, I thought of applying for the post, and to that end made a study of quarantine systems.

ALICE, *to* KURT. That's a lie.

THE CAPTAIN, *boastfully*. The archaic ideas of quarantine held by the authorities were not shared by me. I, in fact, was on the side of the Neptunists—as we called them, because they favoured the water method.

KURT. I beg your pardon! I remember very well that it was I who preached water on one occasion, and you, fire.

THE CAPTAIN. Did I? What rot!

ALICE, *loudly*. Yes, I remember that too.

THE CAPTAIN. You do?

KURT. I remember it all the more clearly because . . .

THE CAPTAIN, *cutting him short*. Well, that may be, but it makes no odds. *Raising his voice*. In any case . . . we have now reached the point when a new state of affairs . . .

KURT *tries to break in.*

don't interrupt! . . . a new state of affairs has arisen, and
the quarantine system is about to take a giant step forward.

KURT. Apropos, do you know who it is who writes those silly
articles in the newspaper?

THE CAPTAIN, *getting red.* I don't know; but why do you call
them silly?

ALICE, *to* KURT. Take care! It was he who wrote them.

KURT, *to* ALICE. He? *To* THE CAPTAIN. Well, shall we say—not
very intelligent.

THE CAPTAIN. You're no judge of that.

ALICE. Do you mean to quarrel?

KURT. Oh no!

THE CAPTAIN. It's hard to keep the peace here on the island,
but we ought to set a good example.

KURT. Yes. Now can you explain this to me? When I came
here I made friends at once with all the officials and was
on confidential terms with the lawyer—as confidential, that's
to say, as one can be at our time of life. Well, after a time
—it was just after you got well again—one and then another
began to cold-shoulder me, and yesterday the lawyer cut
me on the promenade. I can't tell you how hurt I was.

THE CAPTAIN *is silent.*

Have you noticed any coldness towards yourself?

THE CAPTAIN. No, on the contrary.

ALICE, *to* KURT. Don't you realise he has stolen your friends?

KURT, *to* THE CAPTAIN. I wondered if it could be due to that
new issue of shares I refused to have anything to do with.

THE CAPTAIN. No, no. But can you tell me why you wouldn't
subscribe?

KURT. Because I'd already put my small savings into your soda
factory. And also because a new issue means that the old
shares are doing badly.

THE CAPTAIN, *irrelevantly.* That's a superb lamp you have.
Where on earth did you get it?

KURT. In the town, of course.

ALICE, *to* KURT. Keep an eye on your lamp, Kurt.

KURT, *to* THE CAPTAIN. You mustn't think I'm ungrateful or haven't confidence in you, Edgar.

THE CAPTAIN. Well, it doesn't show much confidence when you want to back out of a business you helped to start.

KURT. My dear fellow, common prudence requires one to save oneself and what one has, while there's still time.

THE CAPTAIN. Save? Is there danger pending? Do they mean to rob you?

KURT. Why put it so crudely?

THE CAPTAIN. Weren't you pleased when I helped you to invest your capital at six per cent?

KURT. Yes, I was grateful too.

THE CAPTAIN. You are *not* grateful. It's not in your nature to be, but you can't help that.

ALICE, *to* KURT. *Listen* to him!

KURT. There are plenty of shortcomings in my nature and my fight against them is pretty unsuccessful, but I do recognise obligations. . . .

THE CAPTAIN. Show it then! *Puts out his hand and picks up a newspaper.* Look! What's this? . . . An announcement. *Reads.* Death of the Medical Superintendent.

ALICE, *to* KURT. He's already speculating on the corpse.

THE CAPTAIN, *as if to himself.* This will bring about . . . certain changes.

KURT. In what respect?

THE CAPTAIN, *rising.* We shall soon see.

ALICE, *to* THE CAPTAIN. Where are you going?

THE CAPTAIN. I think I'd better go into town.

He catches sight of an envelope on the writing-table, picks it up as if unconsciously, reads the address, and puts it back. Excuse me for being so absent-minded.

KURT. No harm in that.

THE CAPTAIN. Here's Allan's geometry set. Where is the boy?

KURT. He's out playing with the girls.

THE CAPTAIN. That great boy? I don't like it. And Judith ought not to run about like that. . . . You keep an eye on your young gentleman, and I'll look after my young lady. *Passing the piano, he strikes a few notes.* Superb tone, this instrument. A Steinbech, eh?

KURT. Bechstein.

THE CAPTAIN. Yes, you're well off, Kurt. Thanks to me, who brought you here.

ALICE, *to* KURT. That's a lie. He tried to prevent you coming.

THE CAPTAIN. Goodbye for the moment. I'll take the next boat. *On his way out, he examines the pictures on the walls. Exit.*

ALICE. Well?

KURT. Well?

ALICE. I don't understand yet what he's scheming. But—tell me one thing. That envelope he looked at . . . who was the letter from?

KURT. I'm sorry to say, it was my one secret.

ALICE. And he smelt it out. You see, he's a wizard, as I told you before. . . . Is anything printed on the envelope?

KURT. Yes, it says: "Electors' Association."

ALICE. Then he's guessed your secret. I understand—you want to get into Parliament. And now you'll have to watch *him* getting in instead.

KURT. Has he ever thought of that?

ALICE. No, but he's thinking of it now. I read it in his face while he was looking at the envelope.

KURT. Is that why he's going to town?

ALICE. No. He made that decision when he saw the obituary.

KURT. What has he to gain by the death of the Medical Officer?

ALICE. You may well ask. . . . Perhaps he was an enemy who got in the way of his schemes.

KURT. If he's as monstrous as you say, one has good reason to fear him.

ALICE. Didn't you see how he wanted to get you into his clutches and tie your hands, on the grounds of obligations which don't exist? For instance, he did not get you the post; on the contrary, he tried to prevent your getting it. He's a man-eater, an insect, a woodworm who will devour you internally, so that one day you're as hollow as a rotten pine tree. . . . He hates you, though he's bound to you by the memories of your early friendship.

KURT. How sharp-witted you become when you hate!

ALICE. How dull-witted one is when one loves! Blind and dull.

KURT. Oh no, don't say that!

ALICE. Do you know what's meant by a vampire? . . . Well, it's the soul of a dead person looking for a body to live in as a parasite. Edgar has been dead ever since that fall of his. He has no interests of his own, no personality, no initiative. But if only he can get hold of somebody, he clings to him, puts out his suckers, and begins to grow and bloom. Now he's making a set at you.

KURT. If he comes too close, I'll shake him off.

ALICE. Shake off a burr—you'll see! . . . Listen. Do you know why he doesn't want Judith and Allan to play together?

KURT. He's afraid their feelings will run away with them, I suppose.

ALICE. Not at all. He wants to marry Judith off—to the Colonel.

KURT, *shocked*. That old widower?

ALICE. Yes.

KURT. How horrible! And Judith?

ALICE. If she could have the General, who is eighty, she'd take him so as to spite the Colonel, who is sixty. To crush, you see, that's her object in life. Trample and crush, that's the password of *that* family.

KURT. Judith? That glorious proud young beauty.

ALICE. Yes, we know about all that. . . . May I sit here and write a letter?

KURT, *tidying the writing-table*. By all means.

ALICE *takes off her gloves and sits at the writing-table*.

ALICE. Now I'll try the art of war. I failed once when I intended to slay my dragon. But now I've learnt how it's done.

KURT. You know you have to load before you shoot?

ALICE. Yes, and with ball cartridges too.

KURT *goes slowly out, right.*

ALICE *ponders, then writes.*

ALLAN *rushes in without noticing* ALICE *and throws himself full length on the sofa, sobbing into a lace handkerchief.*

ALICE *watches him for a moment, then rises and approaches the sofa.*

Gently. Allan!

ALLAN *sits up, embarrassed, and hides the handkerchief behind his back.*

Gently, motherly, with real emotion. You mustn't be afraid of me, Allan. I'm no danger to you. . . . What's the matter? Are you ill?

ALLAN. Yes.

ALICE. In what way?

ALLAN. I don't know.

ALICE. Have you got a headache?

ALLAN. No-o-o.

ALICE. In your heart? Pain?

ALLAN. Yes!

ALICE. Pain, pain, as if your heart were melting away. And dragging, dragging . . .

ALLAN. How do you know?

ALICE. And then you want to die; you wish you were dead and it's all so grim. And you can only think of one thing . . . one person . . . but when two are thinking of the same person, then sorrow is heavy for one of them.

ALLAN *forgets himself and fingers the handkerchief.*

This is the sickness no one can cure. . . . You cannot eat; you do not want to drink; you only want to weep, and how bitterly one does weep—out in the woods for choice, where no one can see you, for people laugh at this sorrow—cruel people. *Shudders.* What do you want of her? Nothing. You don't want to kiss her lips, for you think if you did you would die. You feel as if death were stealing on you when your thoughts fly to her. And it is death, my child, the death which gives life. But you don't understand that yet. . . .

There's a scent of violets. It is she. *Goes up to* ALLAN *and takes the handkerchief gently away.* It is she. Everywhere she and only she. Ah! Ah! Ah!

ALLAN *cannot do otherwise than hide his face in* ALICE'S *arms.*

Poor boy! Poor boy! Oh, how it hurts, how it hurts!

She dries his tears with the handkerchief.

There, there, there! Cry, cry then! That eases the heart. . . . But now, get up, Allan, and be a man, or she won't look at you. That cruel girl who isn't cruel. Has she been tormenting you? With the Lieutenant? Listen, my boy. You must make friends with the Lieutenant, so that you can talk about her together. That's generally some comfort at least.

ALLAN. I don't want to see the Lieutenant.

ALICE. Listen, little boy. It won't be long before the Lieutenant seeks you out so as to talk about her. Because . . .

ALLAN *looks up with a ray of hope.*

Well, shall I be kind and tell you?

ALLAN *nods.*

He is just as unhappy as you are.

ALLAN, *joyfully.* Is he?

ALICE. Yes, truly, and he needs someone to confide in when Judith hurts him. . . . You seem to be rejoicing rather soon.

ALLAN. Doesn't she want the Lieutenant?

ALICE. She doesn't want you either, my dear boy. What she wants is the Colonel.

ALLAN *grows depressed again.*

Oh, raining again, is it? But you can't have the handkerchief, because Judith is careful of her possessions and likes her dozen complete.

ALLAN *looks crestfallen.*

Yes, you see, that's how Judith is. Now sit there, while I write another letter and then you can do an errand for me.

She goes to the writing-table and writes.

THE LIEUTENANT *enters, back. He is melancholy, but without looking at all comical. He does not notice* ALICE, *but makes straight for* ALLAN.

THE LIEUTENANT. Cadet!

ALLAN *rises and stands to attention.*

Do sit down.

ALICE *watches them.*

THE LIEUTENANT *goes over and sits beside* ALLAN. *He sighs, takes out a handkerchief like the other one, and mops his brow.*

ALLAN *surveys the handkerchief enviously.*

THE LIEUTENANT *surveys* ALLAN *sorrowfully.*

ALICE *coughs.*

THE LIEUTENANT *springs to attention.*

ALICE. Do sit down.

THE LIEUTENANT. I beg your pardon, madam.

ALICE. Don't mention it. . . . Please sit down and keep the Cadet company. He feels rather deserted here on the island. *Writes.*

THE LIEUTENANT, *disconcerted, converses in a low tone with* ALLAN.

THE LIEUTENANT. Frightfully hot, isn't it?

ALLAN. Rather!

THE LIEUTENANT. Have you finished the sixth book yet?

ALLAN. I'm just working at the last proposition.

THE LIEUTENANT. Bit of a teaser, that one.

Silence.

Have you . . . *Seeks for words* . . . been playing tennis today?

ALLAN. No-o. The sun was too hot.

THE LIEUTENANT, *in torment, but still in no way comic.* Yes, it's frightfully hot today.

ALLAN, *whispering.* Yes, it's very hot indeed.

Silence.

THE LIEUTENANT. Have you been out sailing today?

ALLAN. No, I haven't found anyone to act as crew.

THE LIEUTENANT. Would . . . er . . . would you trust me to do it?

ALLAN, *respectfully, as before.* That would be too great an honour for me, Lieutenant.

THE LIEUTENANT. Not at all, not at all . . . Do you think the wind will be good today—round about noon? That's the only time I'm free.

ALLAN, *slyly.* At noon the wind drops . . . and at that time Miss Judith has her lesson.

THE LIEUTENANT, *crestfallen.* I see, I see. . . . Er, do you think . . . ?

ALICE. Would either of you young gentlemen care to take a letter for me . . . ?

ALLAN *and* THE LIEUTENANT *look at one another suspiciously.*

. . . To Miss Judith.

ALLAN *and* THE LIEUTENANT *rise simultaneously and approach* ALICE, *although with a certain dignity to conceal their feelings.*

Both of you? Well, it's all the more certain of being delivered. *Hands the letter to* THE LIEUTENANT. Now, Lieutenant, may I have that handkerchief? My daughter is careful of her linen. She has a touch of meanness in her character. . . . Give me the handkerchief! . . . I don't want to laugh at you, but you shouldn't make yourselves ridiculous without good cause. And the Colonel doesn't want to be Othello. *Takes the handkerchief.* Off with you now, young men, and try to hide your feelings as best you can.

THE LIEUTENANT *bows and goes out, followed by* ALLAN. *Calling.* Allan!

ALLAN *reluctantly stops in the doorway.*

ALLAN. Yes, Aunt?

ALICE. Stay here. If you don't want to do yourself more harm than you can stand.

ALLAN. Yes, but he's going!

ALICE. Let him burn his fingers. But you take care!

ALLAN. I don't want to take care.

ALICE. Then it will end in a cry. And I shall have the bother of comforting you.

ALLAN. I want to go.

ALICE. Go then. But if you come back, young madcap, I shall have the right to laugh at you.

ALLAN *hurries after* THE LIEUTENANT.

ALICE *writes once more.*

Enter KURT.

KURT. Alice, I've had an anonymous letter which worries me.

ALICE. Have you noticed that since he's stopped wearing his uniform, Edgar has become another person? I never would have believed a coat could make such a difference.

KURT. You haven't answered my question.

ALICE. It wasn't a question. It was a piece of information. What are you afraid of?

KURT. Everything.

ALICE. He went to town. His journeys to town always bring about something fearful.

KURT. But I can't do anything, because I don't know from which quarter the attack will start.

ALICE *folds up her letter.*

ALICE. We must see if I can't guess.

KURT. Are you going to help me then?

ALICE. Yes. . . . But only as far as my interests allow. Mine —that's to say, my children's.

KURT. I realise that. . . . Alice, listen! How still it is—nature, the sea, everything!

ALICE. But behind the stillness I hear voices . . . murmurs, cries.

KURT. Hush! I hear something too. . . . No, it was only the seagulls.

ALICE. But I—I hear something else. . . . And now I'm going to the post—with this letter.

SCENE 2

SCENE: *The same.*

ALLAN *is sitting at the writing-table, working.*

JUDITH *is standing in the doorway, wearing a tennis hat and holding the handle-bars of a bicycle.*

JUDITH. May I borrow your spanner?

ALLAN, *without looking up.* No, you mayn't.

JUDITH. You're being rude, now that I'm running after you.

ALLAN, *not crossly.* I'm not being anything, but I want to be left in peace.

JUDITH, *advancing.* Allan!

ALLAN. Well, what is it?

JUDITH. You mustn't be angry with me.

ALLAN. I'm not.

JUDITH. Shake hands on it.

ALLAN, *gently.* I don't want to shake hands, but I'm not angry. . . . What do you want with me, really?

JUDITH. You're so stupid.

ALLAN. That may well be.

JUDITH. You think I'm just horrid.

ALLAN. No, I know you're nice too. You *can* be nice.

JUDITH. Well, it's not my fault that . . . that you and the Lieutenant go and cry in the woods. Why do you cry? Tell me.

ALLAN *is embarrassed.*

Tell me. I never cry. And why are you such good friends now? What do you talk about when you're walking arm in arm?

ALLAN *has no answer.*

Allan, soon you will see what I am, and that I can strike a blow for anyone I care about. And one piece of advice I must give you, although I don't want to tell tales. Be prepared!

ALLAN. What for?

JUDITH. For trouble.

ALLAN. From what quarter?

JUDITH. The quarter you least expect.

ALLAN. I'm pretty well used to trouble. I haven't had a very pleasant life. . . . What's brewing now?

JUDITH, *pensively.* You poor boy! Give me your hand!

ALLAN *gives her his hand.*

Look at me. . . . Don't you dare look at me?

ALLAN *hastens out, left, to hide his emotion.*

Enter THE LIEUTENANT, *back.*

THE LIEUTENANT. Excuse me, I thought the Cadet . . .

JUDITH. Listen, Lieutenant. Will you be my friend and confidant?

THE LIEUTENANT. If you will do me that honour.

JUDITH. Well! In a word—don't give Allan up when the disaster comes.

THE LIEUTENANT. What disaster?

JUDITH. You'll soon see—perhaps today. . . . Do you like Allan?

THE LIEUTENANT. That young man is my best pupil, and I value him personally too for his strength of character. . . . Yes, life has moments when that's needed . . . *Emphatically* . . . strength to bear, to endure—in a word, to suffer.

JUDITH. That was more than a word—what you said. However, you approve of Allan.

THE LIEUTENANT. Yes.

JUDITH. Go and find him and keep him company.

THE LIEUTENANT. That's what I came for—*that* and *nothing else.* My visit had no other purpose.

JUDITH. I hadn't imagined anything—in the way you mean. . . . *Pointing left.* Allan went out that way.

THE LIEUTENANT, *going slowly to the door, left.* Yes . . . I'll do that.

JUDITH. Please do.

Exit THE LIEUTENANT, *left.*

Enter ALICE, *back.*

ALICE. What are you doing here?

JUDITH. I wanted to borrow a spanner.

ALICE. Will you listen to me for a moment?

JUDITH. Of course I will.

> ALICE *sits on the sofa.*

> JUDITH *remains standing.*

But say what you have to quickly. I don't like long lectures.

ALICE. Lectures? . . . Very well. Put your hair up and wear long skirts.

JUDITH. Why?

ALICE. Because you're no longer a child. And you're too young to need to make out you're younger than you are.

JUDITH. What does this mean?

ALICE. That you're old enough to be married. And your way of dressing shocks people.

JUDITH. Then I'll do it.

ALICE. So you have understood?

JUDITH. Yes, of course.

ALICE. And we're agreed.

JUDITH. Absolutely.

ALICE. On all points?

JUDITH. Even on the sorest.

ALICE. And at the same time will you stop playing about—with Allan?

JUDITH. This is to be serious then?

ALICE. Yes.

JUDITH. Then we'd better begin at once.

> *She puts down the handle-bars, lets down her bicycling skirt, and twists her plait up into a knot, which she fastens with a hairpin taken from her mother's hair.*

ALICE. One doesn't do one's toilet in other people's drawing-rooms.

JUDITH. Am I all right like this? . . . Then I'm ready. Now, come who dares!

ALICE. Now at least you look decent. . . . And now—leave Allan in peace!

JUDITH. I don't understand what you mean by that.

ALICE. Don't you see how he's suffering? . . .

JUDITH. Yes, I think I have noticed it, but I don't know why. I'm not suffering.

ALICE. That's your strength. But wait a little—oh, yes, one day you'll know well enough! . . . Go home now, and don't forget you're wearing a long skirt.

JUDITH. Must one walk differently then?

ALICE. Try to.

JUDITH, *trying to walk like a lady.* Oh, I have fetters on my feet! I'm imprisoned. I can no longer run.

ALICE. No, child, now the walking begins—the slow way towards the unknown—which one knows already and yet must pretend not to know. . . . Shorter steps, and slower, much slower. Children's shoes must go and you must have boots, Judith. You don't remember when you gave up wearing babies' socks and had shoes; but I remember.

JUDITH. I shall never be able to stand this.

ALICE. All the same, you must. Must.

     JUDITH *goes up to her mother and kisses her lightly on the cheek.*

JUDITH. Goodbye.

     She goes out in a dignified manner like a lady, forgetting the handle-bars.

     Enter KURT, *right.*

KURT. Are you here already?

ALICE. Yes.

KURT. Has *he* come back?

ALICE. Yes.

KURT. What like?

ALICE. In dress uniform. So he has been at the Colonel's. Two orders on his breast.

KURT. Two? I knew he was to get the Order of the Sword when he retired. What's the other one?

ALICE. I don't know, but it's a white cross inside a red one.

KURT. Portuguese in that case. . . . Let's think. . . . Ah, didn't his newspaper articles describe Quarantine Stations in Portuguese harbours?

ALICE. Yes, so far as I remember.

KURT. And has he ever been to Portugal?

ALICE. Never.

KURT. But I have been there.

ALICE. You shouldn't be so communicative. His hearing is very acute and he has an excellent memory.

KURT. Don't you think it was Judith who got him this decoration?

ALICE. No, really Kurt—there are limits! *Rises*. And you have overstepped them.

KURT. Are we going to bicker now?

ALICE. Depends on you. Don't interfere with my interests.

KURT. If they cross mine, I have to interfere with them, even if with a very cautious hand. . . . Here he comes!

ALICE. It's now that it will happen.

KURT. What will happen?

ALICE. You'll see.

KURT. May it be an attack then, for this state of siege has got on my nerves. I haven't a friend left on the whole island.

ALICE. Quick now! . . . You sit here on this side . . . he'll take the easy chair, of course, and I can prompt you.

Enter THE CAPTAIN, *back, in full dress uniform with the Order of the Sword and the Portuguese Order of Christ*.

THE CAPTAIN. Good morning. So this is the rendezvous.

ALICE. You're tired. Sit down.

THE CAPTAIN, *contrary to expectation, sits on the sofa, left*. Make yourself comfortable.

THE CAPTAIN. It's so nice here. You're very kind.

ALICE, *to* KURT. Take care! He suspects us.

THE CAPTAIN, *testily*. What's that you said?

ALICE, *to* KURT. He's certainly been drinking.

THE CAPTAIN, *bluntly*. No, he hasn't.

> *Silence.*

> Well? How have you been amusing yourselves?

ALICE. And you?

THE CAPTAIN. Haven't you noticed my Orders?

ALICE. No . . . o.

THE CAPTAIN. I thought not. You're jealous. It's usual to congratulate people when they're decorated.

ALICE. We have the honour to do so.

THE CAPTAIN. We get these things instead of the laurels actresses get.

ALICE. That refers to the wreaths on the wall at home in the tower . . .

THE CAPTAIN. Which you got from your brother . . .

ALICE. Oh, stop!

THE CAPTAIN. And which I've had to kotow to for twenty-five years . . . and which it has taken me twenty-five years to expose.

ALICE. Have you been seeing my brother?

THE CAPTAIN. From time to time.

> ALICE *is taken aback.*

> *Silence.*

> Well, Kurt? You're very silent.

KURT. I'm waiting.

THE CAPTAIN. Listen, I suppose you've heard the big news?

KURT. No.

THE CAPTAIN. Well, it's not very pleasant for me to have to be the one to . . .

KURT. Let's have it!

THE CAPTAIN. The soda factory has gone bust.

KURT. That's very bad news. How do you come out of it?

THE CAPTAIN. I'm all right. I sold out in time.

KURT. You did wisely.

THE CAPTAIN. But how do you come out of it?

KURT. Badly.

THE CAPTAIN. You've only yourself to blame. You should have sold out in time or have subscribed to the new shares.

KURT. Then I'd have lost them too.

THE CAPTAIN. Oh no! Because then the Company would have stayed on its feet.

KURT. Not the Company, but the Board. I regarded the new shares as a collection for the directors.

THE CAPTAIN. Can that point of view save you? That's the question now.

KURT. No, I shall have to give up everything.

THE CAPTAIN. Everything?

KURT. Even the house and furniture.

THE CAPTAIN. That's an appalling state of affairs.

KURT. I have been through worse.

Silence.

THE CAPTAIN. That's what happens when amateurs go in for speculation.

KURT. How can you say that? You know if I hadn't subscribed I'd have been boycotted. . . . "Further means of livelihood for coast-dwellers and sea-workers; unlimited capital, unlimited as the sea . . . philanthropy and national gain." That's what you wrote and had printed. And now you call it speculation.

THE CAPTAIN, *unmoved.* What do you mean to do now?

KURT. I may have to have an auction.

THE CAPTAIN. You would do well to.

KURT. What do you mean?

THE CAPTAIN. What I said. *Slowly.* The fact is, there are going to be certain changes here.

KURT. Here on the island?

THE CAPTAIN. Yes. . . . For instance, your official residence will be exchanged for a simpler one.

KURT. Indeed?

THE CAPTAIN. Yes, it's intended to have the Quarantine Station on the far side of the island, by the water.

KURT. My original idea.

THE CAPTAIN, *drily*. I know nothing of that. . . . I don't know your ideas on the subject. However, it's an excellent opportunity for you to get rid of your furniture—like that, it will scarcely be noticed—the scandal.

KURT. What?

THE CAPTAIN. The scandal. *Working himself up.* For it is a scandal to come to a new place and immediately get oneself into financial difficulties. And it's unpleasant for the relatives—most of all for the relatives.

KURT. Unpleasant most of all for me.

THE CAPTAIN. I'll tell you one thing, my dear Kurt. If you hadn't had me on your side in this affair, you would have lost your job.

KURT. That too!

THE CAPTAIN. You find it pretty difficult to be meticulous. There have been criticisms of you in the service.

KURT. Just criticisms?

THE CAPTAIN. Well, yes. For you are—in spite of your other admirable qualities—a slacker. Don't interrupt me! You're a terrible slacker.

KURT. That's marvellous!

THE CAPTAIN. However! The afore-mentioned charge is likely to happen pretty quickly. And I want to advise you to have the auction at once or try to sell privately.

KURT. Privately? Where could I find a buyer here?

THE CAPTAIN. Surely you don't mean I'm to come and settle myself in among your furniture? That would be a fine story. . . . *Jerkily.* Hm! Specially if one . . . considers what happened . . . at one time . . .

KURT. What's that? Do you mean what *didn't* happen?

THE CAPTAIN, *turning*. You're very quiet, Alice. What's the matter, old girl? You're not in your usual form.

ALICE. I'm just thinking.

THE CAPTAIN. O Lord! Thinking, are you? But you have to think quickly, correctly, and clearly if it's to be of any use. . . . Well, think then! One, two, three! . . . Aha, you can't do it! Well, then I'll have a shot. . . . Where's Judith?

ALICE. She's somewhere about.

THE CAPTAIN. Where's Allan?

ALICE *is silent.*

Where's the Lieutenant?

ALICE *is silent.*

Well, Kurt, what do you mean to do with Allan now?

KURT. Do with him?

THE CAPTAIN. Well, you won't have the means to keep him in the Artillery, will you?

KURT. Perhaps not.

THE CAPTAIN. You must try to get him into some cheap Infantry regiment, up in Norrland or somewhere.

KURT. In Norrland?

THE CAPTAIN. Yes. Or else you must make him go in for something practical, right away. If I were in your shoes, I'd put him in an office. . . . Why not?

KURT *is silent.*

In these enlightened times. Well? . . . Alice is so *unusually* silent. . . . Yes, my children, that's the way life's see-saw goes. Now one's on top, looking confidently around; then one's at the bottom, and then up one comes again. And so on. That's how it goes. Yes. . . . *To* ALICE. Did you say something?

ALICE *shakes her head.*

We may expect visitors here in a few days.

ALICE. Were you addressing me?

THE CAPTAIN. We may expect visitors in a few days. Distinguished visitors.

ALICE. Well, who?

THE CAPTAIN. You see! You're interested. . . . Now you can just sit there and guess who's coming. And while you're guessing, you can take this letter and read it once again.

Gives her an opened letter.

ALICE. My letter? Opened? Back from the post?

THE CAPTAIN, *rising.* Yes. In my capacity as head of the family
and your guardian, I watch over the family's most sacred
interests, and cut with an iron hand every attempt to break
family ties through a criminal correspondence. Yes.

ALICE *is beaten.*

I am not dead, Alice, but don't be angry at this moment,
when I am trying to lift us all out of an undeserved humiliation—undeserved on my part at least.

ALICE. Judith! Judith!

THE CAPTAIN. And Holofernes? Is that to be me? Pah!

Exit, back.

KURT. Who is this man?

ALICE. I don't know.

KURT. We are beaten.

ALICE. Yes . . . without any doubt.

KURT. He has stripped me to the bone, but so cunningly that
I can't accuse him of anything.

ALICE. Accuse? On the contrary, you're under an obligation
to him.

KURT. Does he know what he's doing?

ALICE. No, I don't believe he does. He obeys his nature and
his instincts, and now he seems to be in favour wherever
good and bad luck are meted out.

KURT. It must be the Colonel who is coming here.

ALICE. Probably. And so Allan must go away.

KURT. Do you really think so?

ALICE. Oh yes!

KURT. Then our ways divide.

ALICE, *preparing to go.* For a little while. . . . But we shall
meet again.

KURT. Probably.

ALICE. And you know where?

KURT. Here.

ALICE. You realise that?

KURT. It's easy. *He's* going to take over the place and buy the furniture.

ALICE. That's what I believe too. But don't desert me!

KURT. Not for so slight a cause.

ALICE. Goodbye.

KURT, *as* ALICE *goes.* Goodbye.

ACT II

SCENE: *The same. Some weeks later.*

A cloudy day and rain.

Enter ALICE *and* KURT, *back, in raincoats, carrying umbrellas.*

ALICE. So I've got you here! Kurt, I can't be so cruel as to bid you welcome—in your own home.

KURT. Oh! Why not? I've had the bailiffs in three times—and worse. This means nothing to me.

ALICE. Did *he* send for you?

KURT. A formal summons, but I don't understand on what authority.

ALICE. Quite. He's not your chief.

KURT. No, but he has set himself up as king of this island. And if anyone opposes him, he just invokes the Colonel's name, and they all kotow. . . . Tell me, is it today the Colonel's coming?

ALICE. He's expected—but I don't know anything for certain. Do sit down.

KURT, *sitting.* It's all the same as ever here.

ALICE. Don't think about it. Don't open the wound.

KURT. Wound? I only find it a little strange. Strange—like the man himself. You know, when I first met him in my youth, I ran away from him. But he pursued me. Flattered me, offered his help—and bound me. I tried to escape again, but in vain. . . . Now I am his slave.

ALICE. But why? It's he who's indebted to you; yet you who are under an obligation.

KURT. After I was ruined, he offered to help Allan with his examination.

ALICE. That will cost you dear. . . . Does your candidacy for Parliament still hold good?

KURT. Yes, there's no hitch as far as I can see.

Silence.

ALICE. Is Allan leaving today?

KURT. Yes. If I can't prevent it.

ALICE. That was a brief joy.

KURT. Brief, like everything else, except life itself, which is appallingly long.

ALICE. Yes, that it is. . . . Won't you come and wait in the morning-room? Even if these surroundings don't hurt you, they do me.

KURT. As you wish.

ALICE. I'm ashamed. I'm so ashamed that I could die. But I can't alter things.

KURT. Let's go then, if you like.

ALICE. Besides, somebody's coming.

Exeunt ALICE *and* KURT, *left.*

Enter THE CAPTAIN *and* ALLAN, *back, both in uniform with capes.*

THE CAPTAIN. Sit down here, my boy. I want to have a talk with you.

THE CAPTAIN *sits in the easy chair, and* ALLAN *on a chair, left.*

If it wasn't raining today, I should enjoy sitting here, looking out at the sea.

Silence.

Well? You don't want to go, eh?

ALLAN. I don't like leaving my father.

THE CAPTAIN. Your father, yes. He's rather an unfortunate man.

Silence.

And parents seldom know what's best for their children. That's to say—there are exceptions, of course. Hm! Tell me, Allan, are you in touch with your mother?

ALLAN. Yes, she writes to me sometimes.

THE CAPTAIN. You know she's your guardian?

ALLAN. Oh, yes.

THE CAPTAIN. Now, Allan, did you know that your mother had given me full authority to act on her behalf?

ALLAN. No, I didn't know that.

THE CAPTAIN. Anyway, you know it now. And consequently all discussion of your future is at an end. You are going to Norrland. See?

ALLAN. But I haven't the means.

THE CAPTAIN. I've seen to that.

ALLAN. Then I can only thank you, Uncle.

THE CAPTAIN. At least you're grateful—not everybody is. Hm! *Raises his voice.* The Colonel . . . do you know the Colonel?

ALLAN, *puzzled.* No, I don't.

THE CAPTAIN, *emphasizing each syllable.* The Col-onel is a specially good friend of mine . . . *Speeds up . . .* as you probably know. Hm! The Colonel has shown an interest in my family, including my wife's relatives. Through his good offices, the Colonel has been able to arrange for the means needed for the completion of your course. . . . Now you know your indebtedness—and your father's indebtedness to the Colonel. . . . Have I made myself clear?

ALLAN *nods.*

Now go and pack your things. The money will be handed to you at the gangway. And so, goodbye, my boy.

He rises and holds out one finger for ALLAN *to shake.*

Goodbye.

Exit THE CAPTAIN, *right.*

ALLAN *stands alone, looking miserably round the room.*

Enter JUDITH, *back, wearing a hooded cape and carrying an umbrella. Apart from this, she is beautifully turned out, in a long skirt with her hair up.*

JUDITH. Is it you, Allan?

ALLAN *turns and looks* JUDITH *over from head to foot.*

ALLAN. Is it *you,* Judith?

JUDITH. Don't you recognise me? But where have you been all this time? . . . What are you looking at? My long skirt —and my hair? . . . You haven't seen this before.

ALLAN. Well!

JUDITH. Do I look like a woman?

ALLAN *turns away.*

Gravely. What are you doing here?

ALLAN. I have been taking my leave.

JUDITH. What? Are you—going away?

ALLAN. I'm being transferred to Norrland.

JUDITH, *dumbfounded.* To Norrland? When do you go?

ALLAN. Today.

JUDITH. Who arranged this?

ALLAN. Your father.

JUDITH. I might have known. *Walks up and down, stamping her feet.* I wish you could be here today.

ALLAN. So as to meet the Colonel.

JUDITH. What do you know about the Colonel? Must you really go?

ALLAN. I have no choice. And now it's what I want myself.

Silence.

JUDITH. Why do you want to go now?

ALLAN. I want to get away from here. Out into the world.

JUDITH. It's too cramped here. Yes, I understand, Allan. It's unbearable here. People speculate—in soda and in human beings.

Silence.

With real feeling. Allan, I, as you know, am a happy sort of person who doesn't suffer—but now I'm beginning to.

ALLAN. You . . . ?

JUDITH. Yes. Now I'm beginning to.

She presses both hands to her breast.

Oh, how I am suffering! Oh!

ALLAN. What is it?

JUDITH. I don't know. I can't breathe. I think I'm dying.

ALLAN. Judith!

JUDITH, *crying out.* Oh! Is *this* how it feels? Is it like this? Poor boys!

ALLAN. I ought to laugh, if I were as cruel as you.

JUDITH. I'm not cruel, but I didn't know any better. . . . You mustn't go.

ALLAN. I must.

JUDITH. Go then . . . but give me something to remember.

ALLAN. What have I to give you?

JUDITH, *with deep and genuine feeling.* You! . . . No, this I *cannot* live through. *Cries aloud, clasping her breast.* I'm suffering. I'm suffering. . . . What have you done to me? I don't want to live any longer. Allan, don't go—not alone! We'll go together, and we'll take the little cutter—the little white one—and sail out to sea—but with the sheet made fast —there's a splendid wind—and then we'll sail until we founder—out there, right out where there's no goose-grass and no jellyfish. . . . What do you say? Shall we? . . . But we should have washed the sails yesterday—they should be pure white—I want to see whiteness at that moment. . . . And then you will swim with me in your arms until you grow tired—and then we shall sink. . . . *Turns.* We'll do it in style. Far more style that way than staying here, moping, and smuggling letters for Father to open and scoff at. Allan! *She takes hold of his arms and shakes him.* Are you listening?

ALLAN, *who has been watching her with his eyes shining.* Judith! Judith! Why didn't you say this before?

JUDITH. I didn't know it. How could I say what I didn't know?

ALLAN. And now I must leave you. . . . But it surely is the best and only way. I can't compete with a man who . . .

JUDITH. Don't talk about the Colonel!

ALLAN. Isn't it true?

JUDITH. It's true and it's untrue.

ALLAN. Can't it just be untrue?

JUDITH. Yes, it shall be now. In an hour's time.

ALLAN. Will you keep your word? I can wait; I can endure; I can work. . . . Judith!

JUDITH. Don't go yet! How long must I wait?

ALLAN. A year.

JUDITH, *joyfully*. One? I'll wait a thousand years, and if you don't come then, I'll turn the heavens back to front, so the sun comes up in the west. . . . Hush, someone's coming! Allan, we must part. . . . Hush! . . . Take me in your arms. *They embrace.* But you mustn't kiss me. *Turns her head away.* So go now—go now!

ALLAN *puts on his cape. Then they rush into each other's arms, so that* JUDITH *disappears in the cape, and for one moment they kiss.*

ALLAN *rushes out, back.*

JUDITH *throws herself face downwards on the sofa, sobbing.*

ALLAN *comes in again and falls on his knees beside the sofa.*

ALLAN. No, I can't go. I can't leave you now.

JUDITH, *rising*. If you knew how beautiful you are now, if you could see yourself!

ALLAN. No, no, a man can't be beautiful! But you, Judith! That you . . . that you . . . I see so clearly how when you're kind you seem like another Judith . . . who is mine. . . . But if you deceive me, I shall die.

JUDITH. I think I'm dying anyhow! . . . Oh, that I could die now, at this very moment, when I am happy! . . .

ALLAN. Someone's coming.

JUDITH. Let them come. I'm not afraid of anything in the whole world now. But I wish you would take me under your cape. *She plays at hiding under his cape.* And I would fly with you to Norrland. What shall we do in Norrland? Join the Light Infantry . . . the ones with plumes in their hats . . . that's so smart and would suit you beautifully.

She plays with his hair.

He kisses the tips of her fingers, one after the other, and then her boots.

What are you doing, you crazy boy? You will make your mouth black. *Gets up hastily.* And then I shan't be able to kiss you when you go. . . . Come on, I'll go with you!

ALLAN. No, if you did I'd be arrested.

JUDITH. I'll be arrested with you.

ALLAN. They wouldn't let you be. . . . Now we must part.

JUDITH. I shall swim after the steamer . . . and then you'll jump in and rescue me, and then it will be in the newspaper, and then we can get engaged. Shall we do that?

ALLAN. You can still joke, can you?

JUDITH. One can always cry. . . . Now say goodbye.

They fall into one another's arms. Then ALLAN *draws her gently towards the French windows, which are still open, and they embrace outside in the rain.*

ALLAN. It's raining on you, Judith.

JUDITH. What do I care about that?

They tear themselves apart.

ALLAN *goes.*

JUDITH *stays in the rain and the wind, which ruffles her hair and her dress as she stands waving her handkerchief. Then she rushes in again and flings herself on the sofa, with her face in her hands.*

ALICE *comes in, left, and goes up to* JUDITH.

ALICE. What's the matter? . . . Are you ill? Get up and let me look at you.

JUDITH *straightens up.*

ALICE *gazes at her.*

You're not ill. . . . But I'm not going to console you.

Exit ALICE, *right.*

Enter THE LIEUTENANT, *back.*

JUDITH *rises and puts on her hooded cape.*

JUDITH. Lieutenant, will you be so kind as to accompany me to the telegraph office?

THE LIEUTENANT. If I can be of any service to you, Miss Judith . . . but I don't know if it's quite correct.

JUDITH. So much the better. That's just the object—for you to compromise me—but without having any illusions. . . . You go first.

They go out, back.

THE CAPTAIN *and* ALICE *enter, right. He is in undress uniform. He sits in the easy chair.*

THE CAPTAIN. Call him in.

ALICE *goes to the door, left, and opens it. Then she sits on the sofa.*

Enter KURT, *left.*

KURT. You want to see me?

THE CAPTAIN, *amiably, but a trifle patronisingly.* Yes, I have several matters of importance to tell you. Sit down.

KURT *takes the chair on the left.*

KURT. I am all ears.

THE CAPTAIN. Well then . . . *In a haranguing tone.* You are aware that our quarantine system has been in a parlous state for close on a century . . . hm!

ALICE, *to* KURT. That's the parliamentary candidate speaking.

THE CAPTAIN. But in accordance with today's unprecedented development in . . .

ALICE, *to* KURT. Means of communication, naturally.

THE CAPTAIN. . . . in every possible respect, the Government has been considering a policy of expansion. To this end the Ministry of Health has appointed inspectors, and . . .

ALICE, *to* KURT. He's dictating.

THE CAPTAIN. . . . you may as well know it sooner as later— I have been appointed a Quarantine Inspector.

Silence.

KURT. I congratulate you—and at the same time pay my respects.

THE CAPTAIN. Our personal relationship—due to our family connection—will remain unchanged. But now, to speak of another matter—your son Allan has, at my request, been transferred to an Infantry regiment in Norrland.

KURT. But I don't wish him to be.

THE CAPTAIN. Your wishes in this matter are subordinate to those of his mother . . . and since his mother has authorised me to act for her, I have made the afore-mentioned decision.

KURT. I admire you.

THE CAPTAIN. Is that your only reaction in this moment, when you are about to be parted from your son? Have you any really human feelings?

KURT. You mean I ought to be suffering?

THE CAPTAIN. Yes.

KURT. It would please you if I suffered. You want me to have to suffer.

THE CAPTAIN. Can you suffer? Once I was stricken with illness —you were there—and I can only remember an expression of unfeigned pleasure in your face.

ALICE. That's not true. Kurt sat at your bedside all night, and soothed you when your pangs of conscience became too sharp. But when you recovered, you were ungrateful.

THE CAPTAIN, *without appearing to hear* ALICE. Accordingly, Allan is to leave us.

KURT. Who's to provide the means?

THE CAPTAIN. I have already done so. That is to say, we have —a syndicate, which interests itself in the young man's future.

KURT. Syndicate?

THE CAPTAIN. Yes. And so that you may see that it's all in order, you can take a look at these lists.

He hands KURT *some papers.*

KURT. Lists? *Looks at the papers.* Why, these are begging lists!

THE CAPTAIN. Call them that if you like.

KURT. Have you been begging for my son?

THE CAPTAIN. More ingratitude! An ungrateful person is the heaviest burden the earth has to bear.

KURT. Now I'm done for socially, and my candidature will come to nothing.

THE CAPTAIN. What candidature?

KURT. Why, for Parliament.

THE CAPTAIN. Surely you never dreamt of that? Particularly as you must have had a notion that I, as an older resident, intended to propose myself—whom you appear to have underrated.

KURT. Well, so that's finished, that too.

THE CAPTAIN. It doesn't seem to worry you much.

KURT. Now you've taken everything. Do you want anything else?

THE CAPTAIN. Have you anything else? And have you anything to reproach me with? Think hard now if you have anything with which to reproach me.

Silence.

KURT. In actual fact, nothing. Everything has been done correctly and lawfully, as between honest citizens in daily life. . . .

THE CAPTAIN. You say that in a tone of resignation I would call cynical. But your whole nature has a cynical bent, my dear Kurt, and therefore, at moments, I might be tempted to share Alice's opinion of you—that you are a hypocrite, a hypocrite of the first rank.

KURT, *calmly*. Is that Alice's opinion?

ALICE, *to* KURT. It was once. But it isn't any longer, for to bear what you have borne takes sheer heroism, or—something else.

THE CAPTAIN. I think the discussion may now be considered closed. Go and say goodbye to Allan, Kurt. He's taking the next boat.

KURT, *rising*. So soon? . . . Ah well, I've been through worse.

THE CAPTAIN. Yes, you say that so often that I begin to wonder what you were up to in America.

KURT. Up to? I was just dogged by misfortune. And it is the indisputable right of every human being to meet with misfortune.

THE CAPTAIN, *sharply*. There are self-induced misfortunes. Was it that kind?

KURT. Isn't that a question of conscience?

THE CAPTAIN, *shortly*. Have you got a conscience?

KURT. There are wolves and there are sheep. It's no honour to a man to be a sheep; but I'd rather be that than a wolf.

THE CAPTAIN. Don't you know the old truth that everyone shapes his own destiny?

KURT. Is it a truth?

THE CAPTAIN. And don't you know that it's one's own strength . . .

KURT. Yes, I do know that, since the night when your own strength betrayed you, so you were prostrate on the floor.

THE CAPTAIN, *raising his voice.* A deserving man like yours truly—yes, look at me. I have striven for fifty years against a whole world; but I have in the end won the game through perseverance, attention to duty, energy, and—integrity.

ALICE. You should let others say that.

THE CAPTAIN. Others don't, because they're jealous. However! . . . We're expecting visitors here. . . . Today my daughter, Judith, is to meet her fiancé. . . . Where is Judith?

ALICE. She's out.

THE CAPTAIN. In the rain? Send for her!

KURT. Perhaps I might go now?

THE CAPTAIN. No, you stay! . . . Is Judith dressed? Respectably?

ALICE. Yes, she'll do. . . . Has the Colonel said for certain that he's coming?

THE CAPTAIN, *rising.* Yes—that's to say, he's going to arrive and take us by surprise as it were. I'm expecting his telegram at any moment. *Going, right.* Back soon.

Exit THE CAPTAIN.

ALICE. There you have the man. Is he human?

KURT. When you asked me that before, I said he wasn't. Now I believe him to be one of the commonest types that possess the earth. . . . Perhaps we're a bit like that ourselves. Profiting by other people, opportunists.

ALICE. He has eaten you and yours alive. . . . And you defend him?

KURT. I've been through worse. . . . But this man-eater has left my soul untouched—that he could not devour.

ALICE. What is this "worse" you've been through?

KURT. You ask that?

ALICE. Are you being rude?

KURT. No, I don't want to be so—never ask that again.

Enter THE CAPTAIN, *right.*

THE CAPTAIN. The telegram was there already. Read it please, Alice—my sight is so bad. *Sits down heavily in the easy chair.* Read it! You needn't go, Kurt.

ALICE, *having read it quickly to herself, shows consternation.*

Well? Aren't you pleased?

ALICE *stares silently at* THE CAPTAIN.

Ironically. Who's it from?

ALICE. It's from the Colonel.

THE CAPTAIN, *delighted.* You don't say so! . . . Well, what does he say?

ALICE. He says this: "In view of Miss Judith's impertinent telephone message, I regard our relations as broken off—for good."

She stares at THE CAPTAIN.

THE CAPTAIN. Once more, if you please.

ALICE, *reading loudly.* "In view of Miss Judith's impertinent telephone message, I regard our relations as broken off—for good."

THE CAPTAIN, *turning pale.* This is Judith!

ALICE. And here is Holofernes.

THE CAPTAIN. What are you then?

ALICE. You will soon see.

THE CAPTAIN. This is your doing.

ALICE. No.

THE CAPTAIN, *furiously.* This is your doing.

ALICE. No.

THE CAPTAIN *tries to rise and draw his sword, but has a stroke and falls back into his chair.*

Now you've got what you deserve.

THE CAPTAIN, *whimpering senilely.* Don't be angry with me. I'm very ill.

ALICE. Are you? I'm glad to hear it.

KURT. Let's carry him to bed.

ALICE. No, I won't touch him.

She rings the bell.

THE CAPTAIN, *as before.* Don't be angry with me. *To* KURT. Look after my children!

KURT. That's rich. I'm to provide for his children, when he has stolen mine.

ALICE. What self-deception!

THE CAPTAIN. Look after my children!

He continues to babble incoherently.

ALICE. At last that tongue is stayed. It can brag no more, lie no more, wound no more. . . . You, Kurt, who believe in God, thank Him for me. Thank Him for freeing me from the tower, from the wolf, from the vampire.

KURT. Don't, Alice!

ALICE, *in* THE CAPTAIN's *face.* Where's your own strength now, eh? And your energy?

THE CAPTAIN, *speechless, spits in her face.*

If you can still spit venom, viper, I'll tear the tongue out of your throat.

She gives him a blow on the ear.

The head is off. . . . O Judith, glorious girl, whom I bore like vengeance beneath my heart, you, you have set us free —all of us! If you have any more heads, hydra, we'll take them too!

She pulls his beard.

So there is justice on earth after all! Sometimes I've dreamt of it, but I've never believed it. Kurt, ask God to forgive me for having misjudged Him. Oh, justice does exist! Now I'll become a sheep too. Tell Him that, Kurt. A little good fortune makes us better; it's misfortune that turns us into wolves.

Enter THE LIEUTENANT, *back.*

The Captain has had a stroke. Please help us wheel the chair out.

THE LIEUTENANT. Madam . . .

ALICE. What is it?

THE LIEUTENANT. Well, Miss Judith . . .

ALICE. Help us here first. You can talk about Judith afterwards.

THE LIEUTENANT *wheels the chair out, right.*

Out with the carcass! Out with it and throw everything open! The place must be aired.

She throws open the French windows.

Outside it has cleared.

Ah!

KURT. Are you going to abandon him?

ALICE. A ship that has foundered is abandoned, and the crew saves itself. There's no need for me to lay out a decaying animal. Skinners or scavengers can look after him. A garden plot is too nice a place to receive that barrow-load of filth. . . . Now I'm going to bathe myself—to wash off all this dirt, if I can ever be clean again.

JUDITH *is seen outside by the balustrade, bareheaded, waving her handkerchief towards the sea.*

KURT, *going out, back.* Who's that? Judith! *Calling.* Judith!

Enter JUDITH.

JUDITH, *crying out.* He has gone!

KURT. Who?

JUDITH. Allan has gone.

KURT. Without saying goodbye?

JUDITH. *We* said goodbye, and he sent messages to you, Uncle.

ALICE. Was that how it was?

JUDITH *throws herself into* KURT's *arms.*

JUDITH. He has gone.

KURT. He'll come back, dear child.

ALICE. Or we'll follow him.

KURT, *pointing to the door, right.* And leave him? What would people . . . ?

ALICE. People? Pah! Judith, come and embrace me!

JUDITH *goes up to* ALICE, *who kisses her on the forehead.*
Do you want to follow him?

JUDITH. Need you ask?

ALICE. But your father is ill.

JUDITH. What do I care about that!

ALICE. That's Judith. Oh how I love you, Judith!

JUDITH. Besides, Papa isn't petty, and he doesn't like being coddled. He has at least got some style, Papa.

ALICE. Yes, in a way.

JUDITH. And I don't think he's anxious to see me after that telephone business. . . . But why should he saddle me with an old man? No! Allan, Allan! *She throws herself into* KURT's *arms.* I want to go to Allan.

She pulls herself away again and runs out to wave.

KURT *follows her and waves too.*

ALICE. To think that flowers can grow out of filth!

Enter THE LIEUTENANT, *right.*

Well?

THE LIEUTENANT. Well, Miss Judith . . .

ALICE. Is it now so sweet to feel the sound of her name caressing your lips that you forget a dying man?

THE LIEUTENANT. Yes, but she said . . .

ALICE. She? It would be better to call her Judith. . . . But first, what's happening in there?

THE LIEUTENANT. Oh, in there—it's all over!

ALICE. Over? O God, I thank Thee for myself and for all mankind that Thou hast delivered us from this evil! . . . Give me your arm. I want to go out and breathe. To breathe!

THE LIEUTENANT *offers his arm.*

Checking herself. Did he say anything before the end?

THE LIEUTENANT. Miss Judith's father did say a few words.

ALICE. What did he say?

THE LIEUTENANT. He said: "Forgive them, for they know not what they do."

ALICE. Incredible!

THE LIEUTENANT. Yes, Miss Judith's father was a good and noble man.

ALICE. Kurt!

Enter KURT.

It is over.

KURT. Ah! . . .

ALICE. Do you know what his last words were? No, you don't know. "Forgive them, for they know not what they do."

KURT. Can you interpret that?

ALICE. I suppose he meant that *he* had always done right and died as one wronged by life.

KURT. He's sure to get a beautiful funeral oration.

ALICE. And masses of wreaths. From the non-commissioned officers.

KURT. Yes.

ALICE. A year ago he said something like this: "It looks as if life for us were some monstrous joke."

KURT. Do you think he was pulling our legs on his death-bed?

ALICE. No. . . . But now that he's dead I feel a strange inclination to speak well of him.

KURT. Well, let's then.

THE LIEUTENANT. Miss Judith's father was a good and noble man.

ALICE, *to* KURT. You hear!

KURT. "They know not what they do." How many times have I not asked you if he knew what he was doing? And you thought he didn't know. So, forgive him!

ALICE. Riddles! Riddles! . . . But feel the peace in the house now! The wonderful peace of death. Wonderful as that solemn unrest when a child is coming into the world. I can hear the silence . . . and I can see the marks on the floor of the easy chair which bore him away. . . . And I feel that now my own life is over and I am on the way to dissolution. . . . Do you know—it's very strange, but the Lieutenant's simple words—and he is a simple person—still echo in my mind, but now they mean something. My husband, the love of my youth—yes, you may laugh, but he was a good and noble man—in spite of it all.

KURT. In spite of it all. And a brave one too. How he fought for his own existence and what was his!

ALICE. What anxieties! What humiliations! Which he cancelled out—so that he could pass on.

KURT. He was one who was *passed over*, that's the crux of it. Alice, go in to him!

ALICE. No. I can't. For while we have been talking here, I've had a vision of him when he was young. I saw him—I can see him now—as he was when he was twenty. . . . I must have loved that man.

KURT. And hated.

ALICE. *And* hated. . . . Peace be with him!

She moves towards the door, right, where she stands still, her hands clasped.

SWANWHITE

A Fairy Play in Three Acts

FOREWORD

August Strindberg wrote *Swanwhite* in the spring of 1901 as a betrothal gift for his third wife, Harriet Bosse, the young Norwegian actress who had already played the Lady in *To Damascus* and for whom he had created the part of Eleanora in *Easter*.

In spite of his happiness at having won her hand, for he was deeply in love, Strindberg had followed the penitential dramas *To Damascus* and *Easter* with the masterpiece of horror and hatred *The Dance of Death*. Now he was eager to repeople his stage with spirits and prove the power of love.

In his "Open Letters to the Intimate Theatre" he explains how he had long wanted to blend the fairest and ugliest of Swedish folk-lore into a single picture for the stage. So now he took from the old fairy tales the ubiquitous themes of Prince and Princess and Wicked Stepmother, plucked the Maids, the Gardener, and the Young King from their traditional settings, and, in his own words, "threw them all together into the separator . . . so that the cream poured out and was my own creation. More than ever my own because I lived the story in imagination. A springtime in the winter."

Between the conception of *Swanwhite* and its creation he became a disciple of Maeterlinck's. In his Naturalist period Strindberg had distrusted his Belgian contemporary; but now that he had been through his "inferno," Maeterlinck's philosophy spoke to his condition.

Physical love tormented Strindberg all his life, for it seemed always to bring hatred in its wake. He extolled parental love as the purest form of emotion, and now, sending Harriet Bosse this play, he wrote: "It is through the Flower Test in Swanwhite that the Prince wins her, for his desire is purer and therefore stronger. The other is weakness."

Harriet Bosse did not, however, play the part of Swanwhite. The play was first produced in 1908 in Strindberg's own Intimate Theatre, and by this time he and Harriet Bosse were divorced, although they never ceased to be friends. To the actress Anna Flygare, who created the part of Swanwhite, Strindberg wrote:

> Eros is not the main theme; the symbolism relates to Caritas, the great Love, which suffers everything, overcomes everything, forgives, hopes, and believes however much it is betrayed. This is illustrated by the Stepmother's change of character, but most of all by the final scene: love is stronger than death.

Swanwhite was a success in the Intimate Theatre. In the mid-summer of 1909 or 1910 (the dates given in Swedish books vary), the Company gave an open-air performance in a public park, after which it went on tour to various parts of Sweden.

The play was never again performed during Strindberg's lifetime. In 1913, the year after the author's death, Reinhardt produced it in Berlin, and in 1914 it was revived in Stockholm with the *Swanwhite* music which Sibelius had composed in 1907.

Swanwhite has also been played in Finland, Denmark, and Hungary. The Academy of Music in New York produced it in 1920.

It was broadcast by the B.B.C. for the Strindberg centenary in 1949.

This play is a treasure-chest full of the truth that lies in fairy tales and brimful of magic and romance. It is an invitation to imaginative production as a masque, a chamber opera, a children's play, a ballet, or a film in the vein of Jean Cocteau's *La Belle et la Bête*.

E. S.

CHARACTERS

SWANWHITE

THE YOUNG KING

THE DUKE

THE STEPMOTHER

THE PRINCE

SIGNE ⎫
ELSA ⎬ MAIDS
TOVA ⎭

THE GARDENER

SWANWHITE'S MOTHER

THE PRINCE'S MOTHER

THE EXECUTIONER

THE EQUERRY

THE STEWARD

THE HERB GARDENER

THE FIRST KNIGHT

THE SECOND KNIGHT

THE FISHERMAN

ETC.

SCENE FOR THE WHOLE PLAY

An Apartment in a mediaeval stone castle. The walls and cross-vaulted ceiling are completely white. At the back, three arches open on to a stone balcony. There are rich curtains with which they can be closed. Below the balcony is a garden, and the tops of rose trees can be seen bearing pink and white blooms. In the distance is a glimpse of a white sandy beach and blue sea.

Right of the triple-arched doorway is a small door which, when open, shows a vista of three Closets, opening one into the other. The first is the Pewter Closet, in which are pewter vessels arranged on shelves. The second is the Clothing Closet, in which can be seen gorgeous raiment, and the third is the Fruit Closet, which reveals a store of apples, pears, pumpkins, and melons.

The whole floor is inlaid with black and red squares. In the centre of the Apartment stands a gilded dining-table covered with a cloth; on it are a clock, a dish of fruit, and a single rose in a vase. Over the table hangs a branch of mistletoe, and beside it stand two ornate gilded stools. On the floor in the foreground a lion-skin is spread. Over the small doorway can be seen two swallows' nests. In the foreground on the left is a white bed with a rose-coloured canopy supported at the head by two posts; at the foot are no posts. The bed coverings are white except for one coverlet of palest blue silk.[1]

Behind the bed is a vast wall cupboard. Beside the bed are a small romanesque gilded table (round on a single column) and a lampstand bearing a Roman lamp of gold. Right is a beautifully carved chimney-piece, on which stands a white lily in a vase. Front right is a gilded treasure-chest.

[1] Strindberg includes a filmy white nightdress lying on the bed. I have omitted this, as it disagrees with the text. The only white garment should be the one brought Swanwhite by her mother. E.S.

*In the left arch of the main doorway a peacock is asleep on
a perch with its back to the audience. In the right arch is
a great golden cage containing two sleeping white doves.*

ACT I

As the curtain rises, the three MAIDS *are seen, half-hidden by the doorways of each Closet.* SIGNE, *the false maid, is in the Pewter Closet,* ELSA, *who is tiny and pretty, is in the Clothing Closet,* TOVA, *the ugly faithful maid, is in the Fruit Closet.*

THE DUKE *enters by the main doorway, followed by* THE STEPMOTHER *with a steel whip in her hand.*

The stage is dim as they enter. Outside a horn is blown.

THE STEPMOTHER, *gazing round her.* Is Swanwhite not here?

THE DUKE. You can see. . . .

THE STEPMOTHER. I can see, but I cannot see *her. Calls.* You maids! Signe![2] Elsa! Tova![2]

THE MAIDS *come in, one after the other, and stand in front of* THE STEPMOTHER.

Where is the Lady Swanwhite?

SIGNE *crosses her arms over her breast and is silent.*

You do not know? *Shakes the whip.* Then . . . do you know what I have in my hand? . . . Quick, answer me! *Pause.* Quick! *Swings the whip so that it whistles.* Listen to the whistle of the Falcon. It has claws and a beak of steel. And what is it?

SIGNE. It is the steel whip.

THE STEPMOTHER. Yes, the steel whip. Now—where is the Lady Swanwhite?

SIGNE. I cannot tell what I do not know.

THE STEPMOTHER. Ignorance is a failing, but heedlessness is a

[2] Pronounced Seenya and Toova.

crime. Are you not here to keep watch over your young mistress? Take off your kerchief.

Despairingly, SIGNE *obeys.*

Get down on your knees!

THE DUKE *turns his back in horror at the scene.*

Hold out your neck! Now I shall put such a necklace on it that no young suitor will ever put his lips to it again. . . . Stretch out your neck! Further!

SIGNE. For Christ's sake, have mercy!

THE STEPMOTHER. It is mercy enough that you keep your life.

THE DUKE *draws his sword and tests it first on one of his nails, then on his long beard.*

THE DUKE, *ironically.* Her head should be cut off, put in a sack . . . hung from a tree . . .

THE STEPMOTHER. So it should indeed.

THE DUKE. We are of one mind, you see.

THE STEPMOTHER. We were not so yesterday.

THE DUKE. And perhaps we shall not be tomorrow.

SIGNE, *still on her knees, is stealthily crawling away.*

THE STEPMOTHER. What are you doing? Stay where you are.

She raises the whip and strikes. SIGNE *turns, so that the lash merely cuts the air.* SWANWHITE *comes from behind the bed and falls on her knees. She is simply dressed and has dirty bare feet.*

SWANWHITE. Here I am, Stepmother. I am the guilty one. Signe is innocent.

THE STEPMOTHER. Say "Mother." Say "Mother."

SWANWHITE. I cannot. No human being has more than one mother.

THE STEPMOTHER. Your father's wife is your mother.

SWANWHITE. My father's second wife is my stepmother.

THE STEPMOTHER. You are a stubborn daughter, but this steel is pliant and makes others pliant. *She lifts the whip to strike* SWANWHITE.

THE DUKE, *raising his sword.* Beware! Your head is in danger.

THE STEPMOTHER. Whose head?

THE DUKE. Your own.

> THE STEPMOTHER *recoils in rage, but controls herself and remains silent. Long pause. Then, seeing herself beaten, she changes her tone.*

THE STEPMOTHER. Very well. Now perhaps you will inform your daughter what is in store for her.

THE DUKE, *sheathing his sword.* My beloved child, come and find refuge in my arms.

SWANWHITE, *springing into his arms.* Oh Father, you are like a royal oak tree, and my arms are not long enough to embrace you! But beneath your foliage I can hide from threatening storms . . . *She hides her face in his great beard* . . . and I will swing on your branches like a bird. Lift me up so that I may climb to the very top.

> *He lifts her on to his shoulder.*

Now I have the earth beneath me and the air above. Now I can see out across the rose garden to the white sands and the blue sea, and to all the seven kingdoms. . . .

THE DUKE. Then you can see the Young King, to whom you are betrothed.

SWANWHITE. No, him I cannot see. Him I have never seen. Is he handsome?

THE DUKE. It will depend on your own eyes, dear heart, how he appears to you.

SWANWHITE, *rubbing her eyes.* On my own eyes? . . . All that they see is beautiful.

THE DUKE, *kissing her foot.* Black little foot, foot of my little blackamoor.

> *During this scene* THE STEPMOTHER *has signed to* THE MAIDS *to resume their places in the doorways of the Closets. With the stealthy movement of a panther,* THE STEPMOTHER *goes out through the middle arch.* SWANWHITE *jumps down.* THE DUKE *seats her on the table and sits on a stool beside her.* SWANWHITE *watches* THE STEPMOTHER *disappear and expresses her relief.*

SWANWHITE. Has the sun risen? Has the wind changed to the south? Has spring come back again?

THE DUKE, *putting his hand over her mouth.* Little chatterbox. Joy of my old age—my evening star. Open your rosy ears and shut the little red shell of your mouth. Listen to me. Obey me and all will go well with you.

SWANWHITE, *putting her fingers in her ears.* I hear with my eyes, I see with my ears. Now I cannot see at all. I can only hear.

THE DUKE. Child . . . while you were still in the cradle you were betrothed to the young King of Rigalid.[3] You have never seen him, for such is Court etiquette. Now the day is drawing near when the sacred knot must be tied, but in order to teach you the ways of the Court and the duties of a Queen, the King has sent hither a young Prince, with whom you are to study books, learn to play chess, to dance a measure, and play upon the harp.

SWANWHITE. What is this Prince's name?

THE DUKE. My child, that is something you must never ask, neither of him nor of any other, for it is prophesied that whosoever calls him by his name must love him.

SWANWHITE. Is he handsome?

THE DUKE. Yes—since your eyes see nothing but beauty.

SWANWHITE. But is he not beautiful?

THE DUKE. Yes, he is beautiful. So, set a guard on your young heart, which belongs to the King, and never forget that in the cradle you were made a Queen. . . . And now, my beloved child, I am going to leave you, for I must go to war. Be humble and obedient to your stepmother. She is a hard woman, but your father loved her once, and a sweet nature may melt a heart of stone. *From under his cloak he takes a horn of carved ivory.* If, against her sworn word, her malice should exceed all bounds, then blow upon this horn—and help will come. But do not blow it unless you are in peril, great peril . . . Do you understand?

SWANWHITE. But what am I to do?

THE DUKE. My child, the Prince is below in the Ladies' Chamber. Do you wish to receive him now?

SWANWHITE, *excited.* Do I wish . . . ?

[3] Pronounced Reegaleed.

THE DUKE. Shall I not first bid you farewell?

SWANWHITE. Is the Prince here already?

THE DUKE. He is here already and I am already there—there, far away, where the heron of forgetfulness puts its head under its wing.

SWANWHITE, *throwing herself into* THE DUKE'S *arms and burying her face in his beard.* Don't say such things. Don't say them. You cover me with shame.

THE DUKE, *tenderly.* You should be beaten for forgetting your old father so quickly at the thought of a young Prince. . . . *A horn sounds in the distance. He rises hastily, picks* SWANWHITE *up in his arms, throws her up, and catches her again.* Fly, little bird, fly! High above the dusty earth with the clear air beneath your wings. . . . *He puts her down.* There. Down once more to earth. . . . I am called by war and glory—you by love and youth. *Girds on his sword.* And now hide your magic horn that no evil eyes may see it.

SWANWHITE. Where shall I hide it? Where?

THE DUKE. Inside your bed.

SWANWHITE, *hiding the horn in the bedclothes.* Sleep there. Sleep well, my little herald. When the time comes, I'll waken you. Do not forget to say your prayers.

THE DUKE. And you, child, do not forget my last behest: obey your stepmother.

SWANWHITE. In everything?

THE DUKE. In everything.

SWANWHITE. Not in what is unclean. My mother gave me two changes of linen every week. *She* gives me only one. My mother gave me water and soap—these my stepmother denies me. You have seen my poor little feet.

THE DUKE. Keep pure within, my daughter, and you shall be pure without. You know that holy men who renounce ablutions for a penance grow white as swans, while the wicked turn black as ravens.

SWANWHITE. Then I will grow so white, so white.

THE DUKE. Come to my arms once more—and then farewell! *They embrace.*

SWANWHITE. Farewell, great warrior—my glorious father. May good fortune follow in your train and make you rich in years and friends and victories.

THE DUKE. Amen. May your gentle prayers protect me.

He closes the visor of his golden helmet.

SWANWHITE, *kissing his visor.* The golden gates are shut, but through the bars I see your kind and watchful eyes. *She knocks at the visor.* Open, open, for Little Red Ridinghood! . . . No one is in. "Come in and see," said the wolf, who was lying in the bed.

THE DUKE. Sweet flower of mine, grow fair and fragrant. If I return—so be it, I return. If not, my eyes will watch over you from the starry vault and never again will you be lost to my sight. For there we mortals shall be all-seeing as our Lord Creator.

He goes out firmly, with a gesture forbidding her to follow. SWANWHITE *falls on her knees and prays.*

A wind sighs. All the rose trees sway. The peacock moves its wings and tail. SWANWHITE *rises, goes to the peacock, and strokes its back and tail.*

SWANWHITE. Pavo, dear Pavo, what do you see? What do you hear? Is someone coming? Who is coming? Is it a young Prince? Is he handsome—and kind? Surely you can see with so many, many blue eyes. *She lifts one of the bird's tail-feathers and gazes intently at its eye, then continues in a changed voice.* Oh, are you going to keep your eye on us, you horrid Argus? Do you mean to watch in case the hearts of two young people beat too fast? You stupid creature! I shall draw the curtain, see! *She draws a curtain so that it hides the peacock, but not the landscape. Then she goes over to the doves.* My white doves—oh so white, white, white! You shall see the whitest thing of all. . . . Hush wind, hush roses, hush doves—my Prince is coming!

For a moment she looks out through the arches, then withdraws to the Pewter Closet. She puts on stockings[4] while she peeps out at THE PRINCE, *who does not see her.*

THE PRINCE *enters through the middle arch. He is in black*

[4] Added stage direction, to correspond with the text.   E.S.

*with steel armour. Having carefully observed everything in
the room, he sits down by the table, takes off his helmet,
and studies it. His back is turned to the door where* SWAN-
WHITE *is hiding.*

THE PRINCE. If anyone is here, let him answer. *Pause.* Someone
is here, for I can feel the warmth of a young body wafted
to me like a breeze from the south. I can hear breathing—it
has the fragrance of roses—and gentle as it is, it stirs the
plume on my helmet. *He puts the helmet to his ear.* My
helmet murmurs like a great sea-shell. It is the murmuring
of the thoughts in my head, swarming like bees in a hive.
"Bzz, bzz," they go . . . just like bees. They are buzzing
round their Queen—the little queen of my thoughts and my
dreams. *He puts the helmet on the table in front of him and
gazes at it.* Dark and arched it is, like the night sky—but
starless, for ever since my mother died, the black plume has
spread darkness everywhere. . . . *He turns the helmet
round and stares at it again.* Yet there, deep in the darkness
inside it . . . I see beyond, a shaft of light. Is it a rift in the
heavens? And there in the rift I see—no, not a star, for that
would be a diamond—but a blue sapphire, queen of jewels,
blue as the summer sky, set in a milk-white cloud, shaped
like the egg of a dove. What is it? Not my ring? Now another feathery cloud, black as velvet, passes by. . . .

SWANWHITE *smiles.*

The sapphire is smiling—so sapphires can smile. Now a flash
of lightning, mild and without thunder.

She flashes a startled glance at him.

What are you? Who are you? *He looks at the back of the
helmet.* Not there. Not here. Nowhere at all. *He puts his
face close to the helmet.* As I draw nearer, you go further
away.

SWANWHITE *steals towards him on tiptoe.*

Now there are two . . . two eyes! Young human eyes . . .
I kiss you. *He kisses the helmet.*

SWANWHITE *goes to the table and slowly seats herself opposite* THE PRINCE. *He rises, bows with his hand on his heart,
and gazes at her.*

SWANWHITE. Are you the Prince?

THE PRINCE. The Young King's faithful servant, and your own.

SWANWHITE. What message has the Young King sent his bride?

THE PRINCE. He sends the Lady Swanwhite a thousand tender greetings. He would have her know that the thought of the sweet joys to come will shorten this long torment of his waiting.

SWANWHITE, *looking searchingly at* THE PRINCE. Will you not be seated, Prince?

THE PRINCE. If I were to sit while you were sitting, when you stood up I should have to kneel.

SWANWHITE. Tell me about the King. What is he like?

THE PRINCE. What is he like? . . . *Puts his hand up to his eyes.* How strange! I can no longer see him.

SWANWHITE. How do you mean?

THE PRINCE. He has gone away. He is invisible.

SWANWHITE. Is he tall?

THE PRINCE, *studying* SWANWHITE. Wait—now I can see him. Taller than you are.

SWANWHITE. And beautiful?

THE PRINCE. He is no match for you.

SWANWHITE. Speak of the King, not of me.

THE PRINCE. I am speaking of the King.

SWANWHITE. Is he fair or dark?

THE PRINCE. If he were dark, seeing you he would at once become fair.

SWANWHITE. There is more flattery than sense in that. Are his eyes blue?

THE PRINCE, *glancing at his helmet.* I had better look.

SWANWHITE, *holding her hand up between them.* Oh you, you!

THE PRINCE. Y-o-u—you. Y-o-u-t-h—youth.

SWANWHITE. Are you to teach me spelling?

THE PRINCE. The Young King is tall and fair, with blue eyes, broad shoulders, and hair like a young forest. . . .

SWANWHITE. Why do you wear a black plume?

THE PRINCE. His lips are red as berries, his skin is white, and his teeth would not shame a young lion.

SWANWHITE. Why does your forehead glisten?

THE PRINCE. His mind knows no fear, and his heart is free from guilt.

SWANWHITE. Why is your hand trembling?

THE PRINCE. We were to speak of the Young King, not of me.

SWANWHITE. Is it for you to lecture me?

THE PRINCE. That is my duty—to teach you to love the Young King, whose throne you are to share.

SWANWHITE. How did you cross the sea?

THE PRINCE. By bark and sail.

SWANWHITE. With the wind so high?

THE PRINCE. Without wind one cannot sail.

SWANWHITE. How wise you are, boy . . . will you play with me?

THE PRINCE. I shall do whatever is required of me.

SWANWHITE. Now you shall see what I have in my chest. *She kneels beside the chest and takes out a doll, a rattle, and a toy horse. She brings the doll to* THE PRINCE. Here is my doll. It is my child, my child of sorrow who can never keep her face clean. I have carried her down to the laundry myself, and scoured her with silver sand . . . but she only grew dirtier. I have beaten her, but that did not help either. Now I have thought of the worst punishment of all for her.

THE PRINCE. And what is that?

SWANWHITE, *glancing round.* She shall have a stepmother.

THE PRINCE. But how can that be? She must have a mother first.

SWANWHITE. I am her mother, and if I marry again, I shall be her stepmother.

THE PRINCE. Oh no, that is not the way of it!

SWANWHITE. And you will be her stepfather.

THE PRINCE. No, no.

SWANWHITE. But you must be kind to her even if she cannot

wash her face. Take her. Let me see if you know how to
hold a child.

THE PRINCE *unwillingly takes the doll.*

You do not know yet, but you will learn. Now take this
rattle and rattle it for her. *Gives him the rattle.* I see you do
not know how to do that at all. *Takes back the doll and the
rattle and throws them into the chest. She brings him the
horse.* Here is my steed. It has a saddle of gold and shoes of
silver and it can cover forty miles in an hour. On its back I
have ridden through the forest, over the great moor, across
the King's bridge, along the highway, through the Valley of
Fear to the Lake of Tears. Once it dropped a golden shoe.[5]
It fell into the lake, but up came a fish and along came a
fisherman, and so I got back the golden shoe. That's the end
of that story. *She throws the horse back into the chest and
brings out a chess-board with red and white squares and
chessmen of silver and gold.* If you would like to play with
me, come and sit down on the lion-skin. *She seats herself
and begins to put up the pieces.* Sit down—the Maids
can't see us here.

THE PRINCE *sits shyly down beside her. She runs her hand
through the lion's mane.*

It is like sitting on the grass, not the green grass of a
meadow, but desert grass which has been burned by the
sun. Now you must tell me about myself. Do you like me a
little?

THE PRINCE. Shall we play?

SWANWHITE. Play? What do I care about that? *Sighs.* Oh, you
should teach me something!

THE PRINCE. Alas, what can I teach you other than how to
saddle a horse and carry arms? Such things would be of
small service to you.

SWANWHITE. Are you sad?

THE PRINCE. My mother is dead.

SWANWHITE. Poor Prince . . . My mother is in heaven too—

[5] Strindberg has this discrepancy — "shoes of silver" — "golden
shoe." E.S.

with God. She is an angel now. Sometimes in the night I see her. Do you see your mother?

THE PRINCE, *hesitating.* No.

SWANWHITE. And have you a stepmother?

THE PRINCE. Not yet. It is so short a time since my mother died.

SWANWHITE. You must not be so sad. Everything passes in time. *Pause. She fetches a banner from her chest.* I will give you a banner to gladden your heart. Oh! It is true, I made this one for the Young King—but I will make another one for you. This is the King's, with seven flaming fires—you shall have one with seven red roses. First you must hold this skein of yarn for me. *She takes a skein of rose-coloured yarn from the chest and arranges it over* THE PRINCE'S *hands.* One, two, three. Now I will begin, but you must not let your hands tremble. Perhaps you would like one of my hairs woven into the banner. Pull one out.

THE PRINCE. No, no, I cannot.

SWANWHITE. Then I will do it. *She pulls out one of her hairs and winds it into the ball of yarn.* What is your name?

THE PRINCE. You must not ask that.

SWANWHITE. Why not?

THE PRINCE. Did not the Duke tell you?

SWANWHITE. No. What would happen if I said your name? Something terrible?

THE PRINCE. Surely the Duke told you?

SWANWHITE. I have never heard of such a thing. A person not able to tell his own name!

The curtain behind which the peacock is hidden moves, and a faint sound is heard as of castanets.

THE PRINCE. What was that?

SWANWHITE, *uneasily.* It is Pavo—the peacock. Do you think he understands what we are saying?

THE PRINCE. You never know.

Pause.

SWANWHITE. Tell me your name.

The same sound is repeated.

THE PRINCE. This frightens me. You must not ask me that again.

SWANWHITE. He is snapping his beak, that's all. Keep your hands still. Have you ever heard the story of a Princess who was not allowed to say the Prince's name, for fear something terrible should happen? Do you know what . . . ?

The curtain hiding the peacock is drawn aside. The peacock has turned round and spread his tail. All the "eyes" seem to be gazing at SWANWHITE *and* THE PRINCE.

THE PRINCE. Who drew that curtain? Who told that bird to spy on us with its hundred eyes? You must not ask me that again.

SWANWHITE. Maybe not. Go back and keep quiet, Pavo.

The curtain is drawn again.

There.

THE PRINCE. Is this place haunted?

SWANWHITE. You mean because things like that happen? Yes, many things happen here, but I am used to it. In fact . . . *She lowers her voice* . . . they say that my stepmother is a witch. There, now I have pricked my finger.

THE PRINCE. How did you prick it?

SWANWHITE. There was a splinter in the yarn. When the sheep have been kept in the barns all the winter, that does sometimes happen. Can you take the splinter out?

THE PRINCE. Yes, but we must sit at the table so that I can see.

They seat themselves at the table.

SWANWHITE, *holding out her little finger.* Can you see anything?

THE PRINCE, *rather bolder than hitherto.* What do I see? *He holds her hand up to the light.* The inside of your hand is pink, and through it I see the world and all life in a rosy light.

SWANWHITE. Pull out the splinter. It is hurting me.

THE PRINCE. But I shall have to hurt you. Forgive me first.

SWANWHITE. Yes, yes, but do it now.

THE PRINCE *takes the splinter out of her little finger.*

THE PRINCE. Here is the wretched thing which dared to hurt you.

He throws the splinter on the floor and stamps on it.

SWANWHITE. Now you must suck the blood to keep the wound from festering.

He puts his lips to her finger.

THE PRINCE. Now I have drunk your blood, so I am your foster-brother.

SWANWHITE. My foster-brother. Yes, but you were already that, or how could I have talked to you as I did?

THE PRINCE. Or I to you.

SWANWHITE. Now I have a brother—and that is you. Dear brother, take my hand.

THE PRINCE, *taking her hand.* Dear sister. *He feels the pulse in her finger.* What is it that keeps ticking in there? . . . One, two, three, four . . . *Continues to count soundlessly while looking at the clock.*

SWANWHITE. Yes, what is it that ticks? Tick, tick, tick—so steadily. My heart cannot be in my finger, for it is beneath my breast. . . . Put your hand here and you will feel it.

The doves begin to stir and coo.

What is the matter with my little white creatures?

THE PRINCE, *who has gone on counting.* . . . sixty. Now I know what it is that ticks. It is time. Your little finger is the second-hand. It ticks sixty times for every minute that passes. *Looking at the clock on the table.* Do you think there is a heart inside that clock?

SWANWHITE, *touching the clock.* A clock's works are as secret as a heart's. Feel my heart beating.

SIGNE *enters from the Pewter Closet, carrying the steel whip, which she lays on the table.*

SIGNE. The Duchess commands the Prince and Princess to sit at opposite ends of the table.

They sit as directed. SIGNE *returns to the Pewter Closet.* THE PRINCE *and* SWANWHITE *gaze at each other for a while in silence.*

SWANWHITE. We are far apart, yet nearer even than before.

THE PRINCE. People are never so close as when they are parted.

SWANWHITE. How do you know that?

THE PRINCE. I have just learned it.

SWANWHITE. Now you are beginning to teach me.

THE PRINCE. It is you who are teaching me.

SWANWHITE, *pointing to the dish of fruit.* Will you have some fruit?

THE PRINCE. No, eating is ugly.

SWANWHITE. Yes, it is ugly.

THE PRINCE. Three maids are standing there—one in the Pewter Closet, one in the Clothing Closet, and one in the Fruit Closet. Why are they there?

SWANWHITE. To watch us—lest we do what is forbidden.

THE PRINCE. May we not go into the rose garden?

SWANWHITE. I can only go into the garden in the morning, for my stepmother's bloodhounds are let loose there. And I am never allowed to go down to the sea . . . and so I can never bathe.

THE PRINCE. Have you never seen the sands? Never heard the song of the waves on the beach?

SWANWHITE. No. Only the roaring of the breakers in a storm reaches me here.

THE PRINCE. Have you never heard the murmuring of the winds as they sweep over the water?

SWANWHITE. That cannot reach me here.

THE PRINCE, *pushing his helmet across the table to* SWAN-WHITE. Hold this to your ear and you will hear it.

SWANWHITE, *holding the helmet to her ear.* What is it I hear?

THE PRINCE. The sea singing and the winds whispering.

SWANWHITE. No, I hear human voices. Hush! It is my step-mother. She is talking to the Steward. She is speaking of me —and of the Young King. She is saying evil things. She is swearing that I shall never be a Queen—and she is vowing . . . that you . . . that you shall marry her daughter . . . that ugly, wicked Lena.

THE PRINCE. Can you hear all that in my helmet?

SWANWHITE. Yes, yes, I can.

THE PRINCE. I did not know it had such power. Yet the helmet was a christening present from my godmother.

SWANWHITE. Will you give me a feather from the plume?

THE PRINCE. With all my heart.

SWANWHITE. Shape it into a quill, so that I may write with it.

THE PRINCE. You know how to write?

SWANWHITE. That my father taught me.

Meanwhile she has pushed the helmet back to THE PRINCE *and he has pulled a black feather from the plume. He takes a silver knife from his belt and shapes the quill.* SWANWHITE *brings out an inkhorn and parchment from the drawer of the table.*

THE PRINCE. Who is this Lady Lena?

He gives SWANWHITE *the quill.*

SWANWHITE, *writing*. Who is she? Do you want her?

THE PRINCE. There is evil brewing in this house.

SWANWHITE. Have no fear. My father left me a gift which will bring help in time of need.

THE PRINCE. What was this gift?

SWANWHITE. The magic horn Standby.

THE PRINCE. Where is it?

SWANWHITE. That you must read in my eyes. I dare not speak, for fear of the Maids.

THE PRINCE, *looking into her eyes*. I have seen.

SWANWHITE, *pushing writing materials across to* THE PRINCE. Write it down.

He writes and hands her the parchment.

Yes, that is the hiding-place. *She writes.*

THE PRINCE. What are you writing?

SWANWHITE. Names. All the beautiful names a Prince may have.

THE PRINCE. All but my own.

SWANWHITE. Yours too.

THE PRINCE. No, no, not that.

SWANWHITE. Now I have twenty names—all that I know—so yours must be among them. *She pushes the parchment across to him.* Read!

He reads.

She claps her hands. Oh, I read it in your eyes!

THE PRINCE. Do not say it. For pity's sake, do not say it.

SWANWHITE. I read it in your eyes.

THE PRINCE. But do not say it. Do not say it.

SWANWHITE. But why? What would happen? . . . Is Lena to say it? Your bride, your love.

THE PRINCE. Hush! Oh hush, hush!

SWANWHITE, *rising and beginning to dance.* I know his name. The most beautiful name in all the land.

THE PRINCE *rises, catches hold of her, and holds his hand over her mouth.*

Now I am biting your hand, now I am drinking your blood, now we are brethren twice over. Do you understand?

THE PRINCE. We are of one blood.

SWANWHITE, *throwing back her head.* O-o-o-h! Look, there is a hole in the roof, and I can see the sky, a tiny piece of heaven, a window pane, and behind the window is a face. Is it an angel's face? . . . Look, look . . . it is your face.

THE PRINCE. The angels are young girls, not boys.

SWANWHITE. But it is you.

THE PRINCE, *gazing up.* It is a mirror.

SWANWHITE. Woe to us then! It is my stepmother's magic mirror. She has seen everything.

THE PRINCE. I can see the hearth in the mirror. There is a pumpkin hanging in it.

SWANWHITE, *taking from the hearth a queerly shaped mottled pumpkin.* What can this be? It has the look of an ear. So the witch has heard us too. Alas, alas! *She throws the pumpkin into the fire and runs towards the bed. Suddenly she stops and raises one foot.* Oh, she has strewn the floor with needles. *She sits down and rubs her foot.*

THE PRINCE *kneels to help her.*

No, you must not touch my foot, you must not.

THE PRINCE. Dear heart, you must take off your stocking if I am to help you.

SWANWHITE, *sobbing.* You must not, you must not see my foot.

THE PRINCE. But why, why?

SWANWHITE, *drawing her foot under her.* I cannot tell you, I cannot. Go away. Leave me. I will tell you tomorrow, but today I cannot.

THE PRINCE. But your poor foot is hurting. I must take out the needle.

SWANWHITE. Go away, oh go away! No, no, you must not touch it. Were my mother alive this would never have happened. Mother, mother, mother!

THE PRINCE. I do not understand. Are you afraid of me?

SWANWHITE. Do not ask. Only go away. Oh!

THE PRINCE, *rising, sadly.* What have I done?

Pause.

SWANWHITE. No, do not leave me. I did not mean to grieve you—but I cannot tell you. Oh, if only I might reach the shore, the white sand of the beach. . . .

THE PRINCE. What then?

SWANWHITE. I cannot say, I cannot tell you.

She hides her face in her hands. Once more the peacock snaps his beak and the doves stir. The three MAIDS *enter one after the other. A gust of wind is heard and the tops of the rose trees sway. The golden clouds that have hung over the sea disappear and the blue sea darkens.* SWANWHITE *watches this transformation and then speaks.*

Is this the judgement of heaven on us? There is ill luck in the house. Oh, that my sorrow could bring back my mother from her dark grave!

THE PRINCE, *with his hand on his sword.* My life for yours.

SWANWHITE. Alas, she can even turn the edge of your sword. . . . Oh, that my sorrow could bring back my mother from her grave!

The swallows in the nest twitter.

What was that?

THE PRINCE, *looking at the nest.* A swallows' nest! I had not noticed it.

SWANWHITE. Neither had I. How did it get there—and when? Surely it is a good omen. . . . Yet the sweat of fear is on my brow . . . and I can scarcely breathe. Look, even the rose is withering as that evil woman draws near—for it is she who is coming.

The rose on the table begins to close and drops a petal.

THE PRINCE. But the swallows, where did they come from?

SWANWHITE. Not from that evil woman—for swallows are good. . . . Here she is!

THE STEPMOTHER *enters through the main arch with her panther-like step. The rose droops.*

THE STEPMOTHER. Signe! Take the horn out of the bed.

SIGNE *obeys.*

THE PRINCE *moves towards the door.*

Where are you going, Prince?

THE PRINCE. The day is almost over, madam. The sun is setting and my bark must set sail for home.

THE STEPMOTHER. The day *is* over. The gates are closed and the hounds let loose. Do you know my bloodhounds?

THE PRINCE. Yes, I know them. But do you know my sword?

THE STEPMOTHER. What is there to know?

THE PRINCE. Sometimes there is blood upon it.

THE STEPMOTHER. Ah, but surely never the blood of women. Will you sleep in the Blue Room, Prince?

THE PRINCE. No, by heaven, I will sleep at home in my own bed.

THE STEPMOTHER. Have you many to aid you?

THE PRINCE. Many?

THE STEPMOTHER. How many? As many as these? One, two, three . . .

As she counts, the members of the household begin to pass across the balcony in single file. All appear grim. Some are armed. None look into the room. Among them are THE STEW-

ARD, THE BAILIFF, THE GUARD, THE CHEF, THE EXECU-
TIONER, THE EQUERRY, *and* THE GROOM.

THE PRINCE, *crushed.* I will sleep in the Blue Room.

THE STEPMOTHER. I thought you would. And so I bid you a
thousand times good night—and so too does Swanwhite.

*There is music as of the flight of swans. A swan flies across
the garden. A poppy drops from the ceiling on to* THE STEP-
MOTHER. *She and* THE MAIDS *fall asleep on their feet.*

SWANWHITE, *going up to* THE PRINCE. Good night, Prince.

THE PRINCE, *taking her hand and speaking in a low voice.*
Good night. I am to sleep under the same roof as my Princess. My dreams shall enfold your dreams, and tomorrow we
shall awake to play together and . . .

SWANWHITE, *low.* Now you are the only one I have on earth.
You are my father, for she has robbed me of his great
strength. Look, she is asleep.

THE PRINCE. Did you see the swan?

SWANWHITE. No, but I heard it. It was my mother.

THE PRINCE. Come, fly with me!

SWANWHITE. That we may not do. Be patient. We shall meet
in our dreams, shall we not? But to do this, you must love
me more than all the world. Oh, love me, love me! . . .

THE PRINCE. My King, my loyalty.

SWANWHITE. Your Queen, your heart—this is what I am.

THE PRINCE. I am a knight.

SWANWHITE. But I am not. And so, and so, I take you,
Prince . . .

She puts her hand to his mouth and whispers his name.

THE PRINCE. Alas, what have you done?

SWANWHITE. I have given myself to you through your own
name. With me on your wings you have found yourself
again. You . . . *Whispers his name again.*

THE PRINCE, *with a movement of his hand, as if catching the
word in the air.* Was that a rose you threw to me? *He
throws a kiss to her.* Swanwhite!

SWANWHITE, *catching it and looking in her hand.* You have

given me a violet. It is you. It is your soul. *She puts her hand to her mouth.* Now I drink you in, now I have you in my breast, in my heart.

THE PRINCE. And you are mine. Who then is the owner?

SWANWHITE. We two.

THE PRINCE. We. You and I. My rose.

SWANWHITE. My violet.

THE PRINCE. Rose.

SWANWHITE. Violet.

THE PRINCE. I love you.

SWANWHITE. You love me.

THE PRINCE. You love me.

SWANWHITE. I love you.

The stage grows light again. The rose on the table lifts its head and opens. The faces of THE STEPMOTHER *and* THE MAIDS *are lighted and appear beautiful, kind, and happy.* THE STEPMOTHER *lifts her drowsy head and, with her eyes still closed, appears to be watching the joy of the young people with a sweet smile.*

Look, look! The cruel one is smiling as at a memory of youth. See how false Signe is transformed by truth and hope. How ugly Tova has become beautiful, and little Elsa has grown tall.

THE PRINCE. This is the power of our love.

SWANWHITE. Can love do this? Praise be to God, mighty God the Creator!

She falls on her knees and weeps.

THE PRINCE. Are you weeping?

SWANWHITE. Yes, for I am so full of joy.

THE PRINCE. Come to my arms, and smile.

SWANWHITE. In your arms I shall die.

THE PRINCE. Smile then and die.

SWANWHITE, *rising.* If I might die . . .

THE PRINCE *takes her in his arms.* THE STEPMOTHER *awakens. On seeing the young people embracing, she strikes the table with the whip.*

THE STEPMOTHER. I must have fallen asleep. Ah, so this was your trick! Did I say the Blue Room? It was the Blue Tower I meant. That is where you shall sleep, Prince—with the Iron Maiden. Signe! Elsa!

The three MAIDS *awaken.*

Show the Prince the nearest way to the Blue Tower, and if in spite of your help he should lose his way, call the Guard, the Executioner, the Equerry, and the Groom.

THE PRINCE. There will be no need for them. Wheresoever I go, through fire or water, beneath the earth or above the clouds, there I shall meet my Swanwhite. She will be with me always, and so now I go to meet her—in the Blue Tower. How is that for witchcraft, Witch? Can you surpass it? I think not—for in you there is no love.

He and SWANWHITE *gaze long at one another. Then he goes out, followed by* THE MAIDS. SWANWHITE *approaches* THE STEPMOTHER *with a pleading gesture.*

THE STEPMOTHER. What is it? Do not waste words, but tell me briefly what you wish.

SWANWHITE. Most of all I want pure water in which to bathe my feet.

THE STEPMOTHER. Is the water to be cold or warm?

SWANWHITE. If I may choose, I should like it to be warm.

THE STEPMOTHER. What else do you desire?

SWANWHITE. A comb to take the tangles from my hair.

THE STEPMOTHER. A golden comb or one of silver?

SWANWHITE. Are you—oh, are you being kind to me?

THE STEPMOTHER. Is it to be gold or silver?

SWANWHITE. Wood or horn would do well enough for me.

THE STEPMOTHER. What else do you wish?

SWANWHITE. A clean shift.

THE STEPMOTHER. Of silk or of linen?

SWANWHITE. Of linen.

THE STEPMOTHER. Ha! Now I have heard your wishes, listen to mine. You are to have no water, neither cold nor warm. You are to have no comb, neither of wood nor of horn, still less of gold or of silver. This is my kindness. You are to have no clean shift, but to get you into the closet and cover your body with a coarse black smock. These are my orders. If you were to leave this apartment, which in any case you cannot do, you would be trapped to your death. And if you escaped that, I would mark your pretty face with the steel whip, so that neither Prince nor King would ever look at you again. Now, get yourself to bed!

THE STEPMOTHER *strikes the table with the whip and goes out through the centre archway. She closes the doorway with a golden grille, which squeaks and rattles as she locks it.*

ACT II

SCENE: *As before. The golden grille is still closed. The peacock and the doves are sleeping. Clouds, landscape and sea are dark.*

SWANWHITE *is asleep on the bed in a garment of black homespun.* THE PRINCE's *helmet still lies on the table.*

In the doorways of the Closets stand the three MAIDS, *their eyes closed and lighted Roman lamps in their hands.*

A swan flies over the garden. Music of swans' flight as in Act I.

THE MOTHER OF SWANWHITE *appears outside the grille, clothed in white. Over one shoulder is the plumage of a swan and she carries a small golden harp. As she touches the grille, it opens of its own accord. She enters and it closes behind her.*

She takes off the plumage and puts the harp on the table. She looks round the room and, as she sees SWANWHITE, *the harp begins to play.* THE MAIDS' *lamps go out one after another, beginning with that furthest away. Then the three Closet doors close one after another, the innermost first.*

Slowly the clouds grow golden.

THE MOTHER *lights the lamp beside the bed and kneels down.*

The harp continues to play during the following scene.

THE MOTHER, *still kneeling, takes off* SWANWHITE's *stockings. She bends over her daughter's feet as if bathing them with her tears, then wipes them with a white cloth and kisses them. She puts sandals on* SWANWHITE's *feet, which now appear shining white.*

She takes a comb of gold and smooths SWANWHITE's *hair, then lays a garment of white linen beside her on the bed. She kisses her daughter on the forehead and prepares to leave. A white swan flies past and the swan music is repeated.* THE PRINCE's MOTHER *appears. She too is clothed in white and enters the grille in the same way as* SWANWHITE's MOTHER, *taking off her swan plumage.*

SWANWHITE's MOTHER. Well met, my sister. How long before cock crow?

THE PRINCE's MOTHER. Not long, I fear. The dew is rising from the roses, the corn-crake calls, and the breath of dawn is wafted from the sea.

SWANWHITE's MOTHER. We must make haste with what we have to do.

THE PRINCE's MOTHER. You called me here for our dear children's sake.

SWANWHITE's MOTHER. Yes. I remembered how, as I walked in the green fields of the land that knows no sorrow, I met you —whom I had always known, but never seen before. You were lamenting the fate of your poor child, left alone down here in the vale of sorrow. You opened your heart to me and stirred my own thoughts, which shunned the earth they hated. Then my mind turned once more to earth and sought out my poor deserted daughter. I found her destined to marry the Young King, who is a cruel man and evil.

THE PRINCE's MOTHER. And so I said to you: "Like unto like. May Love, the all-powerful, prevail and join these two lonely hearts so that they may find comfort in each other."

SWANWHITE's MOTHER. And now their hearts are joined, and the soul of each enfolds the other. May sorrow turn to joy and the earth rejoice at their young happiness!

THE PRINCE's MOTHER. If this is granted by the Powers on high.

SWANWHITE'S MOTHER. Their love will be tested in the fire of suffering.

THE PRINCE'S MOTHER *takes* THE PRINCE'S *helmet in her hand and changes the black feathers for white and red ones.*

THE PRINCE'S MOTHER. May sorrow turn to joy this very day when he has mourned his mother for a year!

SWANWHITE'S MOTHER. Give me your hand, my sister, and let the test begin.

THE PRINCE'S MOTHER. Here is my hand and with it goes the hand of my son. Now we have pledged them.

SWANWHITE'S MOTHER. In chastity and honour.

THE PRINCE'S MOTHER. I go to open the Blue Tower, that the young lovers may fly to each other's arms.

SWANWHITE'S MOTHER. In chastity and honour.

THE PRINCE'S MOTHER. And you and I shall meet again in the green meadows that know no sorrow.

SWANWHITE'S MOTHER, *with a gesture towards* SWANWHITE. Listen, she is dreaming of him. . . . Oh, foolish cruel woman who believes that lovers can be parted! . . . They are holding one another by the hand as they walk in the Land of Dreams under whispering pines and singing limes. They are laughing and playing . . .

THE PRINCE'S MOTHER. Hush! The dawn is breaking. I hear the robins calling and the stars are fading from the sky. Farewell, my sister.

SWANWHITE'S MOTHER. Farewell.

THE PRINCE'S MOTHER *goes out, drawing her swan's plumage about her.* SWANWHITE'S MOTHER *passes her hand over* SWANWHITE *in blessing, takes her plumage, and leaves. The grille opens and closes as before.*

The clock on the table strikes three. The harp is silent for a moment, then begins to play a new melody, sweeter even than before.

SWANWHITE *awakes, gazes round her, and listens to the harp. She rises, runs her fingers through her hair, and looks with joy at her white feet. She sees the white garment on the bed. She sits at the table where she sat before, and seems to see someone sitting opposite her in* THE PRINCE's *place. She looks into his eyes and smiles and holds out her hands. Her lips move as if she is speaking, and then she seems to be listening to a reply.*

She points meaningly at the red and white plume on the helmet and bends forward as if whispering. Then she leans her head back and breathes deeply as if inhaling some fragrance. She catches something in the air, kisses her hand, and blows the kiss back. She picks up the quill and caresses it as if it were a bird, then writes and pushes the parchment across the table. She appears to be watching him as he writes an answer; then she takes back the parchment, reads it, and hides it in her dress. She strokes her black dress as if commenting on the sad change in her appearance, then she smiles as if at an answer and finally bursts into ringing laughter. She indicates in mime that her hair has been combed. She rises and goes a little way away from the table, shyly holding out one of her white feet. She stays for a moment like this, awaiting an answer; when she hears it, she is puzzled and hastily hides her foot.

She goes to the chest and takes out the chess-board and men. She places them on the lion-skin with a gesture of invitation, then lies down, puts up the men, and begins to play with an invisible partner.

The harp is silent for a moment, then starts a new melody. The game of chess ends and SWANWHITE *seems again to be talking to her invisible companion. Suddenly she draws away as if he is coming too close. With a warning gesture, she springs lightly to her feet. She gazes long and reproachfully at him, then takes the white garment and hides behind the bed.*

THE PRINCE *appears outside the grille. His hair has grown grey, his cheeks are pale. He tries in vain to open the grille. He raises his eyes to heaven with an expression of despair.*

SWANWHITE, *coming forward.* Who comes with the rising of the sun?

THE PRINCE. Your love, your Prince, your heart's desire.

SWANWHITE. Whence comes my love?

THE PRINCE. From the Land of Dreams, from the flush of

dawn behind the rose-tipped hills, from the whispering pines and singing limes.

SWANWHITE. What did my love in the Land of Dreams behind the rose-tipped hills?

THE PRINCE. He laughed and played. He wrote her name. He sat on the lion-skin at a game of chess.

SWANWHITE. With whom did he laugh? With whom did he play?

THE PRINCE. With Swanwhite.

SWANWHITE. Then you are he. Welcome to my castle, to my table, to my arms.

THE PRINCE. Who will open the golden grille?

SWANWHITE. Give me your hand. . . . It is as cold as your heart is warm.

THE PRINCE. My body slept in the Blue Tower, while my soul escaped to the Land of Dreams. In the Tower it was cold and dark.

SWANWHITE. I will warm your hand against my breast. I will warm you with my gaze and with my kisses.

THE PRINCE. Lighten my darkness with the radiance of your eyes.

SWANWHITE. Are you in darkness?

THE PRINCE. In the Blue Tower there is neither sun nor moon.

SWANWHITE. Rise, sun! Blow warmly, wind! Rock gently, waves! Oh, golden grille, you believe you can hold apart two hearts, two hands, two pairs of lips—but nothing can divide them!

THE PRINCE. Nothing.

Two doors slide in front of the grille and close, so that SWANWHITE *and* THE PRINCE *can no longer see one another.*

SWANWHITE. Alas, what word has fallen? Who heard? Who punishes?

THE PRINCE. I am not parted from you, dear love, for the sound of my voice still reaches you. It goes through copper, steel and stone to touch your ear in sweet caress. In my thoughts you are in my arms; in my dreams I kiss you, and nothing on this earth can part us—nothing.

SWANWHITE. Nothing.

THE PRINCE. I see you, although I cannot see you with my eyes. I taste you, for you fill my mouth with roses.

SWANWHITE. Oh, that I could hold you in my arms!

THE PRINCE. I am in your arms.

SWANWHITE. Alas, I ache to feel the beat of your heart against my own! I yearn to fall asleep within your arms. Oh, grant us each other, dear God, grant us each other!

The swallows chirp. A small white feather falls to the ground. SWANWHITE *picks it up and finds that it is a key. She opens the gates of the grille.* THE PRINCE *enters.* SWANWHITE *springs into his arms and they kiss.*

Why do you not kiss me?

THE PRINCE, *kissing her again.* I kiss you, I kiss you.

SWANWHITE. I cannot feel your kisses.

THE PRINCE. Then you do not love me.

SWANWHITE. Hold me close. I cannot feel your arms.

THE PRINCE. I shall crush the life out of you.

SWANWHITE. I am still breathing.

THE PRINCE. Give me your soul.

SWANWHITE. I have given it to you. So give me yours.

THE PRINCE. Here is my soul. Now I have yours, and you have mine.

SWANWHITE, *breaking away.* I want my soul again.

THE PRINCE, *uneasily.* And I want mine.

SWANWHITE. Search for it.

THE PRINCE. Each of us is lost. You are me and I am you.

SWANWHITE. We are one.

THE PRINCE. God, who is merciful, has heard our prayer. We have each other.

SWANWHITE. We have each other, yet you are no longer mine. I cannot feel the touch of your hand or the caress of your lips. I cannot see your eyes, or hear your voice. You have gone from me.

THE PRINCE. But I am here.

SWANWHITE. You are here on earth. I must meet you in the Land of Dreams.

THE PRINCE. Then let us fly upon the wings of sleep.

SWANWHITE. With my hand in yours.

THE PRINCE. In my embrace.

SWANWHITE. Within your arms.

THE PRINCE. For this is bliss.

SWANWHITE. Eternal bliss without flaw or end.

THE PRINCE. Can any part us now?

THE PRINCE. Are you my bride?

SWANWHITE. Are you my bridegroom?

THE PRINCE. Bridegroom and bride are we in the Land of Dreams—but here we are not.

SWANWHITE. Here? Where are we then?

THE PRINCE. We are below, down below on earth.

SWANWHITE. Where the clouds gather and the ocean rages, where each night the earth sheds its tears upon the grass, waiting for the sun to rise. Where the hawk destroys the dove and the swallow kills the fly, where leaves fall and turn to dust, where hair grows white and cheeks grow hollow, where eyes lose their lustre and hands lose their strength. Down here on earth below.

THE PRINCE. Let us fly.

SWANWHITE. Yes, let us fly.

THE GARDENER *suddenly appears behind the table. He wears cap, apron, and breeches, one side entirely green, the other entirely blue, and has shears and a knife in his belt. He carries a small sack, from which he scatters seed around.*

THE PRINCE. Who are you?

THE GARDENER. I sow, I sow.

THE PRINCE. What do you sow?

THE GARDENER. Seeds, seeds, seeds.

THE PRINCE. What kind of seeds?

THE GARDENER. Onefold and twofold. One pulls this way, the other pulls that way. When the bridal dress is on, unity has gone. In discord I shall sow, and in concord you shall reap. One and one make one, but one and one also make three. One and one make two, but two make three. Do you understand?

THE PRINCE. Earth-worm, mouldwarp. You who live with your nose to the ground and turn your back on heaven—what can you teach me?

THE GARDENER. That you are a mole and an earth-worm. And that since you turn your back on the earth, the earth will turn its back on you. Good day to you.

THE GARDENER *disappears behind the table.*

SWANWHITE. What was that? Who was he?

THE PRINCE. It was the Green Gardener.

SWANWHITE. Green? Surely he was blue.

THE PRINCE. He was green, my love.

SWANWHITE. Why do you say what is not true?

THE PRINCE. Beloved, I said only what is true.

SWANWHITE. Alas, he does not speak the truth!

THE PRINCE. Whose voice is this? Not my Swanwhite's.

SWANWHITE. Who is this my eyes behold? Not my Prince, whose name alone once charmed me like the spell of the water sprite, like the song of a mermaid in green deeps. . . . Who are you, you stranger with evil eyes—and hair grown grey?

THE PRINCE. You see it only now—my hair that turned grey in the Tower, in a single night mourning the loss of Swanwhite, who is no more.

SWANWHITE. But here is Swanwhite.

THE PRINCE. No. I see before me a black-clad maiden whose face too is dark.

SWANWHITE. Did you not see before that I was clad in black? Then you do not love me.

THE PRINCE. Love her who stands there hard and cruel? No.

SWANWHITE. Your vows were false.

THE PRINCE. When I made my vows, another one stood there. Now—now you are filling up my mouth with nettles.

SWANWHITE. Your violets smell of stinkweed—faugh!

THE PRINCE. Now I am punished for betraying my Young King.

SWANWHITE. Would I had awaited the Young King!

THE PRINCE. Wait. He will come.

SWANWHITE. I shall not wait. I shall go and meet him.

THE PRINCE. I will not stop you.

SWANWHITE, *moving towards the doorway.* And this was love.

THE PRINCE, *distraught.* Where is Swanwhite? Where, where is she? The loveliest, the kindest, the most fair.

SWANWHITE. Seek her!

THE PRINCE. Alas, she is not here!

SWANWHITE. Seek her then elsewhere.

She goes sadly out.

Left alone, THE PRINCE *seats himself at the table, covers his face with his hands, and weeps. A gust of wind sets the draperies and curtains fluttering, and a sigh is heard from the strings of the harp.* THE PRINCE *rises and goes over to the bed. He looks at the impression of* SWANWHITE's *head on a pillow, then picks it up and kisses it. A clamour is heard outside. He hastily seats himself at the table again.*

The doors of the Closets fly open. The three MAIDS *are seen with darkened faces.* THE STEPMOTHER *comes through the arch; her face too is dark.*

THE STEPMOTHER, *sweetly.* Greeting, dear Prince. Did you enjoy a good night's sleep?

THE PRINCE. Where is Swanwhite?

THE STEPMOTHER. She has gone to marry the Young King. *Pause.* Is there no such thought, Prince, in your own mind?

THE PRINCE. In my mind is but one thought.

THE STEPMOTHER. Of young Swanwhite?

THE PRINCE. Is she too young for me?

THE STEPMOTHER. Grey hairs should keep company with good sense. I have a daughter of good sense.

THE PRINCE. And I, grey hairs?

THE STEPMOTHER. He does not know. He does not believe it. Maids! Signe, Elsa, Tova, come look at the young suitor with his grey hairs!

THE MAIDS *laugh and* THE STEPMOTHER *joins in.*

THE PRINCE. Where is Swanwhite?

THE STEPMOTHER. Follow the clues. Here is one.

She hands him a parchment.

THE PRINCE, *reading.* Did she write this?

THE STEPMOTHER. You know the hand—it is hers. What has she written?

THE PRINCE. That she hates me and loves another—that she was only playing with me—that she will spew out my kisses and throw my heart to the swine. My only desire now is to die—for I am dead.

THE STEPMOTHER. A knight does not die because a wench makes a fool of him. He shows his mettle and takes another.

THE PRINCE. Another? When there is only one?

THE STEPMOTHER. There are two at least, and my Magdalena has seven casks of gold.

THE PRINCE. Seven?

THE STEPMOTHER. And more beside.

Pause.

THE PRINCE. Where is Swanwhite?

THE STEPMOTHER. Magdalena is skilled in many crafts.

THE PRINCE. In witchcraft too?

THE STEPMOTHER. She could bewitch a young Prince.

THE PRINCE, *gazing at the parchment.* Did Swanwhite write this?

THE STEPMOTHER. Magdalena would not write in such a way.

THE PRINCE. Is Magdalena kind?

THE STEPMOTHER. Kindness itself. She does not play with sacred feelings, or seek revenge for little slights. She would be true to the one she . . . *Hesitates, cannot say the word "loves"* . . . cares for.

THE PRINCE. Then she is fair.

THE STEPMOTHER. She is not fair.

THE PRINCE. Then she cannot be kind. Tell me more of her.

THE STEPMOTHER. See her for yourself.

THE PRINCE. Where?

THE STEPMOTHER. She shall come here.

THE PRINCE, *looking at the parchment.* But did Swanwhite write this?

THE STEPMOTHER. Magdalena would have written tenderly.

THE PRINCE. What would she have written?

THE STEPMOTHER. That . . . *Hesitates.*

THE PRINCE. Say the word. Say the word "love" if you are able to.

THE STEPMOTHER *stammers and cannot say it.*

You cannot say that word.

She tries again.

No, no, you cannot say it.

THE STEPMOTHER. Magdalena can say it. Shall she come to you?

THE PRINCE. Let her come.

THE STEPMOTHER, *rising and speaking to* THE MAIDS. Blindfold the Prince, then he will find in his embrace a Princess who has no peer within the seven kingdoms.

SIGNE *comes forward and binds* THE PRINCE's *eyes.*

THE STEPMOTHER *claps her hands. Pause.*

Why does she not come?

The peacock snaps his beak, the doves coo.

Has my art deserted me? What has happened? Where is the bride?

Four YOUNG GIRLS *come through the arches, carrying baskets of pink and white roses. Music is heard from above.* THE GIRLS *strew the bed with roses. Two* KNIGHTS *enter with closed visors. Between them is* THE BRIDE, *deeply veiled.*[6]

With gestures THE STEPMOTHER *bids all depart except the bridal pair. She herself leaves last of all, closing the curtains and locking the grille.*

THE PRINCE. Is my bride here?

THE BRIDE. Who is your bride?

[6] Stage direction slightly altered to agree with Act III.   E.S.

THE PRINCE. I have forgotten her name. Who is your bridegroom?

THE BRIDE. He whose name may not be spoken.

THE PRINCE. Speak it if you can.

THE BRIDE. I can, but I will not.

THE PRINCE. Speak it if you can.

THE BRIDE. Speak my name first.

THE PRINCE. Seven casks of gold. Hunchback, Harelip, Hatred. What is my name? Say it if you can.

THE BRIDE. Prince Greyhair.

THE PRINCE. You are right.

THE BRIDE *throws off her veil, and* SWANWHITE *is revealed, dressed in white with a wreath of roses on her hair.*

SWANWHITE. Now who am I?

THE PRINCE. You are a rose.

SWANWHITE. You are a violet.

THE PRINCE, *taking the scarf off his eyes.* You are Swanwhite.

SWANWHITE. And you . . . you are . . .

THE PRINCE. Hush!

SWANWHITE. You are mine.

THE PRINCE. But you went away. You fled from my kisses.

SWANWHITE. I have come back—because I love you.

THE PRINCE. You wrote cruel words.

SWANWHITE, *tearing up the parchment.* I have destroyed them —because I love you.

THE PRINCE. You called me false.

SWANWHITE. What does that matter since you are true?—And I love you.

THE PRINCE. You wished to go to the Young King.

SWANWHITE. But came instead to you—because you are my love.

THE PRINCE. Now tell me how I have offended.

SWANWHITE. I have forgotten—because you are my love.

THE PRINCE. If I am your love, are you my bride?

SWANWHITE. I am your bride.

THE PRINCE. May heaven bless our union.

SWANWHITE. In the Land of Dreams.

THE PRINCE. In my arms.

> THE PRINCE *leads* SWANWHITE *to the bed, on which he places his sword. She lies down on one side of the sword and he on the other. The clouds become rose-coloured, the tree-tops murmur, the harp plays softly and sweetly.*

Good night, my Queen.

SWANWHITE. Good morning, oh my soul's beloved! I hear the beating of your heart. I hear it beating like the waves of the sea, like the hoofs of a steed, like the wings of an eagle. Give me your hand.

THE PRINCE. Here is my hand. Now we will take wing.

> *Pause. Music.* THE STEPMOTHER *enters with the three* MAIDS, *carrying torches. All four have become grey-haired.*

THE STEPMOTHER. Now I shall see my work accomplished before the Duke returns. Magdalena, my daughter, is plighted to the Prince, and Swanwhite is shut up in the Tower. *Approaches the bed.* They are asleep in one another's arms. Bear witness to this, Maids!

> *They approach.*

What is this I see? The hair of all three of you is grey.

SIGNE. Your hair too is grey, madam.

THE STEPMOTHER. Mine? Let me see.

> ELSA *holds up a mirror.*

This is the work of evil powers—then perhaps the Prince's hair is no longer grey. . . .

> THE MAIDS *hold their torches so that they light up the bed.*

Great heaven, that is so! Look! How beautiful they are! But the sword? Who placed the sword between them to sever a plighted troth?

> *She tries to remove the sword, but, without waking,* THE PRINCE *clings to it.*

SIGNE. Here is some devilry, madam.

THE STEPMOTHER. How so?

SIGNE. This is not the Lady Magdalena.

THE STEPMOTHER. Who is it? Give my eyes some help.

SIGNE. See—it is the Lady Swanwhite.

THE STEPMOTHER. Swanwhite? Is this some devilish apparition, or have I done what I least wished?

THE PRINCE, *still sleeping, turns his head so that his lips touch* SWANWHITE'S.

THE STEPMOTHER *is suddenly moved by the beauty of the sight.*

Never have I seen a sight more fair. Two roses blown together by the wind, two stars falling from heaven and joining as they fall. This is beauty itself. Youth, beauty, innocence, love . . . What memories this awakens, what sweet memories of the days when I lived in my father's house and was loved by *him. Breaks off in astonishment.* What did I say?

SIGNE. You said, madam, that you were loved . . .

THE STEPMOTHER. Then I did speak that word of power. Beloved. So he called me once, when he was setting forth for war—Beloved. *She is lost in thought.* He went away . . . and they married me to another, whom I could not love. . . . Now my life is drawing to its close, and I must watch joy and happiness I have never had myself. I must find joy in others' happiness, some kind of joy at least—in others' love . . . some kind of love at least. . . . But my Magdalena, what joy is there for her? O love omnipotent, O eternal God the Creator, how you have softened my heart, my tiger's heart! Where is my power? Where is my hatred, where my vengeance? *She sits on the bed and looks long at the sleeping pair.* I remember a song, a love-song which *he* sang when I was young—which he sang on that last evening. . . . *Suddenly she rises as if waking from a dream and flies into a rage. Shouts:* Here, men of the Castle—Guards, Bailiff, Executioner—all of you, come here! *She tears the sword from the bed and throws it behind her.* Come, all of you, come here!

Clamour. The members of the household enter as before.
Behold! The Prince, the Young King's vassal, has defiled his master's bride. Bear witness to the shameful deed. Let the

traitor be taken in chains and irons to his lord—and into the spiked cask with the hussy.

THE PRINCE *and* SWANWHITE *awaken.*

Grooms and Executioner, seize the Prince!

They take hold of him.

THE PRINCE, *struggling.* Where is my sword? Not against evil, but for innocence I fight.

THE STEPMOTHER. Whose innocence?

THE PRINCE. My bride's.

THE STEPMOTHER. The hussy's innocence! Prove it.

SWANWHITE. O Mother, Mother!

The white swan flies past.

THE STEPMOTHER. Bring scissors, Maids! I will cut off the harlot's hair.

SIGNE *brings scissors.*

Now I will cut off your beauty and your love.

THE STEPMOTHER *catches hold of a lock of* SWANWHITE'S *hair and tries to cut it, but the blades of the scissors will not close. She is suddenly seized with panic, which spreads to the men and* THE MAIDS.

Is the enemy upon us? Why are you trembling?

SIGNE. Madam, the dogs are barking and the horses neigh. Strangers are approaching.

THE STEPMOTHER. Quick, to the drawbridge, one and all! Man the ramparts! Fire, water, sword, and axe!

Amid great turmoil the curtain falls.

ACT III

The three MAIDS *are standing in the Closets at their work:* SIGNE *in the Pewter Closet,* ELSA *in the Clothing Closet,* TOVA *in the Fruit Closet.*

THE GARDENER *enters and beckons to* SIGNE, *who comes out to meet him.*

THE GARDENER. Signe, my daughter, I need your help.

SIGNE. First tell me who it was that came with so much din and clamour? Was it the Duke, our master, returning from the war?

THE GARDENER. No, it was not the Duke. It was an Envoy from the Young King, Lady Swanwhite's bridegroom, and with him a great armed retinue. Misfortune is upon us. There will be war—and this domain will blaze with fire.

SIGNE. Your seed has grown, your seed of discord. This is the harvest of your sowing.

THE GARDENER. False Signe, it was you who betrayed us, when you obeyed the Duchess and seized the guardian horn Standby.

SIGNE. A faithful servant must be false to her mistress's enemies.

THE GARDENER. But now, if the Duke does not come, the castle will be razed to the ground. How will he get here in time?

SIGNE. Time brings its own solution. However, now there is to be a banquet. I am polishing the pewter, Elsa is arranging the robes, and Tova is preparing the fruit. Are you sure the Young King has not come himself?

THE GARDENER. Only the Envoy and his retinue.

SIGNE. Where then is the Young King?

THE GARDENER. Who knows? Disguised perhaps among the retinue.

SIGNE. And the Prince?

THE GARDENER. In the Tower. Why do you hate him?

SIGNE. Hate him? I do not hate him. Oh no, no!

THE GARDENER. Perhaps you . . . ?

SIGNE. Do not say it.

THE GARDENER. Can one hate the man one loves?

SIGNE. Yes, when one cannot have him.

THE GARDENER. When one cannot have him? But the Lady

Swanwhite cannot have her Prince, yet she loves him unto death and beyond death.

SIGNE. Is the Prince to die?

THE GARDENER. You know that.

SIGNE. No. O God in heaven, he must not die! Save him, save him!

THE GARDENER. How can I?

SIGNE. By the secret passage—you know the way. Here is the entrance to it, here in the floor.

THE GARDENER. The Duchess has already had the secret passage flooded.

SIGNE. You must find a way through. Oh, save him, save him, before it is too late! Get him to a boat and out to sea.

THE GARDENER. I go to mend what I have broken. If I do not come again, you will know I have atoned.

SIGNE. May God protect you on your journey!

SWANWHITE *enters by the archway.*

SWANWHITE. You evil man, why are you here?

THE GARDENER, *falling on his knees.* I am here to right the wrong I did.

He rises and sows seed.

SWANWHITE. How can you do that? You sowed the seed of discord. What are you sowing now?

THE GARDENER. I sow Concord, Heartsease, Peace, Good to all and ill to none. Do not condemn me, Lady, for your dispute was not my fault.

SWANWHITE. Dispute? You mean as to whether you were green or blue?

THE GARDENER. Even so. Look at me now, Lady, with both your lovely eyes.

SWANWHITE. I am looking.

THE GARDENER, *spinning round.* Then see, I am green on one side, and blue upon the other.

SWANWHITE. So you are both colours. Old simpleton, you have taught me wisdom, and I thank you for it.

He goes to the trapdoor.

But where are you going now?

THE GARDENER. To rescue the Prince.

SWANWHITE. You? Can evil turn to good?

THE GARDENER. Not always. . . . Now I shall take the secret passage—and return with him, or not return at all.

SWANWHITE. The blessing of God go with you and protect you on this journey.

THE GARDENER *goes out through the trapdoor in the floor.* THE EXECUTIONER *rolls the spiked cask on to the terrace and stands beside it, half hidden.*[7] SWANWHITE *watches, then turns to* SIGNE.

Have you betrayed your father?

SIGNE. No, not my father.

SWANWHITE. The Prince then?

SIGNE. No, not the Prince.

SWANWHITE. Then me?

SIGNE *is silent.*

Then me?

SIGNE. My young mistress, disaster is upon us all. One alone can save us now—the Duke, your father.

SWANWHITE. Yes, the Duke, my mighty father. But he does not hear us in our need, because you betrayed me and gave the horn into the hands of the Duchess.

SIGNE. Do you know where she has hidden it?

SWANWHITE. Let me think. *She thinks.*

SIGNE. Where?

SWANWHITE. Hush! *Pause.* Now I can see it. . . . It is behind the mirror . . . in . . . in her silver closet.

SIGNE. Then I will fetch it.

SWANWHITE. You will do this—for my sake?

SIGNE. Do not thank me. Disaster is upon us. No, do not thank me.

SWANWHITE. You will not betray us?

SIGNE. Us? Neither all, nor one, nor any if I know it. He whom

[7] Added stage direction. E.S.

one loves, one hates—though not always. But he whom one hates, one does not love—ever. I am quite confused. We shall see Standby. . . . I shall stand by and be perhaps a bystander.

She goes out.

SWANWHITE. She speaks in riddles. Elsa, Tova, come in here!

They obey.

Here, stand close to me, for someone is listening to us. My pretty Elsa, my faithful Tova, stay by my side. I fear something which I cannot explain. Something is coming which I do not know. I hear with the ears of my heart, I see with the eyes of my breast—danger. I feel a breath as cold as ice. A brutal hand clutches at my breast like a bird of prey swooping on a dove. Woe is me, nettles and goatsbeard, foul flesh and all that reeks! . . . He has come, the Young King.

THE YOUNG KING *enters, full of lust and drink.* ELSA *and* TOVA *stand close together, with* SWANWHITE *behind them.* THE KING *comes up to them insolently.*

THE YOUNG KING. Ha, three of you! Do you know who I am?

ELSA. Knight of the wine barrel.

THE YOUNG KING. Impertinent chit. Give me a kiss, for you are little and bad, but pretty. *To* TOVA. You are good, I know, but plain. Tell me where the Princess Swanwhite is.

ELSA. Can you not guess?

THE YOUNG KING. Are you she? . . . Aha! But your hands are red—you are no Princess. Do you know my name?

ELSA. Lord Goat.

THE YOUNG KING. I like impudent girls. You little scamp, come to my arms!

ELSA. Here? Now?

They flirt.

THE YOUNG KING. Think if the Princess were to hear us.

TOVA. She does not hear such things. She has ears only for the song of the nightingales, for the whisper of leaves, for the murmur of the wind and the waves.

THE YOUNG KING. Don't be so long-winded, ugly one. You talk

too much at a time. Remember your manners, chits, and tell me where the Princess is. Or else, by Satan and all his devils, the Stepmother's steel whip shall rain down fire upon your backs. Where is the Princess Swanwhite?

SWANWHITE, *coming forward.* She is here.

THE YOUNG KING, *gazing at her.* She? *Pause.* Impossible. I saw her portrait, and it was beautiful—but that was painted by the wily Prince so as to deceive me. You have no nose, my girl. You are cross-eyed and your lips are too thick. . . . I ask you—is this Swanwhite?

SWANWHITE. I am she.

THE YOUNG KING, *sitting down.* So it is true, well, well . . . Can you dance, play, paint, sing? *Pause.* You can do nothing. And for this nothing, I am about to storm the castle, burn, sack . . . *Pause.* Can't you at least speak? Can you while away a long evening in conversation? *Pause.* Not that either.

SWANWHITE, *whispering.* I can speak, but not to you.

THE YOUNG KING. Your voice is toneless as a feather brush. Perhaps you are deaf?

SWANWHITE. Certain voices do not reach my ears.

THE YOUNG KING. And blind, and lame as well. *Pause.* This is too great a venture for too small a gain. Go in peace—or rather let me go. Prince Faithless may pluck his goose with the plaintiff. And with me.

He strides out. SWANWHITE, ELSA, *and* TOVA *lift their hands in joy. A melody sounds from the harp.*

THE PRINCE *comes up through the trapdoor.* SWANWHITE *springs into his arms. The harp continues to play.* ELSA *and* TOVA *go out through the arch.*

THE PRINCE *and* SWANWHITE *try to speak to each other, but cannot find words.*

THE YOUNG KING *is seen stealing into the Clothing Closet, where he stands hidden, spying and listening.*

SWANWHITE. Is this farewell?

THE PRINCE. Do not say that word.

SWANWHITE. He is here—he has been here, the King, your King.

THE PRINCE. Then it is farewell—for ever.

SWANWHITE. No. He did not see me. He did not hear me. He did not like me.

THE PRINCE. But he seeks my life.

SWANWHITE. All of them seek your life. . . . Where will you go?

THE PRINCE. Down to the shore.

SWANWHITE. Out on the sea in the storm of winds and waves? You who are my love, my heart's delight.

THE PRINCE. In the waves I shall drink our marriage cup.

SWANWHITE. Then I shall die.

THE PRINCE. And we shall meet never to part, never never more to part.

SWANWHITE. Never more. But if I did not die, my sorrow would bring you back from the grave.

The stage begins to darken.

THE PRINCE. For each tear that is shed from your bright eyes, there is a drop of blood in my coffin. Each hour you walk on earth in happiness fills it with petals of roses.

SWANWHITE. It is growing dark.

THE PRINCE. I walk in light, in your light, because I love you.

SWANWHITE. Take my soul, take my life!

THE PRINCE. I have yours. Take mine, take mine! Now my body must depart, but my soul stays here.

SWANWHITE. My body must stay here, but my soul departs—with you.

As before, THE PRINCE *and* SWANWHITE *try to speak, but their lips move soundlessly.* THE PRINCE *goes down through the trapdoor.* THE YOUNG KING *has witnessed the scene with growing emotion. He sees* SWANWHITE *as she really is. He is first ashamed, then enraptured. When* THE PRINCE *has gone,* THE YOUNG KING *hastens out and falls on his knees.*

THE YOUNG KING. Swanwhite, fairest work of God's hand, do not fear me, for now I have seen you in all your perfection, and heard your voice as of silver strings. But it was with *his* eyes that I saw and with *his* ears that I heard. Alone, I had

no powers, for I have not your love. . . . Your stony gaze
tells me that you do not see me, that you do not hear my
words, that you exist for him alone—that if I took you, it
would be a corpse that I held in my arms. Forgive what I
have destroyed. Forget that I ever was. Believe that I would
never dare defile you by one impure thought, though the
memory of you will pursue me and be my punishment. One
thing alone I ask. Give me your voice in farewell, that I may
carry its echo within my heart. One word to remember, one
only.

Pause.

SWANWHITE, *harshly.* Go!

THE YOUNG KING, *springing up.* Raven! Now hear my answer:
Blood! *He draws his sword.* None shall possess you, save
only I. I will have the raven. I love the strong, the fierce,
the cruel. The dove is not the bird for me.

SWANWHITE, *retreating behind the table.* Help me, my father!
Standby, come to me, come, come!

THE YOUNG KING, *falling back.* There it comes. The silver voice.
The sound of the Angelus on some saint's day. My strength
is gone from me.

SWANWHITE, *half singing.* Come, come, come!

THE YOUNG KING. Your voice is so lovely that my sword weeps
for shame. Go in and hide yourself. No sword then, but fire.
Fire to the castle, death to the traitor.

TOVA *steals in with the horn.*

Who is there?

TOVA. Here it is. Take it, take it!

SWANWHITE, *taking it.* You have brought it, not Signe?

TOVA. I took it from Signe. She was faithless still.

SWANWHITE *blows the horn. Another horn answers in the
distance.* THE YOUNG KING, *panic-stricken, shouts to his unseen men.*

THE YOUNG KING. To horse! Let loose the reins, press in the
spurs, ride for dear life!

He rushes out.

SWANWHITE *blows the horn again, and the other horn answers.*

TOVA. He is coming, the glorious hero. He is coming.

After a pause SWANWHITE *blows again and* THE DUKE *enters.* TOVA *goes out.*

THE DUKE. Sweet treasure of my heart, what is at stake?

SWANWHITE. Your child's life is at stake, Father. Look at the spiked barrel there.

THE DUKE. What has my child done to deserve such a fate?

SWANWHITE. I learned the Prince's name in the way that only those who love can learn. I spoke it and lost my heart to him.

THE DUKE. This does not merit death. What more?

SWANWHITE. I slept beside him—with the sword between.

THE DUKE. Nor does this merit death, although it was not wise. What more?

SWANWHITE. That is all.

THE DUKE, *to* THE EXECUTIONER. Away with the spiked barrel! *He obeys.*

And now, my child, where is the Prince?

SWANWHITE. Sailing for home in his coracle.

THE DUKE. Now in this raging storm? Alone?

SWANWHITE. Alone. Oh, what will befall him?

THE DUKE. That is in the hand of God.

SWANWHITE. Is he in danger?

THE DUKE. Fortune sometimes favours the brave.

SWANWHITE. Oh, he deserves it!

THE DUKE. If he is innocent.

SWANWHITE. He is, he is, more innocent than I.

THE STEPMOTHER *enters.*

THE STEPMOTHER, *to* THE DUKE. How did you come here?

THE DUKE. By the shortest way. Would I had been here sooner.

THE STEPMOTHER. Had you come sooner, your daughter would have escaped this injury.

THE DUKE. What injury?

THE STEPMOTHER. The one for which there is no remedy.

THE DUKE. Have you proof?

THE STEPMOTHER. I have eye-witnesses.

THE DUKE. Call the Steward.

THE STEPMOTHER. He knows nothing of this.

THE DUKE, *grasping the hilt of his sword.* Call the Steward!

THE STEPMOTHER *shudders. She claps her hands four times.* THE STEWARD *enters.*

Have a pie prepared without delay—a pie of beasts' entrails, seasoned with fennel, roots, rank herbs, and fungus.

THE STEWARD *glances at* THE STEPMOTHER.

Why this glance? Obey me instantly.

THE STEWARD *goes out.*

To THE STEPMOTHER. Now call the Herb Gardener.

THE STEPMOTHER. He is ignorant.

THE DUKE. And shall remain so. But come he must. Summon him.

THE STEPMOTHER *claps her hands six times.* THE HERB GARDENER *enters.*

Bring me three lilies—one white, one red, one blue.

THE HERB GARDENER *glances at* THE STEPMOTHER. THE DUKE *touches his sword.*

Have a care of your head.

THE HERB GARDENER *goes out.* THE DUKE *turns back to* THE STEPMOTHER.

Now call the witnesses.

THE STEPMOTHER *claps her hands once.* SIGNE *enters.*

What did you see? Give evidence. But choose your words with care.

SIGNE. I saw the Lady Swanwhite and the Prince together in one bed.

THE DUKE. With the sword between?

SIGNE. There was no sword.

SWANWHITE. Signe, Signe, you are bearing false witness against me—I who saved you from the steel whip! You do me such wrong, such wrong. *Pause.* You betrayed me that night—you know it. Why did you do this to me?

SIGNE. I did not know what it was I did. I did what I had no
will to do. I did the will of another. Now I no longer wish
to live. Forgive me for our Saviour's sake.

SWANWHITE. I forgive you. Do you also forgive yourself, for
you are without guilt since an evil will possessed you.

SIGNE. Punish me, punish me!

SWANWHITE. Is not your repentance punishment enough?

THE DUKE. I do not think so. . . . Are there more witnesses?

The two KNIGHTS *enter.*

Were you the Bride's escort? Give your evidence.

THE FIRST KNIGHT. I escorted the Lady Magdalena to her bridal
couch.

THE SECOND KNIGHT. I escorted the Lady Magdalena to her
bridal couch.

THE DUKE. What is this? A snare that shall entrap the snarer.
The next witness.

Enter ELSA.

Give your evidence.

ELSA. I swear, by God the Just, I saw the Lady Swanwhite
and the Prince, fully clothed and with the sword between
them.

THE DUKE. One for and one against . . . and two not relevant.
I leave it to God to judge.

TOVA *enters.*

The flowers shall testify.

TOVA, *coming forward.* My gracious master, noble Lord . . .

THE DUKE. What have you to tell me?

TOVA. That my sweet Lady is innocent.

THE DUKE. Oh child, child, do you know this? Then let us
know it too.

TOVA. I have said what is true.

THE DUKE. And no one believes you. Yet when Signe says what
is not true, she is believed. And what does Swanwhite say
herself? Does not her pure brow, do not her candid eyes
and innocent mouth declare that she is slandered? Do not

my own eyes, the eyes of a father, tell me this too? Now Almighty God shall judge, so that all men may believe.

THE HERB GARDENER *enters, carrying the three lilies in narrow vases of glass.* THE DUKE *places them in a semi-circle on the table.* THE STEWARD *enters with a huge platter, on which is a steaming pie.* THE DUKE *places the platter within the semi-circle of flowers.*

For whom does the white lily stand?

ALL, *except* SWANWHITE *and* THE STEPMOTHER. For Swanwhite.

THE DUKE. And the red lily?

ALL, *except* SWANWHITE *and* THE STEPMOTHER. For the Prince.

THE DUKE. And the blue?

ALL, *except* SWANWHITE *and* THE STEPMOTHER. For the Young King.

THE DUKE. So be it. Tova, my child, you who believe in innocence because you are innocent yourself, interpret God's judgement for us. Tell us the subtle secrets of these flowers. What do you see?

TOVA. What is evil I cannot speak.

THE DUKE. I shall do that—you speak the good. In the reek of the burning wild beasts' blood, in the vapours of those sensual herbs, what do you see?

TOVA *gazes at the three lilies, which behave as she describes.*

TOVA. The white lily closes its petals against defilement. This flower is Swanwhite's.

ALL, *as before.* Swanwhite is innocent.

TOVA. The red flower, the Prince's lily, closes too. But the blue, the Young King's flower, opens wide to breathe the sensual fumes.

THE DUKE. Well read. What do you see now?

TOVA. The red lily bows its head in reverent love before the white. But the blue flower writhes with envious rage.

THE DUKE. Well read. Who then shall have Swanwhite?

TOVA. The Prince. His desire is purer and therefore stronger.

ALL, *as before.* The Prince shall have Swanwhite.

SWANWHITE *throws herself into* THE DUKE'S *arms.*

SWANWHITE. Father, Father!

THE DUKE. Call back the Prince! Let every horn and trumpet call him. Let every bark on shore set sail. . . . But one thing more—for whom is the spiked barrel?

All are silent.

Then I will tell you. It is for the Duchess, the arch-liar, the destroyer. Now, evil woman, you have seen that for all the power of your spells, they cannot conquer love. Go, and go quickly!

THE STEPMOTHER *makes a movement with her hands, which for a moment seems to stun* THE DUKE. *Then he lifts* SWAN-WHITE *on to his shoulder, draws his sword, and points it at* THE STEPMOTHER.

Out upon you, evil one! My sword will pierce your spells.

THE STEPMOTHER *goes slowly out to the balcony backwards, with the dragging step of a panther.*

Now for the Prince.

THE STEPMOTHER *stops on the balcony as if turned to stone, and opens her mouth as if pouring out venom. The peacock and the doves fall down dead. Then* THE STEPMOTHER *begins to swell. Her clothes become inflated until they hide her head and shoulders; then they seem to be on fire, flaming in a pattern of snakes and branches. The sun begins to rise. The ceiling sinks slowly into the room. Smoke and flame pour from the hearth.* THE DUKE *raises the cross-shaped hilt of his sword towards* THE STEPMOTHER.

Pray, people, pray to Christ our Saviour!

ALL. Christ have mercy upon us!

The ceiling returns to its place, the smoke and the fire cease. The sound of many voices is heard outside.

THE DUKE. What is this? What has happened now?

SWANWHITE. I know. . . . I see. I hear the water dripping from his hair, I hear the silence of his heart. I hear that he no longer breathes. . . . I see that he is dead.

THE DUKE. Where do you see this? And who . . . ?

SWANWHITE. Where? . . . I see it.

THE DUKE. I see nothing.

SWANWHITE. Let them come quickly, since they must come.

Four young MAIDS-OF-HONOUR *enter with baskets, from which they strew the floor with branches of yew and white lilies. Next come four* PAGES, *ringing silver bells of different tones. Then a* PRIEST, *bearing a crucifix, and finally the* PALL-BEARERS, *carrying a bier, on which* THE PRINCE *lies under a white shroud strewn with pink and white roses. His hair is dark again and his face youthful, rosy, and radiantly beautiful. His eyes are closed, but he is smiling.*

The harp begins to play. The sun rises fully. The bewitched shape of THE STEPMOTHER *bursts and she resumes her own form. She steps away.*

The bier is set down in the rays of the sun.

SWANWHITE *throws herself on her knees beside it and kisses* THE PRINCE.

All present hide their faces in their hands and weep. THE FISHERMAN, *who has been standing in the doorway, comes in.*

THE DUKE. Tell us the brief tale, Fisherman.

THE FISHERMAN. Does it not tell itself, my noble Lord? The young Prince had scarcely crossed the Sound when he was seized by such longing for his love—that he must return. Since his bark had lost its rudder, he plunged into the water and swam against spring-tide and wave and wind. I saw his young head top the billows, I heard his voice call out her name. . . . Then his dead body dropped gently on the white sand at my feet. His hair had turned grey that night in the Tower, his cheeks had grown hollow with sorrow and care, his lips had lost their power to smile. . . . Now in death he was young again and beautiful. His dark locks framed his rosy cheeks . . . he smiled, and see, he is smiling still. The people gathered on the shore, awed by this sad sweet sight, and one whispered to another: "See, this is Love!"

SWANWHITE. He is dead. His heart no longer sings, his eyes no longer light my life, his breath no longer sheds its dew on me. He smiles, but not at me—it is at heaven that he smiles. I will join him on his journey.

She kisses him and prepares to lie down beside him.

THE DUKE. Do not kiss a dead man's lips, for they bear poison.

SWANWHITE. Sweet poison if it brings me death, that death which for me is life.

THE DUKE. They say, my child, that the dead do not meet again at will, and that what a man has prized in life has little worth beyond it.

SWANWHITE. But love? Can love not reach to the other side of death?

THE DUKE. Our wise men have denied it.

SWANWHITE. Then he must come back to earth again. O God, dear God, send him back from Your heaven!

THE DUKE. A vain prayer, I fear.

SWANWHITE. I cannot pray. Alas, an evil eye still rules this place.

THE DUKE. You mean the witch whom the sunlight pierced. Let her then be taken to the stake and burned alive.

SWANWHITE. Burned alive? No, no. Let her go in peace.

THE DUKE. She shall be burned alive. You men, build the pyre close to the shore, that her ashes may be strewn to the winds.

SWANWHITE *falls on her knees before* THE DUKE.

SWANWHITE. No, no. I pray for her, my executioner. Have mercy on her, mercy!

THE STEPMOTHER *enters, changed. She is freed from the evil powers that have held her under their spell.*

THE STEPMOTHER. Mercy? Who spoke that sacred word? Who prayed a prayer from the heart for me?

SWANWHITE. I prayed for you. . . . I, your daughter . . . Mother.

THE STEPMOTHER. O God in heaven, she calls me Mother! At whose bidding is this?

SWANWHITE. At the bidding of love.

THE STEPMOTHER. Blessed be love that works such miracles. Ah child, it has the power too to call back the dead from death's dark realm! I cannot do this, for love has been denied me. But you, you can do it.

SWANWHITE, *humbly.* I, what can I do?

THE STEPMOTHER. You can love, you can forgive, and so, mighty child, you can do everything. Learn this from me, who may not use my powers. Go to him. Call the name of your beloved and lay your hand upon his heart. Then with the help of Almighty God—but only with His help—your love will hear your voice—if you can believe.

SWANWHITE. I believe. I will. I pray.

She goes to the bier and lays one hand on THE PRINCE'S *heart and raises the other to heaven.*

With my mind.

She bends down and whispers something in his ear.

With my heart.

She whispers again.

With my soul.

She whispers a third time.[8]

THE PRINCE *awakens. He rises and takes* SWANWHITE *in his arms.*

All kneel in praise and thanksgiving.

The music swells to a climax.

---

[8] Strindberg puts only that Swanwhite whispers three times in the Prince's ear. "With my mind," "with my heart," and "with my soul" have been added to express what is implied: three stages of will. E.S.

THE GREAT HIGHWAY

A Wayfaring Drama with Seven Stations

FOREWORD

The Great Highway was written in 1909, when Strindberg was sixty. It was his last play. Divorced for the third time, he was now living alone in the high Stockholm apartment he called "The Blue Tower." His health was failing and he had the urge to write, as his farewell to life, one more drama of the journey, in which he, as the Hunter, could express the unending conflict in himself between the terrible heights of heaven and the dear but dirty plains of earth. Strindberg's first pilgrimage play, *To Damascus,* written ten years before, was a trilogy, and his autobiographical novels run into many volumes; but now, with the use of poetic imagery, he condensed his soul's experience into a single composition with seven scenes. Chance helped his inspiration: a hand-painted plate for sale, brought by a child to his apartment, suggested the scenery for the Hunter's home; he heard it said that a dying man had "coughed up his heart," and the phrase became a dominant theme; the new North Road out of Stockholm, which passed his present door, so many doors in his past, and also the gate of the cemetery where he had chosen to lie, was known as "The Great Highway," and thus he named his play, adding as sub-title, thinking surely of the Cross, *A Wayfaring Drama with Seven Stations.*

Having written his earliest plays in verse and abandoned this form for terse, realistic prose, and having swung from phantasy to realism and back again, in his last play Strindberg let his inspiration dictate its own form. *The Great Highway* is full of symbolism and imagery; the higher emotional moods are expressed in unrhymed verse, containing some of Strindberg's finest poetry, while the scenes in which he satirizes society, its institutions and its successful men are written in witty colloquial dialogue.

The introduction of a Japanese character in this play reminds one that Strindberg was a considerable sinologist. As a young man, he had taught himself Chinese in order to catalogue a collection of Chinese manuscripts in the Royal Library of Stockholm, which hitherto nobody had been able to do. Doubtless he obtained some knowledge of Japanese at this time too, and all his life oriental philosophy appealed strongly to him. It is with a shock that one comes upon the name that Strindberg gave this Japanese:

> I have travelled, sinned, and suffered by
> the name "Hiroshima," after my native town.

Strindberg gave many proofs of psychic power, but surely his gift of prophecy was never so strangely manifested as in the choice of the name "Hiroshima" for the tragic Japanese figure about to commit hara-kiri.

The Great Highway was given a single performance at Strindberg's own Intimate Theatre in Stockholm in 1910, but after this, was seldom seen until it was revived with a distinguished cast at Stockholm's Royal Theatre to celebrate the centenary of Strindberg's birth in January 1949. Passages from this translation were also read at the Anglo-Swedish Society in London by Michael Redgrave to mark this anniversary. And in September 1950 the play was presented at London's Watergate Theatre. It has now also been seen in many Scandinavian and Continental cities, and Mr. Arvid Paulson's version was given at the Pasadena Playhouse in California in 1952.

I am indebted to Lady Low for her help in translating *The Great Highway*, and to Mr. Arvid Paulson for allowing me to quote from the foreword to his translation, and to print the Japanese poem, in Japanese and in English, as it appears in his version:[1]

. . . it has been discovered that the Japanese poem quoted by Strindberg in Scene IV has been misprinted in the published editions of the play. It is by an unknown Japanese poet and is published in the famous *Kokinshu* collection. It is here reprinted as it appears in this anthology.

E. S.

[1] *The Great Highway*, translated from the Swedish by Arvid Paulson, published in *Modern Scandinavian Plays* by The American-Scandinavian Foundation—The Liveright Publishing Corporation, New York, 1954.

CHARACTERS

In order of appearance

THE HUNTER

THE HERMIT

THE TRAVELLER

MILLER ADAM

MILLER EVE

MILLER ADAM'S WIFE

THE GIRL

THE SCHOOLMASTER

THE BLACKSMITH

THE WAITRESS

THE ORGAN-GRINDER

THE PHOTOGRAPHER

EUPHROSYNE

GOTTHARD

KLARA

THE JAPANESE

MÖLLER THE MURDERER

THE CHILD

THE WOMAN

THE TEMPTER

SCENES

During Scene VII, "The Dark Wood," Chopin's Nocturne 13, Opus 48, 1, is played softly in the distance until the end of the play.

I. IN THE MOUNTAINS

A signpost with two arms, one pointing upward, the other down.

A background of dark thunderclouds. Later the storm breaks.

THE HUNTER *enters and looks at the signpost.*

THE HUNTER. Where have I got to, and how far have I come?
Yes, there the track leads up, and there goes down.
Descent's the common way—I want to rise.
And yet the signpost has thrown out his arms,
as if in warning of the upward way.
Danger then, many dangers
on that path, so narrow and so steep.
That does not scare me—I delight in danger.
But I must pause here for a little while,
and breathe,
and think; gather up
and find myself again,
myself which they stole from me. . . .
I lived too long among humanity
and gave away my soul,
my heart, my thoughts;
the rest they took, they stole—
they fettered me with friendliness,
with gifts I did not want.
Yes, it was warm down there, passing
from home to home, with fair-spread tables,
music and flowers, glasses, light.
But it grew too warm and stifled me—

And so I cast my moorings,
threw overboard my ballast, all that weighed,
however dear—and see, I rose!
Here I can breathe, my heart's seed-leaves,
the tender lungs, can open to the air;
no dust, no smoke, no breath breathed by another
poison my blood.
White, pure snow
of sublimated vapour. Water-diamonds,
you lily flowers crystallised from frost,
you flour of heaven strained through the cloud's black sifter.
O blessed silence, draw your silken quilt
over the head of a tired traveller,
who seeks his bed while whispering this prayer!
What's to the North? A cliff of slate,
a cloud like a schoolroom blackboard, as yet
unwritten on. What a din! Now comes the Teacher
and silence falls upon the class.
Nature is silent when the Great Teacher speaks.
Look now! A lightning flash from East to West—
in flaming ink he writes his name
on blue-black cloud. I know Thee,
eternal, unseen yet seen,
thou stern Compassionate!
The mountain firs bow down,
the brooks are mute and still.
The frightened chamois falls to knee,
the vulture bends his naked head.
All nature trembles
before the mighty Lord Creator,
and I who took his name in vain,
I bow myself in shame,
meanest of all before Thy mighty throne.
Look, the cloud's burst! The curtain's pulled,
is drawn aside. What do I see?
You lovely earth! You temptress,
pulling me down again.
How you have decked yourself!
In green of hope and blue of faith
and the rose-red of love.

The pine tops painted by the setting sun,
the cypresses of tombs and night,
a marble temple set on high
to honour or to happiness,
a grotto, the grey Sybil's home,
who scares the nymphs from olive groves—

Here comes the sun. What a sparkle
of frost's rose-diamonds! The clouds are edged
with silver; the blue-black capes
are hung out in the wind to air.
But what is this? Who veils the sun
and draws a shadow on the pure white snow?
Imperial eagle, gold-breasted chrysaëtos,
knight of the air in gilded mail,
with the knight's chain around your neck—

What? Are you sinking? Do you seek the valley
when wings tire, and your rudder-tail's
no power to steer your course aloft?
Yes. That's his will. Down, down to rest
and breathe the breath of warm humanity,
and smell the fragrance of the cloverfields—
for surely there it's summer still.
There water falls down from the clouds like pearls,
here it's like brilliants, square-cut diamonds;
there the brook chirps, here it's struck dumb,
here wastes of snow, although white flowers—
down there white daisies.
Up here, down there. Hither, thither
one is driven, to equal good and equal ill.

Enter THE HERMIT.

THE HERMIT. Whither? Quo vadis, traveller?
You have come halfway and now look back.
Excelsior! That's been your motto hitherto.

THE HUNTER. It is so still.

THE HERMIT. What are you seeking here?

THE HUNTER. Myself. The self I lost down there.

THE HERMIT. What you have lost down there,
surely you cannot find again up here?

THE HUNTER. That's true. Yet were I to go down,
  I'd lose still more, not find what I have lost.

THE HERMIT. You fear for your skin. . . .

THE HUNTER. Not for my skin, but for my soul. . . .

THE HERMIT. You do not love your fellow beings. . . .

THE HUNTER. Yes, all too much. Therefore I fear them too. . . .

THE HERMIT. To love is to give. Give!

THE HUNTER. But they will not receive—they only take;
  nor will they take the gift without the giver too.

THE HERMIT. The shepherd gave himself for the sheep.

THE HUNTER. Dust unto dust, but the spirit belongs to God.

THE HERMIT. You fence well with your tongue, you ought to
    wield the pen.
  In any case, half of your life has gone.
  Don't force the issue—premature birth
  can never bring you to full growth.
  Live your life out. Return and do not fear.
  The highway's dusty—brush it off.
  Ditches on either side—fall in
  but rise again. Where you find gates,
  jump over, creep under, lift the latch.
  When you meet people take them in your arms—
  they will not bite, but if they bite, what harm?
  If you are ducked, then shake the water off.
  Scatter your coins, they'll come to you again.
  Up here there is not anything to win,
  for stone is stone and snow is snow—
  but human nature is another thing.

THE HUNTER. I know that well. Could I but sit
  among the audience and watch the play!
  But I must mount the stage, take part and act,
  and once I play a part, I'm lost,
  forgetting who I am.

THE HERMIT. Who are you?

THE HUNTER. Well said. Now let us stop.
  Truly it is too cold for me up here.

  Enter THE TRAVELLER.

THE HERMIT. The air is somewhat thin, and it is lonely.
But look, here's company!

THE HUNTER. Queer fellow. Coming from above.
Looks a bit fagged. Halt, you traveller!

THE TRAVELLER. I come from the mountain tops.
I bathed in air, but could not stay in air,
so clad myself again to journey further,
with company or without—but rather with.
What is that country in the distance, Hermit?

THE HERMIT. It is called the Country of Desires.

THE TRAVELLER. Of pious desires?

THE HERMIT. Pious or pagan, whichever . . .

THE TRAVELLER.   . . . whichever they may be.
Well, I'm to have company, I see.
With whom have I the honour?

THE HUNTER. I am a soldier.

During the following speech, THE HERMIT *goes out.*

THE TRAVELLER.   And I a traveller.
One travels best incognito and—mark my words—
one should always make acquaintance,
but never get to know.
In fact one never can—
one only thinks one knows. And so,
in company—neither friend nor enemy—
two steps between us—not too close.
On. And down. The route is clear.
A slope up, a slope down,
an inn, a stop, a little glass—
but keeping always to the southern course.

THE HUNTER. With sun as beacon, we'll not lose our bearings.
It will not fail; that watchman never sleeps—
I think our hermit's left us.

THE TRAVELLER. Well, let him go. He has no place
down there where our way lies.
He has made his choice and bade the world farewell.

THE HUNTER. He may perhaps be right.

THE TRAVELLER.   Don't look up there!
Humanity and vanity rhyme as hither, thither.
But we do not go thither—we go hither!

II. AT THE WINDMILLS

*Against a background of cloudy sky stand two windmills,
known as Adam and Eve.*

THE TRAVELLER *and* THE HUNTER *are sitting at a table outside an inn, drinking.*

THE TRAVELLER. How still it is, here in the valley!

THE HUNTER. Too still to suit the miller,

THE TRAVELLER. sleeping no matter how much water runs,

THE HUNTER. waiting for wind and stormy weather . . .

THE TRAVELLER. which unrewarding business rouses in me a
certain aversion for windmills.

THE HUNTER. Just as it did in the noble knight Don Quixote
de la Mancha,

THE TRAVELLER. who did not, however, trim his sails to the
wind,

THE HUNTER. but quite the reverse,

THE TRAVELLER. which is why he got into difficulties. What
are we doing? Playing Beggar-my-neighbour?

THE HUNTER. Sir Incognito, why do you drink so much?

THE TRAVELLER. As I'm always lying on the operating table,
I chloroform myself.

THE HUNTER. Then we'll ask no more.

THE TRAVELLER. Perhaps I said too much.

THE HUNTER. To think that I can't guess what you are.

THE TRAVELLER. Stop trying to guess. It is far pleasanter.

THE HUNTER. Certainly, yes. . . . . It's been cloudy all day today.

THE TRAVELLER. Let me drink a bit more, then you'll see it's
clearing up. *Drinks.* Do you know Greek? Do you understand what *oinos* means?

THE HUNTER. *Oinos* means wine.

THE TRAVELLER. Yes, it means wine. So you are educated, are you?

THE HUNTER. *Noli me tangere!* Do not touch me! I sting.

THE TRAVELLER. Have you noticed that a grape is like a bottle, and its tendrils like a corkscrew? The implication's clear.

THE HUNTER. But the juice of the grape has none of the characteristics of chloroform—

THE TRAVELLER. till the grapes have been crushed underfoot and rotted in dregs and draff,

THE HUNTER. so the spirit of wine is set free from the filthy body of matter,

THE TRAVELLER. and rises to the surface like sea-foam,

THE HUNTER. out of which Aphrodite was born,

THE TRAVELLER. naked.

THE HUNTER. Without even a vineleaf to cover herself,

THE TRAVELLER. for clothes are only a consequence of sin. Are you always as serious as this?

THE HUNTER. Are you always as frivolous as this?

THE TRAVELLER. Which of us two is the more inquisitive?

THE HUNTER. Now he is stretching out his tentacles,

THE TRAVELLER. obeying the universal law of attraction,

THE HUNTER. followed by mutual repulsion,

THE TRAVELLER. which is why it's best to keep two steps apart and march in open file,

THE HUNTER. according to the agreement made day and date as above. Full stop. Here come the actors.

MILLER ADAM *and* MILLER EVE *appear in the distance.*

THE TRAVELLER. May I borrow your pince-nez? I can't see very well.

Takes THE HUNTER's *glasses.*

What's this on the glass? It's like hoar-frost,
or crystallised water—or salt.
A tear that has dried. Warm at the source,
very soon it cooled and became rock-salt.
The steel of the bridge has rusted.

Ah, he weeps often! But in secret.
Rivulets of tears have carved a course,
down from the eyes to the smiling mouth
to quench the smile that would kindle a laugh.
Poor human being!
Your mask is torn,
and when you show your teeth,
one cannot tell if it's to bite or smile.

THE HUNTER. The play's beginning. An idyll of the windmills.

THE TRAVELLER. A pastoral in minor-major key. We'll watch.

The MILLERS *take the stage.*

MILLER ADAM. True, neighbour, to-day we're both in the same boat, as there's no wind at all. All the same, I'm thinking of having your mill moved, as you interfere with my progress.

MILLER EVE. You mean I take the East wind from you. On the other hand, you take the West wind from me. So we're quits.

MILLER ADAM. But my mill was here first, and yours was just built out of malice. Things go badly for both of us now, so it would be better if they went well for *one* of us.

MILLER EVE. For *you,* you mean?

MILLER ADAM. For you, *you* mean?

MILLER EVE. Yes, of course.

MILLER ADAM. But when I said *one* of us, I meant the better of us, the one who has right on his side.

MILLER EVE. Which would that be?

MILLER ADAM. Is it for us to judge in the matter?

MILLER EVE. I have a better grain-bolter than you, and my Eve grinds quicker, turns more easily, and has new sails.

MILLER ADAM. But my Adam was built before your Eve, and my mill-hopper is made of boxwood—

MILLER EVE. Stop. We'll ask those gentlemen over there.

THE TRAVELLER. So now we're going to be dragged into it.

THE HUNTER. They'll grab us as witnesses, perhaps even as judges—in order, later on, to override our judgement.

Enter the WIFE OF MILLER ADAM.

WIFE. Come along now, husband, and have your dinner.

MILLER ADAM. Wait a bit.

WIFE. I can't do that.

MILLER ADAM. You should learn never to be in a hurry.

WIFE. Never?

MILLER ADAM. Never—so long as the world remains and a word holds good.

WIFE. Then the cabbage will get cold.

MILLER ADAM. Is it cabbage? Well, that's another matter. I'll come at once.

WIFE. Then the world will come to an end, and a word hold good no more.

MILLER ADAM. Did I say that? Then I take it back.

They go out.

THE TRAVELLER. He sold his birthright,

THE HUNTER. for a mess of cabbage.

THE TRAVELLER. And that's that.

THE HUNTER. But now we're to be set on by the Eve miller. Look, now he's spying on us—and hesitating. He wants something out of us—some bit of information to increase his knowledge. Look how he's examining our clothes, shoes, hair, and beards. He's a thief.

MILLER EVE. Excuse me.

THE TRAVELLER. He's trying to trick us into talking. Don't answer.

MILLER EVE. Where have you gentlemen come from?

THE TRAVELLER. That's none of your business.

MILLER EVE. Strictly speaking, no.

THE TRAVELLER. Well, we are speaking strictly, so be off with you.

MILLER EVE. I wasn't going to pinch anything.

THE TRAVELLER. That wouldn't be easy in any case.

MILLER EVE. On the contrary, I was going to give you something.

THE TRAVELLER. We don't need anything.

MILLER EVE. Huh! Well, there it is, I was going to give you gentlemen something—and ask nothing for it—a bit of information, a useful bit of information. *Pause.* They're at work blasting rock just behind here—and one, two, three, we'll get a shower of stones on our heads!

THE TRAVELLER *and* THE HUNTER *spring up.*

THE TRAVELLER. Why on earth didn't you say so at once?

MILLER EVE. You wouldn't listen. But sit down again—there's no rush. The blasters will give the alarm first.

THE TRAVELLER. Look here, is this the way to the Promised Land?

MILLER EVE. This is the straight way.

THE TRAVELLER. Will the weather hold till the afternoon?

MILLER EVE. We can expect more thunder. It's very unsettled in this district.

THE TRAVELLER. All the year round?

MILLER EVE. Always unsettled, the whole year round. Year out, year in.

THE TRAVELLER. What is the next village called?

MILLER EVE. That's none of your business. Certainly it's pleasanter to give than to take, but to be robbed isn't pleasant at all. Thief! Have you a pass?

THE TRAVELLER. What for?

MILLER EVE. There are robbers in the woods, and everyone who won't say where he comes from must be examined.

THE HUNTER. Now we are in it up to our necks.

THE TRAVELLER. And it's not exactly an idyll of the windmills we are in.

MILLER EVE. I'll go and fetch my neighbour and his men. Then we can establish alibis.

THE TRAVELLER. That's a queer idea.

MILLER EVE. Well, you see, I'm the Parish Constable, and my neighbour's the Parish Clerk. *Exit.*

THE TRAVELLER. So now Herod and Pilate have become friends.

THE HUNTER. I really started out to gain my own soul, but he who seeks to gain shall lose. Let's cast ourselves into the throng again . . .

THE TRAVELLER. at the risk of sinking,

THE HUNTER. without reaching the bottom,

THE TRAVELLER. thanks to a certain life-belt which intelligent people wear.

THE GIRL *enters.*

Here comes a woman.

THE HUNTER. As one might expect in the vicinity of Adam and Eve,

THE TRAVELLER. without, however, expecting any paradise.

THE HUNTER. Full stop. Now the scene begins.

THE TRAVELLER. I think it's advisable to take the offensive. What is your name, my pretty child?

THE GIRL. Guess!

THE TRAVELLER. Let me see. Fair, miller's daughter, not very tall, round face . . . Your name's Amelia!

THE GIRL. How did you know?

THE TRAVELLER. By your appearance.

THE GIRL. If I'd been dark and tall, with an oval face, what would I have been called then—as a blacksmith's daughter?

THE TRAVELLER. Jenny, of course.

THE GIRL. That's right.

THE TRAVELLER. Now you've had all this from me, what do I get in return?

THE GIRL. You get . . . tell me, where did you learn this gift of reading people?

THE TRAVELLER. From life, experience, certain books, an innate superior intelligence—and a good portion of acquired acuteness. Now, my dear, why won't you have the son of your neighbour miller?

THE GIRL. So you know that too.

THE TRAVELLER. But you ought to take him. Then the mill problem will be settled out of court. You will sell one of the mills and have it moved to the next parish, where it is so badly needed.

THE GIRL. How wise, how very wise you are!

THE TRAVELLER. But I see you don't want the miller's boy. You'd rather have one of the robbers from the forest, eh? The one with the black eyes and big moustaches. . . .

THE GIRL. I'm beginning to be frightened. Are you a fortune-teller?

THE TRAVELLER. As you see. But I can only tell the fortunes of young people.

THE GIRL. Why is that?

THE TRAVELLER. Because old people are so cunning.

THE GIRL, *to* THE HUNTER. Is that true?

THE TRAVELLER. Don't talk to him—he doesn't want to be involved. Talk to me. Give me something in exchange for all you have learnt in this one short moment. Otherwise you'll be in my debt, and you wouldn't like that.

THE GIRL. Very well, you shall have something, so you will go away from here rewarded, richer than you came, loaded with knowledge, for which I ask nothing.

THE TRAVELLER. That's a likely story.

THE GIRL. To begin with, I'm not called Amelia. . . .

THE TRAVELLER. But Jenny—what did I say?

THE GIRL. No, not that either. Secondly, there is no miller's son. Thirdly, the next parish already has four windmills, so the mill problem would still be unsolved. And now for one or two bits of advice into the bargain. Don't be so familiar with a strange girl—you never know to whom you are talking, however observant you think you are. And don't be disloyal to a friend when a third person comes along, or else, when you are alone again and need him, he may not be there.

THE TRAVELLER. I haven't been disloyal.

THE GIRL. Yes, just now, in order to gain my favour, you tried to make him look ridiculous. That wasn't nice. Now you are on the defensive. And if you were to ask me my name now, I wouldn't answer as you answered the miller when he was trying to save you from the robbers in the forest.

THE HUNTER, *rising*. Won't you have a seat, young lady?

THE GIRL. It's true, I am a young lady. From the manor—and not a miller's daughter. *To* THE TRAVELLER. Go to the miller and give him my compliments—then you'll get the pass. Go on. Just give him my compliments.

THE TRAVELLER. But I must know your name.

THE GIRL, *sitting down.* I don't give my name to strangers, and if you were a respectable man you wouldn't ask for it. Go along.

Exit THE TRAVELLER.

THE GIRL. You are lucky, you, who roam the world, meet people, get to know them . . .

THE HUNTER. Know them?

THE GIRL. True, one cannot know. But one grows acquainted.

THE HUNTER. Scarcely even that. But guessing riddles is a way to pass the time.

THE GIRL. Because what's said does not mean much.

THE HUNTER. Just so. It has to be translated.
For every language is a foreign one,
and foreigners we are, each to the other,
all travelling incognito.

THE GIRL. Incognito even to ourselves.
You have a grief, and yet are not in mourning.

THE HUNTER. You dress as miller-girl, yet are a lady.

THE GIRL. And your companion?

THE HUNTER. Only an acquaintance—and entirely unknown.

THE GIRL. What do you think of him?

THE HUNTER. Everything and nothing.
So far I haven't summed him up.

THE GIRL. What were you doing up there?

THE HUNTER. Breathing and forgetting.

THE GIRL. But why forget? Without memory
our life is nothing but an empty waste.

THE HUNTER. And *with* it—a cargo foundering the ship.

THE GIRL. Ships without cargo most easily capsize. . . .

THE HUNTER. Therefore one takes on ballast . . .

THE GIRL. and takes in the sails.

THE HUNTER. Like a windmill, eh?

THE GIRL. Yes, otherwise the wings would break . . .

THE HUNTER. but it turns better on the heights . . .

THE GIRL. best of all down there, out on the plains . . .

THE HUNTER. where the air is so dense . . .

THE GIRL. that you can see for miles,
can count the country churches with the naked eye.
There all the stars of night appear,

THE HUNTER. not on the horizon,

THE GIRL. but in the zenith.
The zenith is everywhere,
once the horizon has been reached.

THE HUNTER. Tell me—was I once there?

THE GIRL. You are there now—where you strove to get
this very morning. Is it not sweet
to find the new when the old is won?

THE HUNTER. And that country in the distance?

THE GIRL. Press on and you will reach it—
but if you tire, it will recede.
No mortal's reached the Pole star in the zenith;
yet still they journey and return,
and others travel the same road and are forced back.
Do as they do—but learn while on the way.

THE HUNTER. One drags and dredges, nose down in the nadir.

THE GIRL. But eyes from time to time lift to the zenith.

A horn sounds.

THE HUNTER, *alert.* Do you hear?

THE GIRL. I hear, but do not understand.

THE HUNTER. I will translate.
You hear only sound, but I hear words.

THE GIRL. What does the horn say?

THE HUNTER. "Give answer now, where are you, where?"

The horn answers: Here!

THE GIRL. It is someone calling you.

The horn is heard again.

THE HUNTER. "Come hither, come hither, come hither, hither!"

THE GIRL. I hear you are a soldier, I see it rather.
They are calling you. We part as briefly as we met.

THE HUNTER. Not quite so briefly, not so lightly. . . .
Come with me—just a little way—
to the next village.

THE GIRL. And your companion?

THE HUNTER. Such ones are found at the bar of every inn.

THE GIRL. How cruel you are!

THE HUNTER. I have been to war.
There the word's "onward," never "stop"!

THE GIRL. So I must go or else I'll stop.

THE HUNTER. If you go, you will take something with you.

THE GIRL. If I stop, you will have taken something from me.

THE HUNTER, *looking off*. Look! They are quarrelling. In a mo-
ment they'll fight.
They're fighting. And I shall be called as witness.
But you must go. You must not be involved.

THE GIRL. Are you really thinking of me?

THE HUNTER. Of you, for you,
with you and through you. And now farewell.
A flower seen through the garden fence,
for a moment delighting the traveller's eye—
fairest unpicked; its fragrance lingering
a while on the wind—and then it is gone.
And so, onward!

THE GIRL. Goodbye. And so—onward! *Exit*.

THE HUNTER. Now I am sunk. Bound, trapped,
dragged between grind-stones of the law,
wings caught in a web of emotion,
allied with a stranger and involved
in a matter which does not concern me.
Enter THE TRAVELLER.

THE TRAVELLER. Are you still here? I thought you'd gone. You
must really have a faithful disposition.

THE HUNTER. Did you get into the fight?

THE TRAVELLER. I gave the miller a punch on the jaw for making a fool of me. All that stuff about blasting and robbers

in the forest was a pack of lies. And now we're summoned
to appear at the autumn Assizes—I as defendant, you as
witness.

THE HUNTER. Did you give our names then?

THE TRAVELLER. No, I took two names at random.

THE HUNTER. What a risk! Now they can have us up for per-
jury as well. Going and getting oneself tangled up in this
way. What did you call me then?

THE TRAVELLER. I said you travelled under the name Incognito.
That satisfied the yokels.

THE HUNTER. And I am to give evidence against you?

THE TRAVELLER. Yes, in three months' time. Let's make the
most of our liberty and get going. They say there's some
festivity in the next village.

THE HUNTER. What sort of festivity?

THE TRAVELLER. Oh, a kind of battle of flowers—and an Asses'
Gala, at which the biggest dunce in the village gets a crown
of gold paper.

THE HUNTER. How very odd! What's the village called?

THE TRAVELLER. It's called Assesdean. And this one's called
Liarsbourne, because only liars live here.

THE HUNTER. *Enteuthen exelaunei*,[2] and then they
marched, . . .

THE TRAVELLER. *parasangas trêis*, three leagues, . . .

THE HUNTER. and so they did.

They march out together.

III. IN ASSESDEAN

Left, a smithy. Right, in a corner, a bench, on which THE
HUNTER *and* THE TRAVELLER *are sitting.*

THE HUNTER. Now we have travelled quite a way together,

THE TRAVELLER. and not come any closer to each other, not
even so that I have a clue as to who you are.

[2] Literally: "Thence he marched."

THE HUNTER. As I told you, I'm a soldier. I'm always fighting. Fighting to keep my personal independence . . .

THE TRAVELLER. But not always winning.

THE HUNTER. One cannot ask for that,

THE TRAVELLER. specially as lost battles are the most instructive,

THE HUNTER. for the victor,

THE TRAVELLER. but the worst of it is one never knows who's won. In the last war it was the victor who lost most.

THE HUNTER. Which war?

THE TRAVELLER. The one at the windmills.

THE HUNTER. May I borrow your penknife? I lost mine in the mountains.

THE TRAVELLER. One shouldn't be inquisitive. If you just observe this knife, it will tell you a lot. The big blade's scarcely used—so the owner's no craftsman. The little blade, on the other hand, shows traces of lead and coloured crayons. He may therefore be an artist—but perhaps only an amateur. The corkscrew's worn—that we can understand—and the bottle-opener too. But then there's also a gimlet and a saw. Yes, and a skeleton key, which is far more significant. But as it's only thrown in with the rest, taken by and large we have no information.

THE HUNTER. Well! So this is Assesdean.

Enter THE SCHOOLMASTER.

Here comes the schoolmaster. This time we'll hold our tongues so as not to be involved.

THE TRAVELLER. As if that will help.

THE SCHOOLMASTER. Abra-kadabra, abrakadabra, ab-ra-ka-da-bra! *Gazes at the strangers.* No, they did not hear. Again. Abra-ka-dabra, abra-kadabra, abra-ka-da-bra! No, they're superior beings—they have self-control. Gentlemen, he who is silent gives his consent. I've come to ask if you will receive a deputation of the leading intellectuals of the village, who will engage you in a battle of words. If I get no answer, I'll take it as affirmative. One . . . two . . . three!

THE HUNTER *and* THE TRAVELLER. No!

THE SCHOOLMASTER. Fine!

THE TRAVELLER. You're not such a fool, considering you come from Assesdean.

THE SCHOOLMASTER. I'm the only sane fellow in the place—therefore I must make myself out an imbecile, or else they'll shut me up. I had an academic education, and I've written a verse tragedy in five acts called "Potamogeton,"[3] which is so damned silly that I should have won the prize. But the village blacksmith got the better of me. He produced a memorial to the Nation's Destroyer—and so I was passed over. I am one who is always passed over. You gentlemen will think me very egotistical, talking like this about myself, but there are two reasons for it. Firstly, I have to explain myself—and secondly, you wouldn't like it if I talked about you.

THE BLACKSMITH's *steps are heard.*

Here comes the Blacksmith. I must disguise myself, or he'll think me sane and have me shut up.

THE SCHOOLMASTER *puts on asses' ears.*

Enter THE BLACKSMITH.

THE BLACKSMITH. Abra-ka-da-bra, abra-kadabra!

THE SCHOOLMASTER. Good day, Axe-handle!

THE BLACKSMITH. Is that a hit at me?

THE SCHOOLMASTER. Life is a fight, and we're part of it.

THE BLACKSMITH. Are you referring to the emancipation question or to free trade?

THE SCHOOLMASTER. Twice two is four, and six more makes eight. Agreed?

THE BLACKSMITH. I reserve to myself all mathematics, as that is my principal subject, particularly *quatuor species*, which means the four simple rules of reckoning, fractions included, excepting, of course, simple whole fractions and decimal fractions.

THE SCHOOLMASTER. Sometimes even great Homer falls asleep.

THE BLACKSMITH. But six and four make eleven, and if one

[3] NOTE. Pondweed.

moves the decimal two points to the left, it will be straight as a nail. Isn't that so, gentlemen? Am I not right?

THE TRAVELLER. Absolutely right. Six and four make eleven, and not eight.

THE BLACKSMITH. Now we'll pass to lighter matters, or, if I may say so, subjects of conversation. Gentlemen, a subject of conversation is not blown from the nose, if I may so express myself, even if such a subject is light. A light subject of conversation, closely observed, falls into two equal parts —first comes the subject, for everything must have a subject, and then the conversation follows of its own accord. Furthermore, the subjects may be as numerous as . . . as . . . days in the year—or more still—say, as drops in the ocean—or yet more as, let me see, as sands in the desert. True, I have never been in a desert, but I can quite clearly imagine how it looks. On the other hand, I did once do a journey by steamboat. It was expensive, gentlemen—I take it you have never made such a journey—but that wasn't what I meant to say.

THE SCHOOLMASTER. The Guano Islands lie 56 degrees North, 13 degrees East by East to South.

THE BLACKSMITH. If this is a dig at me, I don't like digs.

THE SCHOOLMASTER. But that is nothing compared with Charles the Great.

THE BLACKSMITH. No. But it is harder to shoe a nag so it doesn't go lopsided.

THE SCHOOLMASTER. Hafiz also very rightly remarks in the third sura, page 78 and following: "Eat man! You never know when you'll have the chance again."

THE BLACKSMITH. I only want to explain that one says *pagīna* just as one says Carolīna, Chīna, and so forth. Or does one say *pagna?*

THE SCHOOLMASTER. Yes, yes, yes!

THE BLACKSMITH. Right's right, that's my principle. Now, Schoolmaster, do you know when Julius Caesar was born?

THE SCHOOLMASTER. The year 99 before Christ.

THE BLACKSMITH. Before Christ? That's impossible. The calendar begins at year one, and one can't count backwards, can one?

THE SCHOOLMASTER. Can't one count backwards?

THE BLACKSMITH. Take care, don't begin to argue! Take care. You've such a weak head—anything might happen. Can you tell me the difference between rye and wheat?

THE SCHOOLMASTER. Julius Caesar was born in 99 and died in 31.

THE BLACKSMITH. Look here, how can that be? Did he live backwards? The difference between rye and wheat is first of all the price of grain or the land tax, and secondly free trade—for rye is protected and wheat is free. Isn't that right?

THE SCHOOLMASTER. Yes, yes, yes!

THE BLACKSMITH. But currency, that's another matter. I deal in silver—I won't deny that. The exchange is another matter too, so are quotation rates, and agio again is something different. . . .

THE SCHOOLMASTER. What is it then?

THE BLACKSMITH. What is it? Do I have to stand here and tell you what it is? Haven't I anything else to do? Haven't I paid my taxes? Am I not married? I'm only asking. Only asking. If anyone has any objection to make, I'd like to talk to him in private—in private. Do you know what that means? Behind the stable. Don't speak. I can't stand being answered back. No one must ever answer me back. Now do you consider all these questions settled in my favour, or shall we go behind the stable? I'm a very serious man, I'm not to be trifled with. Now, gentlemen, you see what an ass you have before you. I don't mean me, but the schoolmaster, who believes a man can have been born before the calendar began. You ought to know exactly what kind of a fellow he is.

Well, he's the most miserable ignoramus that ever walked in shoes. He's so ignorant he even believes in the Guano Islands—and there's no such place. *He picks up a bottle and takes a gulp.* He doesn't know the difference between rye and wheat—and he boozes into the bargain. Perhaps you think I booze too, but I only tipple—it can't be called boozing, that's something different. Knowledge, gentlemen, is a virtue, but the schoolmaster knows absolutely nothing—and it's his place to educate children. He's a despot, a tyrant, a domineering wretch, and a bully into the bargain. Now you know what he is.

THE TRAVELLER. Stop a minute. I certainly don't intend to answer you back, because then you'd fight, and I'm not going to cross-examine you, because if I did your knowledge would show its absence. I'm not going to offer you a drink, because that's unnecessary, nor am I going to argue with you, because you wouldn't understand what I meant and you'd never admit my points. But I should like to ask you one thing.

THE BLACKSMITH. Ask, but ask nicely!

THE TRAVELLER. You consider yourself something of a character?

THE BLACKSMITH. Certainly I'm a character, a strong character at that.

THE TRAVELLER. Moreover, you deal in silver?

THE BLACKSMITH. I'm proud to say I do.

THE TRAVELLER. Don't you recognise gold as the standard in the world market?

THE BLACKSMITH. No, not gold.

THE TRAVELLER. Not in private business either?

THE BLACKSMITH. I must think a while. *Aside.* Does he mean to cheat me on the exchange? *Aloud.* I won't answer that. No one can force me to answer it. And although I'm full of sense, I can't make any sense of what you're saying.

THE TRAVELLER. Really? Were you afraid your strong character wouldn't stand the test?

THE BLACKSMITH. Are you slandering me? Don't do that, because I'm the boss here. I'm a despot.

THE TRAVELLER *laughs.*

Don't look at me, for I'm a terrible despot.

THE TRAVELLER. I wasn't looking at you. I was only laughing.

THE BLACKSMITH. Don't laugh. I have a vote in the parish as a tax-paying citizen, and that's no laughing matter. I have

five children, all well educated, very gifted, specially in regard to brains. Two of them, it is true, are in America—but,
well, such things do happen. And one made a false step
. . . but he has paid for it, so there's nothing more to be
said about that, nothing at all.

THE TRAVELLER, *aside.* He's superb.

THE HUNTER. But this must stop. I'm suffocating.

THE BLACKSMITH. I'll just go and get my manuscript; then the
festivities can begin. But you gentlemen mustn't leave. I'm
the Mayor and have authority. The schoolmaster is about
to read from his tragedy "Potamogeton." It's not so bad for
an amateur, but many hounds cause the death of the hare.

THE SCHOOLMASTER. And the lines walk by themselves like
great goslings.

THE BLACKSMITH. Is that a dig at me?

THE SCHOOLMASTER. It scarcely can be, since you are full-
grown.

THE BLACKSMITH. Full-fledged it's called when it's birds. Read
nicely now for the gentlemen, and I'll soon be back. But
don't slander me in my absence.

THE TRAVELLER. But in your presence it's impossible.

THE BLACKSMITH. That's true. Of two evils one must choose
the least. So slander me in my absence and not in my
presence. *Exit.*

THE TRAVELLER. What is this village—a lunatic asylum?

THE SCHOOLMASTER. Yes, they are so ill-natured they've gone
mad.

THE TRAVELLER. And are you an inmate?

THE SCHOOLMASTER. I'm kept under observation because I'm
suspected of being sane.

THE TRAVELLER. Come with us and we'll give them the slip.

THE SCHOOLMASTER. Then all three of us will be caught.

THE TRAVELLER. So it isn't all just folly?

THE SCHOOLMASTER. Evil is folly's mother—and its child at the
same time.

THE TRAVELLER. Who is this smith?

THE SCHOOLMASTER. He is a god of filth such as Isaiah speaks of. He's composed of the hatred, jealousy, and lies of all the rest. The smith became Mayor because the baker was the most deserving man. When I had served faithfully for twenty-five years, the day was made a celebration for the blacksmith. At the last Asses' Gala the smith got the laurel wreath—because he had written the worst verses.

THE HUNTER. Better to run away than lose the battle. We can't win this, so we must run away.

THE TRAVELLER. We're in mortal danger here.

THE SCHOOLMASTER. But most dangerous of all is to run away.

THE TRAVELLER. Can't we trick them, as they're such fools?

THE SCHOOLMASTER. But like all fools, they are cunning.

THE TRAVELLER. We'll try it. *Calls.* Blacksmith!

Enter THE BLACKSMITH.

Abra-kadabra, abra-kadabra!

THE BLACKSMITH. What is it? Are you gentlemen thinking of leaving? Don't do that. On no account do that.

THE TRAVELLER. We're only going to the next village to requisition properties for the show.

THE BLACKSMITH. To do what?

THE TRAVELLER. Requisition properties.

THE BLACKSMITH. Requisition. Well, I suppose requisitions are always welcome. Are there any smithy properties at all?

THE TRAVELLER. There are shoe-nails, axle-boxes, scythes, and spades. . . .

THE BLACKSMITH. Splendid!

THE TRAVELLER. But we must have the schoolmaster to help us carry them.

THE BLACKSMITH. He's so weak and such a simpleton.

THE TRAVELLER. But the properties are only paper, so he'll be able to manage them.

THE BLACKSMITH. Very true, very true . . . but axle-boxes are heavy—they'll be too much for him.

THE TRAVELLER. Property axle-boxes are no heavier than property nails.

THE BLACKSMITH. Very true, very true. Well, go along then— but you must come back.

THE TRAVELLER. Don't you realise that if one goes, one's bound to come back.

THE BLACKSMITH. Wait a minute. What is it that goes and goes and never comes back?

THE TRAVELLER. That's the clock. But we are not clocks, so we will come back.

THE BLACKSMITH. That's logic, and I understand it. But, wait a minute. Don't your clocks come back?

THE TRAVELLER. They aren't clocks, they're watches.

THE BLACKSMITH. Ah, very true! Clocks can strike but watches are something different. And bells strike too, but they do not go.[4] Ergo . . .

THE TRAVELLER. But we're going, that's the main point.

THE BLACKSMITH. Exactly, that's the main point. And it's logical. I like logic in all walks of life, and I can only follow a strictly logical argument.

THE TRAVELLER. Then don't follow us, for we aren't a logical argument.

THE BLACKSMITH. Exactly. So I will stay here at my post and you will go. Go along.

THE TRAVELLER. Sing the praise of the ass, you great rhyme-smith!

Wisest of all animals on earth,
with your long ear-trumpet
you have the finest hearing of them all.
You hear grass growing underneath the stone,
at the same moment you look both east and west,
strong character is shown in your stiff legs,
your own will is your master's law.
When you should stand, you run instead,
when whipped to run, then you stand still.

THE BLACKSMITH. That's really very well said, for the mammal in question has belonged to the world of the unappreciated,

---

[4] NOTE. The Swedish word *klockor* means both "clocks" and "bells." This pun cannot be exactly reproduced in English.

to the camp of the dumb, and deserves to be re-ha-bi- . . .

THE TRAVELLER. . . . litated. But did you ever hear a dumb ass?

THE BLACKSMITH. No, but I don't bother about that. I concern myself with the character, the strong character, and therefore I understand this misunderstood animal. Yes, indeed I do.

THE TRAVELLER. Do you take your stand on that?

THE BLACKSMITH. I take my stand.

THE TRAVELLER. Then we'll be off.

THE BLACKSMITH. Wait a minute. I take my stand, but I don't stand alone. I have public opinion on my side and a party. All right-thinking, enlightened, undeluded people. In short, the whole nation rallies round my banner, and from my standpoint I'll show you you are wrong. For right is right —isn't that logic?

THE SCHOOLMASTER. The highest right is the highest wrong.

THE BLACKSMITH. And the voice of the people is the voice of God. Come in, people! Rally, nation!

A few persons enter.

THE TRAVELLER. Here is the nation—but how few they are!

THE BLACKSMITH. These are few, but you don't see the massed ranks behind them.

THE TRAVELLER. No, I can't see anything like that.

THE BLACKSMITH. You can't see them for the simple reason that they are invisible. That's logical. People! These learned charlatans maintain that there's such a place as the Guano Islands. Is there such a place?

THE PEOPLE. No!

THE BLACKSMITH. Then these gentlemen are either liars or blockheads. Is there any punishment severe enough for such villains who spread lies?

THE TRAVELLER. Yes, there's one more cruel than any other, and that is exile.

THE BLACKSMITH. Not a bad idea. But we must have full evidence against them first. Here is one who asserts that Homer slept.

THE TRAVELLER. At times.

THE BLACKSMITH. At times or all the time, it comes to the same thing. That's mere sophism. Do you people believe that a poet can sleep? Have you ever heard anything so idiotic?

ONE OF THE PEOPLE. But surely he slept at night.

THE BLACKSMITH. At night? Is that an answer? Have I given permission for an answer? Come round behind the stable, and I'll give you the answer, I will.

ONE OF THE PEOPLE. Is it a matter of taking sides?

THE BLACKSMITH. Yes, people must take sides, or else they're just characterless opportunists.

THE SCHOOLMASTER, *to* THE BLACKSMITH. Aren't you going to read from your "Charles the Great" now? Then we can get away from this brawl. The visitors are in a hurry. *Aside to* THE HUNTER *and* THE TRAVELLER. His name isn't Charles the Great, but we must call him that, or else we'll be put in gaol.

THE BLACKSMITH. I heard what you said, and I saw you two sneering. He who sneers is an accomplice. Shut them up! You know what I mean—seize them! His name isn't Charles the Great, but we call him that, because he definitely was great. Give them a punch on the jaw and lock them up until they come to their senses.

THE HUNTER, THE TRAVELLER, *and* THE SCHOOLMASTER *are seized and about to be removed.*

THE HUNTER. But we have been exiled, and we must go to the town to fetch properties.

THE BLACKSMITH. That's quite right. Everything's quite right. You have leave to go, but on your word of honour to come back, and on—or rather against—your promise to be grateful, for an ungrateful person is the heaviest burden on earth. Now I have, it so happens, a wife who has a salon. Yes, it may sound ridiculous, but you see, it is a literary salon, and I shall expect you gentlemen to turn up at the first reception.

THE TRAVELLER. So we are free. But at what a price!

THE HUNTER. Can it be called freedom to be chained by one's word of honour to the forge of a literary salon?

THE BLACKSMITH. Be off with you! But the nation is to stay.

As THE HUNTER, THE TRAVELLER, *and* THE SCHOOLMASTER *go, the curtain falls.*

IV. THE ARCADE IN TOPHET[5]

In the arcade. Right, a café, then a photograph booth, then a shell shop. Left, a fruit and flower stall and a Japanese tea and perfume shop.

THE HUNTER *and* THE TRAVELLER *are sitting outside the flower stall.*

THE TRAVELLER. You're very gloomy.

THE HUNTER. I've come down too far.

THE TRAVELLER. You have been in Tophet before?

THE HUNTER. Yes. I lived here once.

THE TRAVELLER. I could see that.

THE HUNTER. We must get some chloroform. My wounds are beginning to ache.

THE TRAVELLER. *Vinum et circenses.* There'll be plenty of free shows here. This appears to be the town sewer through which everything runs. *He waves towards the café.*

A WAITRESS *brings wine.*

Won't you be recognised here?

THE HUNTER. Impossible. I've let my beard grow and cut my hair. Besides, I washed my hands this morning. In this town one is never recognised if one washes.

THE TRAVELLER. But the waitress is staring at you.

THE HUNTER. Perhaps I resemble one of her former friends.

THE TRAVELLER. Here comes a little entertainment.

Enter THE ORGAN-GRINDER *with a monkey.*

Come along, musician, and we'll redeem our heads for a good sum.

THE ORGAN-GRINDER. Heads?

[5] Hell.

THE TRAVELLER. Well, ears then. You'll get a gold coin here not to play.

THE ORGAN-GRINDER. But the monkey's the chief attraction.

THE TRAVELLER. Then we'll look at him, but without accompaniment.

THE ORGAN-GRINDER. But there's the text too.

THE TRAVELLER. Is it true that all of you in this town are descended from a monkey?

THE ORGAN-GRINDER. What a thing to ask! You'd better take care.

THE TRAVELLER. When I look at you more closely, I believe it is true. I'm sure of it, I could swear to it. May I look at the text? But this head of Zeus looks more like a ram.

THE ORGAN-GRINDER. Yes, it really does. Very well then, so it is.

THE TRAVELLER. Do you really believe that mammal in the red jacket with the gun is the father of the human race?

THE ORGAN-GRINDER. If you're a freethinker, you'd better take care. We're orthodox in this town, defenders of the faith.

THE TRAVELLER. Which faith?

THE ORGAN-GRINDER. The only true one; the doctrine of evolution.

Exit THE ORGAN-GRINDER.

THE HUNTER. Now we'll probably be charged with blasphemy. Where's the schoolmaster got to?

THE TRAVELLER. Having made use of us, he's disappeared of course.

THE HUNTER. Shall we go?

THE TRAVELLER. What's the point? It makes no difference whether we fall into the hands of these people or others.

THE HUNTER. For people lurk like robbers in the ditches ready to spring out upon each other. Look at the café window! That girl's standing there, gazing at you with eyes of entreaty, as if begging you out of kindness or pity to rescue her. She's pretty and could rouse feelings other than pity. Well, suppose you were to decide to free her from her heavy and degrading job, suppose you were to offer her a home and protection from life's worst hardships. What then? Be-

fore long she would have robbed you of your friends, separated you from your family, ruined you with your superiors
and patrons. In a word, she would have devoured you,

THE TRAVELLER. and if I didn't permit that, she would sue me
for cruelty,

THE HUNTER. and for having destroyed her youth. But the
worst thing of all is, that you'd find yourself in a family
that you don't know,

THE TRAVELLER. but can imagine . . . Yes. She's standing there
drawing, sucking—creating a whirlpool. She's spinning a net
that feels like warm air. . . . Wait. I'll go in and destroy it,

THE HUNTER. or be caught in it.

THE TRAVELLER *goes into the café.*

Man overboard!

Enter THE PHOTOGRAPHER *with a camera.*

THE PHOTOGRAPHER. May I take your portrait, sir?

THE HUNTER. No-o-o!

THE PHOTOGRAPHER. Please do me this favour—I'm so poor.

THE HUNTER. Very well, but you mustn't put me in the show-
case or in a packet of cigarettes or on a tablet of soap. And
if I come out like an Australian negro or the latest murderer, you must destroy the plate.

THE PHOTOGRAPHER. How suspicious you are, sir!

THE HUNTER. Not at all. Just a little prudent.

THE PHOTOGRAPHER *beckons to his booth.*

EUPHROSYNE *enters.*

THE PHOTOGRAPHER. Allow me to introduce my wife. She helps
with the developing and printing. Come along, Euphrosyne,
I have promised to take an outdoor picture of this gentleman, although I'm so busy. You talk to him, while I do the
job.

EUPHROSYNE, *sitting down.* You must have been born lucky,
sir, to meet such an artist as my husband. He's the cleverest
one I've ever seen, and if this picture isn't good, then you
can say *I* don't understand art. So you must appreciate his
work and not behave as if you're doing us a favour.

THE HUNTER. Wait a minute . . .

EUPHROSYNE. No, you mustn't look so haughty. When you beg a favour of someone, you must be grateful.

THE HUNTER. Stop a moment . . .

THE PHOTOGRAPHER, *calling*. Gotthard! Come here! You've put the plate in back to front.

Enter GOTTHARD.

GOTTHARD. I didn't put the plate in.

EUPHROSYNE. Are you answering your father back? Your own father.

GOTTHARD. I don't know anything about cameras. Shells are my job. I . . .

THE PHOTOGRAPHER. Your job, yes. But do you sell any? Ask this gentleman if he wants any shells. I think he said something just now about shells.

THE HUNTER. I never mentioned shells. I only mentioned cigarettes and soap. . . .

EUPHROSYNE. Gotthard, bring some cigarettes! Didn't you hear the gentleman say he wanted some?

THE HUNTER. I wanted to avoid having my face on a cigarette packet or a soap wrapper. . . .

GOTTHARD, *sitting down*. You're difficult to deal with, I see, sir, but let's reason a little, then we'll get it straight.

EUPHROSYNE. You're right, Gotthard. When he gets to know our ways, he'll understand. Tell Klara to come out.

GOTTHARD, *calling*. Klara!

Enter KLARA, *the flower-seller*.

EUPHROSYNE. You try and sell a flower to this gentleman. He's so economical—or rather, mean—that he won't buy a single shell, although Gotthard has the most beautiful ones *I've* ever seen.

KLARA, *sitting down*. Perhaps he can be talked round, although he looks so haughty. Is he a hunter?

EUPHROSYNE. You can see he is.

KLARA. He looks cruel—like all drunkards. . . . Yes, anyone who drinks in the morning is a drunkard. He kills animals. He shouldn't do that; it's a sin.

THE HUNTER, *to* KLARA. What have you done with your husband?

KLARA *is terrified.*

It's a sin to kill people. Don't you know that?

KLARA. Is that your opinion?

THE HUNTER. Yes, that's my opinion.

KLARA. You hear, witnesses. That's his opinion.

ALL. Yes, we heard.

THE HUNTER. May I say one word? Just one?

GOTTHARD. No. Why should you?

THE HUNTER. I'm not going to say what you think, but something quite different.

EUPHROSYNE, *curious.* Say it then.

THE HUNTER. Has Möller been arrested yet?

All rise in horror.

THE TRAVELLER, *entering from the café.* What's going on now?

THE HUNTER. Has Möller been arrested yet?

All scatter but look threatening.

For the third time—has Möller been arrested yet?

All disappear.

THE TRAVELLER. What was all that about?

THE HUNTER. It's the town's secret. Everyone knows the last murder was committed by Möller, but no one dares denounce him, as there isn't sufficient evidence. As the result of the bomb I've dropped, we must take ourselves off at once. Come on!

THE TRAVELLER. I can't.

THE HUNTER. Caught?

THE TRAVELLER. In a bar. Dregs in glasses, matches and cigar ash, pawed by young men, soiled with smoke and night life —yet, in spite of all that, in spite of everything, caught.

THE HUNTER. Break loose!

THE TRAVELLER. I can't.

THE HUNTER. Let's run for it!

THE TRAVELLER. I can't.

THE HUNTER. Very well then, stay!

THE TRAVELLER. I can't. I can't do anything.

THE HUNTER. Then I must bid you farewell.

THE TRAVELLER. We shall meet again.

THE HUNTER. That's always so, when one's met once.

THE TRAVELLER. Then—goodbye.

Exit THE TRAVELLER *into the café.*

Left alone, THE HUNTER *walks a few steps in the arcade, and stops aimlessly in front of* THE PHOTOGRAPHER's *show-case.*

THE HUNTER. This place was once my own . . .
   but long ago. On rainy days
   I walked beneath this roof of glass;
   when murky days lay heavy on my heart,
   in here the lights were always lit;
   flowers and fruits rejoiced my eyes,
   shells murmured fairy tales from seas.
   In this case are portraits of acquaintances
   and near acquaintances—
   companions of my solitude.
   One look, one expression was enough
   for me to feel my kinship with these mortals.
   There they still are. . . . Here is my oldest friend;
   he must be growing grey, but his portrait,
   like leaves in autumn,
   has just grown yellow.
   Here I see relatives, previous relatives—
   a brother-in-law, brother-in-law no more—
   and here—O Saviour of the world, preserve me,
   for I grow faint—my child!
   My child, who is no longer mine,
   my child, who was, but is no longer mine.
   Another's child who is yet mine . . .
   And here was my café—
   our table. For a long time now
   all this has ceased to be,
   yet it exists—in memory.
   That fire which never can be quenched,
   which burns, but does not warm,
   which burns, but does not burn away.

The old JAPANESE *enters from the teashop. He has the appearance of a dying man.*

THE HUNTER *goes up and supports him.*

THE JAPANESE. A human being at last. Where from? Where going?

THE HUNTER. From the great highway. How can I be of service?

THE JAPANESE. Help me to die.

THE HUNTER. One can always die.

THE JAPANESE. Do not say that. I can live no longer, but I have no one to turn to for the last services, for in this Tophet there are no human beings.

THE HUNTER. What services do you mean?

THE JAPANESE. You must hold my sword, while I . . .

THE HUNTER. That I will not do. Why do you want to die?

THE JAPANESE. Because I can live no longer.

THE HUNTER. Tell me the long tale then in a few short words.

THE JAPANESE. Yes . . . yes. I left my country because I had committed an offence. I came here absolutely determined to become an honest man by strictly observing the laws of honour and conscience. I sold good wares at a reasonable price, but the inhabitants of this place only wanted bad wares at a low price. So I had but one choice, if I were not to perish. Instead of distilling the perfume of flowers, I gave them chemicals, and instead of tea leaves I gave them leaves of sloe or cherry. At first my conscience was silent—I had to live. But one day, fifteen years ago, I woke up. Then it was as if all I had been, and all I had done, was written in a book—and now the book was opened. Day and night, night and day, I read all the false entries, all the irregularities. I struggled, but in vain. Death alone can liberate me, for the evil is in my very flesh. My soul I have purified by suffering.

THE HUNTER. In what way can I help you?

THE JAPANESE. This way. I shall take a sleeping draught and become as one dead. You will have me put in a coffin, which will be carried to the crematorium.

THE HUNTER. But if you were to wake?

THE JAPANESE. That is just what I am counting on. For a moment I shall feel the purifying redeeming power of the fire. For a short while I shall suffer—then feel the bliss of deliverance.

THE HUNTER. And after that?

THE JAPANESE. After that you will gather the ashes in my most precious vase.

THE HUNTER. And put your name upon it. . . . What is your name?

THE JAPANESE. One moment. I have travelled, sinned, and suffered by the name "Hiroshima," after my native town. But in my country it is the custom, when a man dies, for him to give up his old, cursed, sullied name, and to be given a new one, which is called his Eternity Name. This name alone is put upon his tombstone with an epitaph. And then a bough of the sakaki tree is burned for him.

THE HUNTER. Have you these things ready?

THE JAPANESE. I have. Look at this.

THE HUNTER, *reading*. What does this name mean?

THE JAPANESE. *Harahara to*. It means "rustling leaf, whispering silk," but it also means "falling tears."

THE HUNTER. And the epitaph?

THE JAPANESE. *Chiru hana wo*
Nani ka uramin
Yo no naka ni
Waga mi mo tomo ni
Aran mono kawa.

THE HUNTER. And this interpreted?

THE JAPANESE. The blossoms are falling. . . .
Why should I feel aggrieved?
The gods have willed it;
And I, too, must—as the flowers—
Turn to dust some day. . . .

THE HUNTER. I will carry out your last wish. But have you no heirs?

THE JAPANESE. I had once. I had a daughter who came here three years ago, when she thought I was going to die. She came for the inheritance. But when I did not die, she grew angry, could not hide her feelings—and went away again. Since then she has been dead to me.

THE HUNTER. Where is this that we have talked of to take place?

THE JAPANESE. Outside the town—at the crematorium.

THE HUNTER. Are we to go together, or to meet there?

THE JAPANESE. We shall meet in the arbour of the inn—very shortly. I have only to bathe myself and shave.

THE HUNTER. Very well. We will meet there.

THE JAPANESE, *going towards his shop.* Here comes the murderer. Be on your guard!

THE HUNTER. Is that he?

THE JAPANESE. Be on your guard! He is the most powerful man in the town.

Exit THE JAPANESE.

Enter MÖLLER THE MURDERER. *He is stiff and pompous; his arms dangle awkwardly. He stares at* THE HUNTER.

THE MURDERER. Is it . . . ?

THE HUNTER. No, it's not.

THE MURDERER. Oh, then it is!

THE HUNTER. No, it was. The one you mean is no more.

THE MURDERER. Then you are dead?

THE HUNTER. Yes. Twelve years ago I committed hara-kiri. I executed my old self. The one you see here now, you do not know and can never know.

THE MURDERER. Yes, I remember. You were fool enough to put yourself in the pillory. On that blood-red carpet, you publicly confessed all your faults and failings. . . .

THE HUNTER. And the whole community revelled. Everyone felt themselves better people—as if they were vindicated by my social death. No one said a single word of compassion or of approval of my action.

THE MURDERER. Why should they?

THE HUNTER. However, when after ten years of suffering I had atoned and put everything right again, it occurred to me that I ought to confess your sins as well. Then the tune was changed.

THE MURDERER. Devil take you!

THE HUNTER. You who have, for example, committed murder. . . .

THE MURDERER. You can't say a thing like that . . . when you have no evidence.

THE HUNTER. I know you are the most powerful man in the community, that you bully the Grand Duke himself through the agency of a Freemason gang which . . .

THE MURDERER. What's that?

THE HUNTER. You know very well. A league which is not the holy one.

THE MURDERER. And what about you?

THE HUNTER. I've never belonged to the league, but I recognise it by certain signs. . . .

THE MURDERER. Look in the window of that paper-shop and you'll see who you are!

THE HUNTER. You mean that caricature? That's not me, that's you. That's how you look—inside. That's your creation. You're welcome to it.

THE MURDERER. You have a great talent for shaking off your vermin.

THE HUNTER. Do the same yourself in the same way—but not on to me. Execute yourself, as I did, as I had to do, when you made me into a scapegoat, on to whom you loaded all your guilt.

THE MURDERER. What are you talking about?

THE HUNTER. Take an example. Once a certain heretic wrote this piece of idiocy—that if he were standing alone on Gaurisankar, and the Flood came and drowned the whole human race, no harm would have been done at all, so long as *he* remained alive. At the next Carnival, Gaurisankar was carried in the procession, and on its summit stood not the heretic, but *I*. What have you to say about that? And on my birthday, *he* had the celebrations. When I invented the new insulators, *you* received the prize—but when you com-

mitted murder, *I* was accused. Moreover, when sugar shares
went up, people blamed my insulators, although you had
received the prize for the invention. To think of anything
as perverse, you would have first to stand on your head and
then turn yourself back to front.

THE MURDERER. Have you any evidence—that you dare call me
a murderer?

THE HUNTER. Yes, I have.

THE MURDERER *appears amazed.*

But I dare not use it before a jury of your friends. They
would deny the facts and have me arrested. Now tell me
something. Who is that girl in there who caught my companion?

THE MURDERER. She is your daughter.

THE HUNTER *clutches his heart and his face grows white. He
presses a handkerchief to his mouth. It becomes red with
blood.*

THE HUNTER. That child—who has been brought up by you!
. . . Now I must go to the crematorium.

He goes out.

V. IN THE ARBOUR OUTSIDE THE CREMATORIUM

*Outside the Columbarium. Back, an avenue of cypresses.
A bench, a chair, a table.*

Enter THE HUNTER.

THE HUNTER. What's this I see? Row upon row of urns,
but all alike?
A chemist's, a museum? No.
A columbarium, a house for doves,
but with no doves, no olive branch—
only chaff; the corn must grow elsewhere.
In the urns, ashes, so all must be alike,
as dust resembles dust.
Once human destinies, these now
bear numbers and are labelled—
"Here rests . . ." Yes, I knew you,

but you would never learn to know yourself . . .
and you, you went disguised through life,
your long and heavy life;
when I unmasked you, then you died.
Idolator! That was your name,
your character. One had to worship
your wretched wife and hateful children—
had to, or else be victimised—
each Saturday cut to pieces with a flint-knife,
or lynched, or by the Sunday press
deprived of bread and honour.

THE MURDERER, *who has been listening, enters.*

You light of Tophet's State, around your bier
you called the nation, and though dead,
counted the wreaths and threatened vengeance
on those who stayed away.

THE MURDERER. Nice things to say at a grave!

THE HUNTER. This is no grave. It's a jar with a bit of dirt in it.
No, a stone. He has become slowly petrified. . . .

THE MURDERER. You mean he died of calcification—

THE HUNTER. Yes, he turned into limestone.

THE MURDERER. Tell me a little about yourself.

THE HUNTER. I did that thirteen years ago, so you're tired of
the subject. But here are the ashes of one of whom I could
speak well, although—or, rather, because—he was murdered
by you. This victim of yours never did evil for evil's sake,
only in self-defence. And when he refused to become an
accomplice, he was killed and stripped of all he had.

THE JAPANESE *appears in the background.*

THE MURDERER. You go round with that rascally Japanese?

THE HUNTER. Do you mean to strike me down now, as that
tycoon did?

THE MURDERER. Don't speak evil of the dead. Say "poor man."

THE HUNTER. You say that about rascals who stick their fingers
in the sugar bin, but never about your victims. Now be off
with you . . . quick!

THE MURDERER. I shall go when I wish.

THE HUNTER *displays his bloody handkerchief, and* THE
MURDERER *turns to go.*

I can't bear the sight of blood. That's one of my peculiarities.

THE HUNTER. Since the fourth of April.

THE MURDERER *slinks out.*

To THE JAPANESE. Are you ready for your journey now?

THE JAPANESE. I am, but let us sit down here,
   until the furnace has been heated up.

THE HUNTER. Gladly.

They sit.

Tell me, now life lies at your feet,
like hunted game, pursued and won,
how does the journey look?

THE JAPANESE, *after a pause.* A line with many coils,
   like the image of a script
   on blotting paper. Back to front—
   forward and back and up and down—
   but in a mirror you can read the script.

THE HUNTER. What has been hardest to bear—
   of all the stones your foot has knocked against?

THE JAPANESE, *after reflection.* Once I spared an enemy,
   and afterwards he stabbed me.
   To have to wish a good deed never done
   can be the hardest.
   Another time I gave good counsel
   to one oppressed. He turned my enemy,
   took from me all I had,
   and I was helpless in the hopeless fight,
   for he—he had it written by myself
   that he was the better of us two.
   And yet all that is nothing,
   nothing compared with life's own facts—
   the humiliation of living,
   a mere skeleton in a dress of flesh,
   set going with tendons, strings,
   by a small motor in the chest's
   engine-room, run by the heat
   the belly's furnace can get up.

And the soul, the spirit, sits there in the heart,
like a bird in the bosom's cage,
in a hencoop or a fish-creel.

You little bird, soon I shall open the cage,
and you can fly—to your own land,
to the glowing sunlit isles
where I was born,
but may not die.

Look! Here's my best vase, a family heritage
which now will house the mortal dust of dust,
but once held flowers,
and decked a table for a feast.

Young eyes and rosy cheeks
were mirrored in the gold-rimmed glass,
and a small hand served the children
with the treasures of the house.

Then you became a flask of tears, dear vase!
For all the good life gave us,
came later to be mourned.

I remember at the turning of the year,
the children held their festival of dolls—
with us, all dolls pass on from kin to kin.

A child!
What is so perfect in its kind
as this small being?
Not man, nor woman,
yet both and neither—
A human being in miniature.

Say, traveller—I had forgotten you
in my own sorrows—say a word
about yourself—about your fate.

How do you look on life, how did you look?
What did you find most hard, most bitter?

THE HUNTER. What I found bitterer than death,
was having to take the great joke seriously
and treat as holy what was coarse.

When I smiled at the joke, I soon must weep,
when coarseness made me coarse,
humiliation was my lot.

Then this.
I was a preacher:
in the beginning I spoke well of human nature,
brought forward all the goodness that I knew,
and set high standards up for life—
ideals, they are also called—
those bright banners on the signal posts,
calling mankind to joyfulness.
But now—how bitter! The beauty of my thoughts
and words I must take back.
Beauty does not exist in life,
cannot materialise down here.
The ideal is never found in practice.

THE JAPANESE. I know. But it's a memory,
a hope, a beacon for one's course—
and so: send up the signals!
Let the banners blow!
They're high, but so seen all the better.
They point the upward way—towards the sun.

THE HUNTER. The furnace now begins to glow . . .

THE JAPANESE. And on the cypress tops it throws
a rosy light like flush of dawn
when the sun is rising.
Welcome, day! Farewell, you night
of heavy dreams!
For the last time I strip
and go to rest, to sleep—

And when I wake—my mother will be there,
my wife, my children, and my friends.
Good night, poor human being!

*The stage lights up, and the same image as in the first scene
—the Country of Desires—appears in the clouds.*

VI. AT THE LAST GATE

*Back, two white gates opening to a low sandy beach and
blue sea.*

Left, a wooden house, painted red (THE HUNTER's home),

*in a beechwood. It has an orchard and a box hedge. Left
of the house, a small table, decorated for a child's birthday
party.*

*A shuttlecock is seen being thrown up and down beyond
the hedge.*

A blue-hooded baby carriage stands by the gate.

THE HUNTER *enters, lost in meditation.*

THE HUNTER. Yes. Alone. That's how it ends
  if one tries to preserve one's life,
  and not to barter and haggle
  to get a position;
  not to let oneself be stolen,
  not to let oneself be cowed. . . .
  When first my brain awoke,
  and I grew conscious
  that I was shut up in a madhouse,
  a penitentiary, sanatorium,
  then I wished myself out of my mind,
  that no one should guess
  my thoughts. . . .
  "Thelō, thelō manēnai!"[6]
  I desired, desired to be mad!
  Then wine became my friend—
  I hid, I veiled myself in drunkenness,
  in the fools' garb of drunkenness forgotten,
  and none guessed who I was.
  Now that has changed;
  the drink of oblivion has become the drink of memory.
  Everything I remember, everything.
  The seals are broken, the books lie open
  and read themselves aloud—
  and when my ears are weary, then I see.
  Everything, everything I see.
  Waking from his thoughts.
  Where have I come to? The sea?
  The beechwood and the hunter's home.
  A shuttlecock rises in the air and falls,

[6] "I desire, I desire to go mad."

and here's a wicker carriage with a newborn child—
the blue hood arching like the sky
over the sleep of innocence.
Behind the shutters of that small red house
a man and woman hide their happiness—
for happiness exists, it's true,
but brief as lightning,
sunshine, or convolvulus,
one blossom and *one* day,
and then it's gone.
Smoke rises from the kitchen—
beyond's a well-stocked larder,
a little cellar underneath . . .
a verandah full of light, facing the wood . . .
I know just how it all must be—
just how it was. . . .

And here's a birthday table gaily spread
for a young child.
A little altar to all childhood,
to hope, to innocent joy built
on its own happiness,
and not on others' ruin.
And there's the beach,
with white, clean, soft, warm sand,
with shells and pebbles
and the blue water to dabble in
with naked feet. . . .
Garlands of leaves, the paths all raked—
for friends are coming to a children's party.
They have watered the flowers,
the flowers of my childhood—
blue monkshood with two doves inside,
fritillary bearing a diadem,
a sceptre, and an orb.
The passion flower of suffering
in white and amethyst with cross
and lance and nails,
sipped by the bee, which from its heart
draws honey, where we find only gall.

And here, loveliest of trees
in a child's garden,
from dark green leaves peep out in pairs
the white-heart cherries, red and white,
young children's faces, sister and brother,
playing, caressing, swinging in the wind.
Between branch and stem a warbler
has built his nest—
unseen singer, song on wings . . .
Hush! The gravel's crunched beneath small boots.
Here comes the sovereign!

THE CHILD *enters, takes* THE HUNTER's *hand, and leads him to the baby carriage.*

THE CHILD. Walk quietly and you can look at the doll. There's the doll. That's what we call her. But you mustn't walk on the gravel, because it's been raked. Ellen raked it, for we're going to have visitors. It's my birthday today. . . . Are you sad?

THE HUNTER. What's your name, child?

THE CHILD. I'm called Mary.

THE HUNTER. Who lives in that house?

THE CHILD. Papa and Mamma.

THE HUNTER. May I look at your birthday table?

THE CHILD. But we mustn't touch anything.

THE HUNTER. No, I won't touch anything, little one.

THE CHILD. Do you know what we'll have for dinner today? We'll have asparagus and strawberries. Why are you sad? Have you lost your money? You can take a cake from the table, but you mustn't take the big one—that's for Stella. Do you know, Stella had crumbs in her bed last night, and she cried—and then there was thunder and we were frightened, so Mamma shut the damper. Yes, she'd been eating a sandwich in bed and it broke in pieces—it was that sort of crisp bread you get in the town. . . . Now shall we have a fairy story? Can you tell stories? What's your name?

THE HUNTER. My name is Cartaphilus.[7]

---

[7] Cartaphilus, later called Ahasuerus: The Wandering Jew.

THE CHILD. No, you're not called that.

THE HUNTER. Ahasuerus then—the one that's always wandering.

THE CHILD. Shall we talk about something else? Are your eyes hurting?

THE HUNTER. Yes, child, they hurt so much, so much.

THE CHILD. You mustn't read in bed by candlelight. That makes one's eyes hurt.

A horn sounds.

Papa's coming!

Exit THE CHILD.

THE HUNTER. My child! *My* child! She did not know me. How fortunate—how fortunate for us both!

Farewell, sweet vision.
I will not stand in the sun's path
and cast a shadow on the youngest's plot.
I know the father here—the mother too—
a lovely image, an image
wavering but lovely.
A memory perhaps, or more than that—
a hope—a summer's day out in the woods
beside the sea—a birthday table and a cradle.
A beam of sunlight from a child's eyes,
a gift from a child's hand—
and so on again and out—into the darkness.

VII. THE DARK WOOD

THE HUNTER. Alone!—I have lost my way—
In the darkness.
"And Elijah sat down under the juniper tree and he wished himself dead and said: It is enough! Take my life, O Lord!"

THE VOICE OF THE WOMAN, *in the darkness.* He who seeks to lose his life shall find it.

THE HUNTER. Who are you that speaks out of the darkness?

THE VOICE OF THE WOMAN. Is it dark?

THE HUNTER. Is it dark?

THE WOMAN *enters.*

THE WOMAN. I ask, because I cannot see. I am blind.

THE HUNTER. Have you always been blind?

THE WOMAN. No. When the tears ceased to flow, my eyes could no longer see.

THE HUNTER. It is good to be able to weep.

THE WOMAN. But I hear instead, and I know your voice. I know who you are—and I believe in you.

THE HUNTER. You must not believe in me, nor in any human being. You must believe in God.

THE WOMAN. I do that too.

THE HUNTER. But in God alone. The children of man are not to be believed in.

THE WOMAN. Weren't you once a lawyer, for the defence?

THE HUNTER. I was the defender of the only True One against the idolators. You always wanted to worship yourselves, your relatives, your friends, but you never respected simple justice.

THE WOMAN. Sometimes you abandoned the case you were fighting.

THE HUNTER. When they tricked me into pity for an unrighteous man on the pretext that he was poor, I abandoned the case of the unrighteous.

THE WOMAN. You were an evangelist once too, but you tired of that.

THE HUNTER. I did not tire, but when I found I could not live what I taught, I stopped preaching in order not to be called a hypocrite. And when I discovered that nowhere was there any putting into practice of those beautiful doctrines, I left their realisation for the land of fulfilled desires.

THE WOMAN. And now—are you dead?

THE HUNTER. Yes, socially, but not spiritually. I'm a fighter and so I live. But *I* don't exist—only what I have done. Good and evil. The evil, I confessed and suffered for—with the good, I tried to do good.

THE WOMAN. Would you still plead the human cause?

THE HUNTER. When it was right, not otherwise. Once, misled by the gratitude I owed a man, I fought a case for him, and in so doing caused great injury to an innocent person. That's how it is with even our best feelings. They beguile us into evil.

THE WOMAN. You are accusing—prosecutor!

THE HUNTER. Whom am I accusing?

THE WOMAN. The ruling powers.

THE HUNTER. Get thee behind me, Satan, before you tempt me to blasphemy.

THE WOMAN. Satan?

THE HUNTER. Yes, Satan!

THE WOMAN. No one was as black as you.

THE HUNTER. Because you blackened me, so that I should be like you. And explain this to me: when I confessed my sins, you felt yourselves guiltless and thanked God you were not as I—and yet you were just as bad. Once when I was a child I saw an execution. What a bunch of hypocrites the crowd was! On the way home they lamented his fate, then they went to the taverns and spoke ill of the dead man and felt better themselves. And after that, some of them went back to the gallows and took the dead man's blood—to cure epilepsy. They dipped their handkerchiefs in his blood! Look at this one! Oh, of course, you are blind. Feel it then. Your eye is in your hand. *Gives her the bloody handkerchief.*

THE WOMAN. It feels like red. And it is sticky. It smells like—butcher's meat. No, I know what it is. I had a relative who died recently. He coughed up first his lungs and finally the heart itself.

THE HUNTER. Did he cough up his heart?

THE WOMAN. Yes.

THE HUNTER, *looking at the handkerchief.* I believe it. The goat, as we know, is not a clean animal, yet on the great day of atonement he had to bear the sins of all, and thus burdened, he was driven out into the desert to be devoured by wild beasts. That was the scapegoat.

THE WOMAN. Do you mean that you have suffered for the sins of others?

THE HUNTER. For my own and others'. And so for others.

THE WOMAN. Weren't you something else, before you became a lawyer?

THE HUNTER. Yes, I was an architect. I built many houses. They weren't all good, but when I built well, they were angry with me because they were good. So they gave the work to others who did it worse. That was in the town of Tophet, where I built the theatre.

THE WOMAN. That is considered very fine.

THE HUNTER. Remember it then when I have ceased to be— and forget me.

THE WOMAN. "*I* don't exist. Only the good I did remains." Why did you have no pity for your fellows?

THE HUNTER. The question's wrongly put. Did you see any pitying me? No. Then how could I reciprocate an emotion not granted me? Besides, who was it who first preached: "Mankind is to be pitied"?

THE WOMAN *disappears.*

She's gone. They always go when one seeks to defend oneself.

THE TEMPTER *enters.*

THE TEMPTER. So now I have met you! Well, we will have a talk, but as it's rather dark here, we'll make a nice light . . . *It grows lighter* . . . so that we can see one another. It's essential to see one another if we're to talk sense. This from the Grand Duke. He admires your talents and offers you the appointment of Court Architect, with a salary of so-and-so, living quarters with fuel, etc., all found. You understand?

THE HUNTER. I don't want an appointment.

THE TEMPTER. Wait a minute! There are certain conditions. . . . Well, yes, in a word, you must conduct yourself like a human being, an ordinary human being.

THE HUNTER. I would like to hear more. It would interest me to know how an ordinary human being conducts himself.

THE TEMPTER. Don't you know that? Why do you look so distraught?

THE HUNTER. I can answer the last question in two words. I look distraught because I'm utterly confused. You see, to begin with, I was one of those people who believe what they are told—and therefore I was stuffed with lies. Everything I believed in was a pack of lies—and so my whole self is falsified. I have gone round with false opinions about people and about life; I have reckoned in false terms, passed off false coin without knowing it was false. And so I am not what I am. I can't mix with other people, can't talk, can't quote another's words of appeal to any statement, for fear it is a lie. Many times over I became an accomplice in that forge known as society, but when I grew like the rest, I went out and became a highwayman, a robber in the woods.

THE TEMPTER. All that's just twaddle. Let's get back to the Grand Duke, who is asking for your services.

THE HUNTER. He's not asking for my services, he's asking for my soul.

THE TEMPTER. He's asking you to take an interest in his great enterprise.

THE HUNTER. That I cannot do. Leave me now. I haven't long to live and I want to be alone to make up my accounts.

THE TEMPTER. Aha! If pay day is at hand,
then I will come with invoices,
with bills and summonses—

THE HUNTER. Yes, come! Come with despair,
you tempter, trying to gull me
to a coward's denial of the Good Giver.
From the height's pure air, I came down here
to walk a while yet among the sons of man
and share in their small cares.
But here there was no open road—
a ravine among thorns,
one was caught in the thicket,
leaving a shred here, a shred there.
People offered—so as to take back with interest,
gave—so as to make the gift a debt,

served—in order that they might rule,
set free—in order to confine.
I lost my companion on the way . . .
one snare was followed by another . . .
I was drawn between grindstones
and came out on the other side.
A beam of light from a child's eyes
led me here into this darkness.

THE TEMPTER *disappears.*

Now you are bringing out the bills—
What? Even he has disappeared!

So I am alone,
in night and darkness,
where the trees sleep and the grass is weeping
from the cold when the sun has set.
But some beasts wake, although not all—
the bat is weaving his cabals,
the snake coils under poison plant,
the light-shy badger makes a move
after a day of sleep.
Alone! And why?
A traveller in another's land
is always stranger and alone.
He goes through towns and villages,
stays, pays, and passes on,
until the journey's end—then he's at home.
But this is not the end . . .
I still can hear . . . a withered branch
cracks—an iron heel rings on a rock—
it is the awful blacksmith,
the idolator with his flint-knife
looking for me,
and the miller with his grindstones,
into which I was drawn
and nearly crushed.
The people in the arcade, that arcade—
a lobster pot, easy to enter
but hard to get out of.
And the murderer Möller,

with bills and summonses
and alibis and libels—
infamous man!
What do I hear now? Music!
I know your tunes—and your dear hand,
I do not want to meet you. . . .
A little way off the fire warms,
but not too near, for then it burns.
And now—a child's voice in the darkness,
you little child, last memory of light
to follow me into the dark night wood,
on the last stage to that distant land—
the land of fulfilled desires.
A vision seen from the mountain tops,
but in the valley veiled
by dust from roads and chimney smoke.
Where did you go, fair vision—
land of longing and of dreams?

If but a vision, let me see you again
in the crystal air on the snow-white height.
There with the hermit I will stay
and wait for the release.
Surely he will grant me a grave
beneath the cold white blanket,
and will write in the snow a fleeting epitaph:
Here Ishmael rests, the son of Hagar,
whose name was once called Israel,
because he fought a fight with God,
and did not cease to fight until laid low,
defeated by His almighty goodness.
O Eternal One, I'll not let go Thy hand,
Thy hard hand, till Thou bless me.

Bless me, Your creature,
who suffers, suffers from Your gift of life.
Bless me, whose deepest suffering,
deepest of human suffering, was this—
I could not be the one I longed to be.